ROUTLEDGE LIBRARY EDITIONS:
SOCIOLOGY OF EDUCATION

Volume 24

THE CHANGING CULTURE
OF A COLLEGE

THE CHANGING CULTURE
OF A COLLEGE

JOHN FRAIN

Routledge
Taylor & Francis Group

LONDON AND NEW YORK

First published in 1993 by The Falmer Press

This edition first published in 2017
by Routledge
2 Park Square, Milton Park, Abingdon, Oxon OX14 4RN

and by Routledge
711 Third Avenue, New York, NY 10017

Routledge is an imprint of the Taylor & Francis Group, an informa business

British Library Cataloguing in Publication Data
A catalogue record for this book is available from the British Library

ISBN: 978-0-415-78834-2 (Set)
ISBN: 978-1-315-20949-4 (Set) (ebk)
ISBN: 978-1-138-22248-9 (Volume 24) (hbk)
ISBN: 978-1-138-22250-2 (Volume 24) (pbk)

Publisher's Note
The publisher has gone to great lengths to ensure the quality of this reprint but points out that some imperfections in the original copies may be apparent.

Disclaimer
The publisher has made every effort to trace copyright holders and would welcome correspondence from those they have been unable to trace.

The Changing Culture of a College

John Frain

The Falmer Press

(A member of the Taylor & Francis Group)
London • Washington, DC

UK   The Falmer Press, 4 John St, London WC1N 2ET
USA   The Falmer Press, Taylor & Francis Inc., 1990 Frost Road, Suite 101,
        Bristol, PA 19007

First published in 1993

**A catalogue record for this book is available from the British
Library**

**Library of Congress Cataloging-in-Publication Data are available on
request**

ISBN 1 85000 907 4 (cased)

Cover design by Caroline Archer

Typeset in 10/12 pt Times
by Graphicraft Typesetters Ltd., Hong Kong

Contents

Contents

Abstract

In the early nineteen eighties, the Liverpool City Council decided to reorganize its further education provision. This emanated from a number of social and economic factors including the declining number of sixteen to nineteen year olds, a reduced resource base and a declining employment base. This last factor gave rise to grave, continuing decline in some traditional areas of further education provision. The eight existing colleges were reorganized to form four new colleges and began to operate from 1st September 1986. The colleges were, broadly, of equal size, each with defined specialist provision and a pattern of general and community education. The reorganization involved substantial transfers of technological and other work. The colleges were expected to make a purposeful, cost effective response to changing environmental conditions of enough complexity to constitute, in social science terminology, a 'turbulent field'. This called for management decision-making both skilful and professionally self-confident.

This book records the progress of one of the four new colleges, South Mersey College during the four-year period from September 1986 to August 1990. Its findings derive from an action research project which utilized the non-reactive research technique of participant observation supported by other unobtrusive research measures. The research paid particular attention to the development of the College's curriculum, its organization and management structures and the quality and cost effectiveness of its provision. Importantly, the research was grounded in the belief that the processes of strategic management need to be understood as a cultural process. Throughout the four-year period the researcher studied the relationship between the changing culture and the diversification and development of the College.

The purpose of the research and its methodology are described in Chapter 1 of the book. Chapters 2 and 3 outline the environmental conditions acting upon the College and challenges these constituted for its strategic management. The processes of strategic analysis and strategic choice which culminated in the establishment and organization of the College are explained in Chapter 4.

Abstract

The research examined the larger theories and ideas emanating from industrial and commercial settings. It assessed these for their value if applied in an educational context. Chapters 5 to 8, inclusive, relate these constructs to the narrative history of the College's development during the review period.

Chapter 9 summarizes the principles found expedient for strategic change. While the focus of the research centred on the management process the powerful influence of students and staff is also outlined.

Fundamentally also, the book is offered as evidence that action research, in which a practitioner theorizes about his practice, can be used to interrogate larger theories about the working of systems and public policy. It can also counter the mutual distrust between researchers and practitioners which emanates from their traditional division of labour.

Preface

To read any of the works of J.K. Galbraith is to be enlightened and intrigued by his formidable intellectual energy. Yet modestly he has said that authorship of any sort is a fantastic indulgence of the ego and that it is well, no doubt, to reflect on how much one owes to others. This is a happy construct on which to base the Preface to this book — which records four years of research into the development of a college within a rapidly changing economic, political and social context.

Apart from those identified in the dedication there are many people for me to thank: My wife, Patricia, and the children, for their love and forbearance in the face of yet another project, yet another book; My secretary, Sue Bioletti, for her dedication and sunny disposition — the latter a powerful antidote to the loneliness of the research worker; My publisher, Malcolm Clarkson and two members of his editorial staff Jackie Day and Carol Saumarez, at Falmer Press, whose interest and support throughout was of a kind about which most authors can only fantasize; importantly, the management and staff of the two former colleges, Riversdale and Childwall, for what they handed on to us — one establishment noted internationally for its technological strengths, another whose community ethos had become a model for others.

In his preface to the English Dictionary, Samuel Johnson talked of those unhappy mortals whose fate was:

> *to be exposed to censure, without hope of praise; to be disgraced by miscarriage, or punished for neglect, where success would have been without applause, and diligence without reward*

This is no bad description of Liverpool and its people except that they are not unhappy mortals — rather do they find in adversity yet more resilience, yet more humour, yet more care and concern.

I hope as you read this book, within the formal method of its chapters, you will be able to discern these people and come to appreciate them, as I did.

John Frain
Liverpool
February 1993

List of Figures

Chapter 1

Introduction

In the 1985/86 Academic Session, when the Liverpool City Council reorganized its further education service, it made clear its view that staff development had an important role in increasing the effectiveness of its Colleges. The national and local funding available for staff development was, moreover, to provide programmes for *all* academic staff, including College Principals.

The Principal of South Mersey College participated in a number of short, self-contained staff development initiatives, but he also elected to conduct an action-research programme spanning four years in the corporate life of his own College. The objectives of the research were these:

1 to provide, for archival purposes, a narrative history of the College's development and diversification and of the context in which it operated, in the period under review;
2 to evaluate the processes by which the College adapted to changing 'boundary conditions';
3 to examine the larger theories and ideas about the workings of organizations derived from industrial and commercial settings and to assess these for their value, if applied.

In this research, the unit of enquiry was a organization as a whole, not the individuals comprising it. Reactive methods of data collection (questionnaires, interviews, experiments) seemed hardly appropriate. Moreover, since the researcher was also the Principal of the College, the dangers of respondent bias present in the administration of reactive techniques would have increased markedly. If respondents on occasion answer as they think they are expected to answer, rather than answer objectively, the manager-managed relationship must surely have increased the possibilities of such conscious behaviourism. Given the political and financial problems of Liverpool at this time, reactive research would also have generated doubts and uncertainties with industrial relations facets, such as 'Why is the Principal asking these questions?' 'What use will he make of the information?'

Participant Observation

The context of the research, its scale, its time-span and the need to safeguard objectivity all pointed to the efficacy of a non-reactive research approach — to the use of methods based upon the interpretation of observed phenomena and extant data. The word 'observed' should be noted. In this context it has a particular coinage. *Observation* has been widely used in scientific studies. It has been described as 'the classical method of investigation'.[1] In the literature, its use as a primary tool of social enquiry has been widely reported. Early commentators in the UK have included Madge and Huxley[2] who, in their work on the Mass-Observation studies of the 1930s argued for its effectiveness, since there were very many areas of knowlege in which people would not answer correctly, either because they did not know the correct reply or because they would be unwilling to respond correctly, either from embarrassment or for various reasons of prestige.

Participant observation is an intense form of the approach and derives from the work of anthropologists and ethnologists. It requires the observer to deal with sources of empirical evidence by joining in the daily life of the group or organization being studied. The researcher attends to the life of the community as a whole — its activities, its institutions, the relationship between its members. It is the type of study typical of social anthropology and seemed particularly fitting for the research objectives the author had in mind. Notably, for example, observational techniques have frequently been used in survey work concerned with industrial relations. Lupton's (1963) study 'On the Shop Floor' and the 1954 study by Liverpool University on industrial relations and morale in the local docks were early examples.[3] The Tavistock Institute of Human Relations has also been a devotee of participant observer methods. In the context of his own research, therefore, it seemed to the author that a premium could be charged to the method.

The community studied by the participant observer may be as small as a family or as large as a city. It may be a 'closed' community such as a family or a tribe, or an 'open' one such as a factory, a college, a town or a village. The important difference is that in the open community an observer can sometimes remain unnoticed. In a closed community this is impossible. The observer's task is to place himself in the best position to obtain a complete and unbiased picture of the community. As Moser and Kalton[4] indicate, if the observer can become so accepted as part of the community that its members are unaware of being observed, he will naturally obtain a more authentic, because less self-conscious, picture of its behaviour. As Chisnall[5] asserts, while no research method is without bias, the dangers can be minimized by intelligent planning in the early stages of designing a research strategy. From the onset, for example, the author felt strongly that his role as College Principal would automatically secure him the best position to obtain a complete picture of the organization. His acceptance as a member of the community would clearly pose no problem either. At the same time, observation might suffer from the observer's biases and expectations and his dual role as Principal and researcher could add significantly to this danger.

Advantages and Limitations of the Technique

At the planning stage, several points emerged in favour of the participant observer approach, with the College as its setting. They were as follows:

- The college constituted a large 'block' sample (approximately 300 staff and 10,000 students) capable of yielding data of much richness and variety;
- A non-reactive research method, such as participant observation, would enable data to be obtained not achievable by the standardized reactive methods of social surveys;
- The key drawbacks of the observation technique — time and cost — would be surmounted by the unique circumstances of the survey (the Principal as researcher), so that although no external funding was available for the research, a significantly long period (four years) could be devoted to it even so;
- The strength of participant observation as a method of data collection is its objectivity, although there are potential pitfalls. These are outlined below:

    - A risk with participant observation is that the role adopted by the observer will restrict his understanding of the situation. This biased-viewpoint effect derives from the fact that in playing a clearly defined role in the community, the observer's understanding of the situation is thereby restricted. He will have access only to sources of information associated with that role;
    - The observer's preconceptions of how people normally behave may also distort the objectivity of the study: instead of recording what he actually observes, the researcher may fit this into stereotypes to which he is accustomed;
    - There is the difficulty of distinguishing between objectivity and inference. Researchers observing the same phenomena may well describe these differently. Participant observers become so much part of their subject matter that they may fail to see it objectively. Their vision may be distorted by what they are used to seeing, or what they expect to see, and consequently they may find it hard to present a report in which observation is satisfactorily distinguished from inference and interpretation;

3

- As in all social science research, there is the danger of informant bias. At the planning stage, the author recognized that in the study he had in mind, this had two aspects: 1) bias arising from the conscious behaviourism of informants, i.e. due to their answering as they felt they were expected to answer, rather than answering objectively — a danger heightened in this study by the manager-subordinate relationship, described earlier; 2) distortion arising from the 'Hawthorne effect', in that to examine phenomena is to disturb them — attitudes, behaviour, performance could all be affected by the respondents' knowledge of being part of a research process: effort expended may be less or more than effort normally expended and therefore may not be safely generalizable for theoretical purposes (Roethlisberger and Dickson[6] *q.v.*).

Because of these factors, the success of the approach depends very much on the skill and competence of the researcher. As Moser and Kalton[7] have written in this connection:

> ... the method enables him to present a picture more vivid, complete and authentic than is possible with other procedures. But any defects in his approach and ability can easily arouse suspicion and so undermine his position and its possibilities. Participant observation is a highly individual technique.

In devising a conceptual framework for the study, the author bore these points in mind. He found his role of Principal of the institution a help rather than a hindrance in overcoming the biased-viewpoint effect, which can arise from the restricted role of the researcher. By contrast the author was able to enter into the life of the College at very many different levels, and his sources of information were legion. Coupled with the four-year time scale of the study, this enabled him to obtain a comprehensive picture perhaps rarely, if ever, obtained by a single observer.

The difficulty of distinguishing between objectivity and inference was a substantial one. Here, two points must be stressed. First, as will be explained more fully below, the research was kept confidential between the researcher and the Local Authority. Because of this, each meeting, formal or informal, from those of the College Academic Board to those of small groups within Faculties became in effect, a group discussion. In such discussions, the origins, complexities and ramifications of staff attitudes to the issues of reorganization, change, development and diversification could be explored in order to clarify what coordinates of behaviour were to be observed. The Principal had his own 'item pool' of concepts he felt worthy of investigation, but in the best social science tradition he recognized these would not be the only or perhaps the most significant ones. Taking a neutral, non-directive stance in these discussions, as far as possible, would enable him to safeguard the objectivity of both the conceptual framework and its processes of observation. This coalesced with his perception of his own role as substantially that of germinating ideas and then relying on 'change-heroes', the key personnel within the organization structure who would implement change. This would also increase participation and enrich jobs.

A third point fundamental to the quality of the research was that apart from the appropriate officer of the Local Education Authority, through whom the research was arranged, no one was told it was to be conducted. This certainly applied to virtually every member of the College staff (two senior members were told, in confidence, late in the research project). This was not only to prevent needless concern of an 'industrial relations' nature ('Why is this survey being conducted?') but also to ensure that informant-bias, due either to conscious behaviourism or to the Hawthorne effect, did not distort the research findings.

Finally, as Moser and Kalton have indicated, participant observation is a process demanding a great deal of skill and competence on the part of the researcher. Which raises the question as to how far the College Principal was fitted for the task. In fact, he possessed three University higher degrees. Within the structure of each of these, the use of social science research techniques had played a significant part. He was also the author of a number of published works in which the use of these techniques had been described, including the ways in which distortion and bias could enter into the administration and interpretation of survey work. Throughout the four-year period of the research he kept the threats to objectivity constantly in mind and so arranged his observations and the compilation of his material to minimize these dangers.

Unobtrusive Measures

No research method is without the danger of bias and it is difficult to eliminate entirely the effects of measurement on the subjects of an enquiry. While these dangers can be minimized by intelligent planning in the early stages of the conceptual analysis they have to be recognized as ever-present tendencies.

Because of this, some writers (for example, Webb, Campbell, Schwartz and Sechrest[8]) have called for a multi-technique approach to research so that research outcomes are not dependent on the results produced by a single, potentially fallible technique. Webb and others were particularly concerned with reactive measurement errors and therefore underlined the desirability of using several different methods which together make up a sound research strategy.

The problem of reactive measurement errors is pervasive and it increases the complexity of research. To reduce this form of bias, researchers have developed techniques which Webb and his colleagues have classified as

unobtrusive measures. Like observation techniques conducted in secrecy, unobtrusive measures allow investigations to be carried out without the subjects
being aware of them. Such measures include the study of records, of official
publications and of economic, demographic and organizational data of various kinds.

In this research project unobtrusive measures have been used extensively both to provide a framework for the survey and to substantiate the
findings emanating from the participant observation process. These measures
included statistical data prepared by the College and its predecessor institutions. These were public data in that they were subject to scrutiny by the
Department of Education and Science, the District Audit Service, the Liverpool Education Authority and the Governors of the College. It should be
noted that much use had also been made of the Principal's reports to the
Governors submitted during the four years of the survey. Significantly, however, these reports were not prepared exclusively by the Principal. His own
role was largely to provide appropriate introductory remarks, a concluding
summary and to ensure that they had uniformity of style and presentation.
This was part of a strategy of ownership of change in which Heads of Faculty
also made presentations to Governors' meetings. While the reports do contain
important issues brought to Governors' attention by the Principal, their generic
content comprises public reports written by the individual Heads of Faculty
unaware that they would also be used for research purposes. Perhaps it is not
too far-fetched to suggest that these Principal's reports might legitimately be
added to the list of unobtrusive measures examined and employed for research
purposes.

Mention has already been made of the large number of formal and
informal meetings which the Principal was able to utilize as proxy discussion
groups within the research. The Principal would claim that his own research
background, qualifications and experience have provided him with interpretive
skills which were adequate enough for the objective analysis of the viewpoints
and responses made by the staff and students during these many meetings.

What this means, therefore, is that the claims made in the body of this
work in respect of the marked diversification and development of the College
in the four-year review period can be substantiated from more than a single
source. When attention is drawn to the organizing power of a particular
concept or to the value of some particular theoretical insight, such proposi-
tions derive from a triangulation of research methods — observation, documentation, discussion.

The argument for the safeguarding of objectivity by such 'multiple
operationism' has been neatly summarized by Campbell and Fiske:[9]

> When a hypothesis can survive the confrontation of a series of com-
> plementary methods of testing it contains a degree of validity un-
> attainable by one tested within the more constricted framework of a
> single method.

Action Research

The final comment in this outline of the methodology for the research is perhaps the most important. In this introduction the survey was described as an action-research programme. An explanation is necessary.

In Meighan's[10] commentary on conducting research in educational institutions, he describes the psychological distance which too frequently separates practitioners and researchers. The image of the researcher is that of an outsider looking in, motivated by concerns different from those which engage the subjects of the survey. In effect, the researcher is often perceived as remote or coldly detached from the everyday struggles, ambitions and troubles of those at work in the establishments and the classrooms being investigated.

The exclusion of educational practitioners from the process in which research problems are selected and formulated almost inevitably produces a chain of consequences which either distort the research or render its practice futile. This kind of exclusion is based upon, or lends support to, the view that analysis and practice (i.e. researching and educating) are distinct, separate activities requiring different skills and techniques and involving different perceptions of the establishments and classrooms in which they take place. Analysis is concerned with theory; practice is to do with action. Since teachers have neither the time, the opportunity nor (presumably) the skills to pursue research, it follows that theory is something created by educationalists and researchers. Meighan believes that once this absurd division of educational labour is given currency the path which leads initially to mutual disregard between practitioners and researchers and eventually to mutual distrust becomes dangerously seductive.

An approach developed as a direct attempt to confront this issue has been variously described as 'classroom-based research', the 'teacher-researcher' movement, and 'teacher-based research' or, more frequently, 'action research'. It is inspired by the pioneering work of the late Lawrence Stenhouse and begins with the assumption that teachers are already problem-solvers, inquirers and self-evaluating professionals. The approach of 'action research' is to activate and extend the idea that the work of practitioners theorizing about their practices can be enhanced by research methodology and can contribute to the creation of theory which focuses on practical interaction and which can be used to interrogate larger theories and ideas about the working of systems or public policy.

Writing in 1983 Ebbutt[11] outlined 'action research' as:

> about the systematic study of attempts to improve educational practice by groups of participants by means of their own practical actions and by means of their own reflection upon the effects of those actions.

This is a reasonable definition of the objectives of this investigation. It also provides a fitting description of the author's role as both observer and participant. A seminal management study of the part played in productivity by social and psychological factors was the one conducted at the Glacier Metal Company by Dr. Elliott Jaques and his colleagues from the Tavistock Institute, who acted as participant observers. The first of a large number of publications emanating from that extended applied research study of organization and management in an industrial setting was entitled *The Changing Culture of a Factory*. Given the context, objectives and time span of this author's study, it seemed entirely appropriate to title it *The Changing Culture of a College*.[12]

Notes

1 MOSER, C.A. and KALTON, G. (1971) *Survey Methods in Social Investigation*, 2nd Edition, London: Heinemann Educational Books Ltd., p. 244.
2 MADGE, C. and HUXLEY, J. (1937) 'Mass-Observation', in WORCESTER, R. and DOWNHAM, J. (Eds) (1986) *Consumer Market Research Handbook*, 3rd Edition, London: McGraw Hill, p. 267.
3 MOSER, C.A. and KALTON, G. Op. cit., p. 31.
4 MOSER, C.A. and KALTON, G. Op. cit., p. 249.
5 CHISNALL, P.M. (1986) *Marketing Research*, 3rd Edition, Maidenhead, Berks: McGraw-Hill Book Company (UK) Ltd., p. 27.
6 ROETHLISBERGER, F.J. and DICKSON, W.J. (1949) *Management and the Worker*, Cambridge, Massachusetts: Harvard University Press.
7 MOSER, C.A. and KALTON, G. Op. cit. p. 251.
8 WEBB, E.J., CAMPBELL, D.T., SCHWARTZ, R.D. and SECHREST, L. (1966) *Unobtrusive Measures: Nonreactive Research in the Social Sciences*, Chicago, Illinois: Rand McNally and Company.
9 CAMPBELL, D.T. and FISKE, D.W. (1959) 'Convergent and discriminant validation by the multi-trait-multimethod matrix', *Psychological Bulletin*, **56**, pp. 81–105.
10 MEIGHAN, R. (1986) *A Sociology of Educating*, 2nd Edition, London: Cassell Educational Ltd., p. 283.
11 EBBUTT, in HOPKINS, D. (1985) *A Teacher's Guide to Classroom Research*, Milton Keynes, Bucks: Open University Press.
12 JAQUES, E. (1951) *The Changing Culture of a Factory*, London: Routledge & Regan Paul.

Chapter 2

A College and its Environment

A College of Further Education: The Organization and its Environment

The province of this research project includes an extended examination of South Mersey College as an organization: its structure, functioning and behaviour. To paraphrase John Donne, no organization is an island, entire of itself. It is located within a setting which management theorists describe as its 'causal texture' or, more generally, its environment.

The organizational environment includes all elements existing outside the boundaries of an organization which have the potential to affect it. This external environment may usefully be thought of as comprising two layers. The outer layout is variously described in the literature as the general or indirect action environment. It is a widely dispersed layer and includes demographic, economic, technological, and political elements that may be thought of as influences on the climate in which the organization operates.

The environment's inner layer, typically called the task- or direct-action environment is made up of elements which have a close working relationship with the organization and so exert a direct influence on its actions. In the case of a Further Education College prominent among these elements would be its 'stakeholders' (its students; client industrial, commercial and public sector organizations; the local education authority; the community at large), its competitors and its suppliers.

Each organization also has an internal environment (one made up of elements within the organization's boundaries). Among these elements, current employees, production technology, organization structure, physical facilities, and especially corporate culture are prominent. Figure 2.1 is an attempt to represent, diagrammatically, the environmental make-up of a Further Education College.

Figure 2.1:   The environmental make-up of a Further Education College

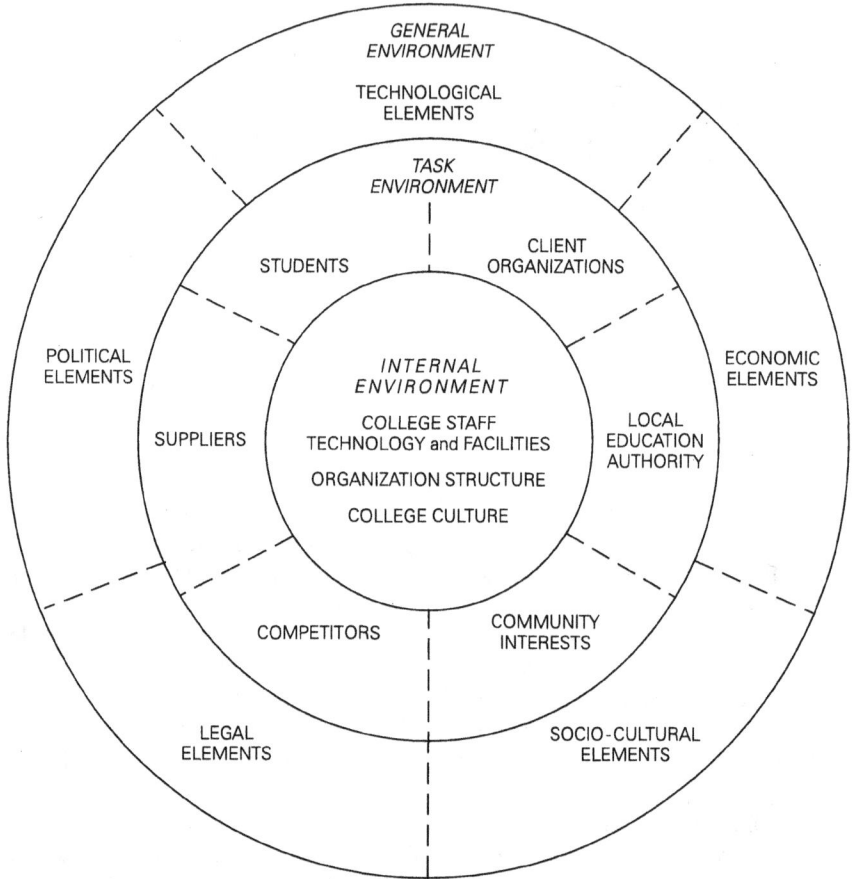

The City of Liverpool: Its Recent Economic and Social History

In order to understand fully the specific environmental make-up (internal and external) of the South Mersey College, it is important, in the first instance, to provide a narrative history of the background against which the 1985/86 further education reorganization took place. This is set out below. Following that is an outline of the reorganization itself in terms of the strategic analysis preceding it and the strategic choices made in the light of the City Council's declared policy objectives for the service.

Immediately prior to the reorganization eight Further Education establishments were being maintained by the Liverpool Education Authority. These were:

The Central Liverpool College of Further Education
The Childwall Hall College of Further Education
The Colquitt Technical and Nautical Catering College
The Mabel Fletcher Technical College
The Millbrook College of Commerce
The North-East Liverpool Technical College
The Old Swan Technical College
The Riversdale College of Technology

Although the eight Colleges provided some courses for which there was a national market in the performing arts, maritime studies and nautical catering, the pattern of demand on Colleges of further education is an intensively local one. The fortunes of the eight Colleges were closely linked to the City they were established to serve. It is therefore important to describe the social and economic context in which they were operating immediately prior to their reorganization.

By 1914, Liverpool was Britain's second port (after London) and handled one third of Britain's exports. Its population grew in response and in 1937 reached its peak of 867,000. However, the impact of the 1930s depression upon world trade had already revealed the problems caused by Liverpool's over-dependence upon the port. By the early 1930s unemployment in the City had reached a level of 28 per cent. Throughout the rest of that decade it was always at least one and a half times the national average. Trade through the docks decreased in the post-war period (to 75 per cent of the 1914 level) and rapidly continued to decrease. Consequently unemployment also appeared in related industries and small businesses, so that by the late 1940s it had risen to two and a half times the national average.

Attempts to attract new manufacturing industry to Liverpool were partially successful but were dogged by industrial relations difficulties, closures and withdrawals and a continuing loss of jobs in the ports. Liverpool's geographical position had given it an advantage when much of Britain's trade was with the Americas and the old Empire and Commonwealth. It was a drawback when Britain joined the European Community, and the port's problems were exacerbated by the new dynamics of distribution, which included the rapid growth of containerization and air freight services.

Throughout the 1970s and 1980s a significant number of new firms chose to locate in the South-East of Britain, particularly near the M25 motorway around London. The building of the Channel tunnel was another development predicted to increase Liverpool's problems (though some would say it will bring increased opportunity). The City's decline was at the root of the demographic, economic and social changes which followed. Some of these are now described.

i *Total Population*   1937   867,000
                         1961   745,000
                         1986   484,000

Loss since 1937 (382,600): 44 per cent

Liverpool's loss of population was the highest of any urban area in England and Wales, for example, almost twice that of Manchester in the same period. According to Liverpool's City Planning Officer[1] most of this loss was due to 'outmigration', itself the result of slum clearance, and reduced job opportunities. Current population decline is now approximately 6500 per year.

ii *Population Profile — Changes 1961–83*

That this change in the population has not been constant for all sections is demonstrated by the following statistics, which relate to two decades since the early 1960s:

Total population	*34 per cent decline*
Pre-school (0–5)	54 per cent decline
School age	46 per cent decline
Working age	32 per cent decline
Elderly (under 75)	29 per cent decline
Elderly (over 75)	31 per cent decline

Although Liverpool's annual overall loss of population has slowed down, it is still significantly high. Moreover, the City Planning Officer states that: 'Most of the people moving out into the rest of Merseyside or to other parts of the country tend to be younger skilled or professional workers and their families, consequently the proportion of the population that is unemployed, older or retired, is rising'.[2]

He adds that for the City Council this means that a higher proportion of the population is dependent on it for services, so that there has been no reduction in the level of needs or resource requirements. Moreover, it is not practicable to adjust the level of services in direct relationship to loss of population. A decrease in the school-age population cannot be immediately followed by closure of surplus schools.

Schools reorganization is complex, lengthy and, if only in the short-term, costly. Other statistics available from the City Planning Officer, which it is beyond the scope of this work to examine in detail, demonstrate that the decrease in population did not result in a concomitant reduction in the number of households so that the level of certain services, for example, refuse collection, could not be justifiably related to the reduced population levels.

In serving the needs of the people of Liverpool, the City Council was faced with the reduction in income derived from rates, due to this loss of population. With the advent of the Conservative national government in 1979, income was further reduced, as this new government acted upon its declared intention to reduce significantly the Public Sector Borrowing Requirement. When making decisions about its annual budgets, therefore, Liverpool had to contend with a number of problems, including: high levels of unemployment, significant losses of population, transition to a 'more dependent' population, and reductions in funding from central government. The table and the figures below illustrate the points which have been made in the foregoing summary.

In June 1986, the City Planning Officer, in his report, 'Urban Decline and Deprivation' reviewed five national studies concerned with the relative incidence of deprivation and/or economic performance. A number of trends were identified:

1 Urban problems associated with decline are clearly apparent in Britain;
2 Where problems of urban decline are evident they are related to the poor performance of the regional and national economies;
3 Urban decline and deprivation in Britain are strongly associated with loss of population and high unemployment;
4 The largest concentrations of deprivation occur in conurbation core cities, and particularly in Liverpool;
5 Without exception, Liverpool appears at or near the top of the deprivation league in each of the studies examined.[3]

Figure 2.6 indicates that four of six European urban regions with the highest problem scores related to these trends are British. Port cities represent a high number of those European cities with problems. The strong link between population loss and level of problems is also clear, except that in certain circumstances population growth correlates closely to a high problems level, as is the case with Southern Italian cities. Finally, what has been said in this Section is neatly summarized by Eversley and Begg in their study of 'Deprivation in the inner city'. They conclude that:

> ... falling populations are in every case associated with falling job opportunities. Both public and private investment is withdrawn. As the population loses purchasing power, retail trades and personal services decline. Private housebuilding virtually ceases. Professional services deteriorate as individual practitioners choose greener pastures. It becomes increasingly difficult to staff educational, social and health services. Relatively high concentrations of ethnic minorities, unemployed people, one parent families, tenants of unfurnished accommodation and pensioners living alone are not good for business.

Figure 2.2a: The main components of change, 1961–85

	Numbers				% Change			
	1961	1971	1981	1985	1961–71	1971–81	1981–85	1961–85
Dwellings	208,196	204,152	200,705	200,396	−1.9	−1.7	−0.2	−4.7
Households	217,594	197,628	189,158	189,622	−9.2	−4.3	−0.2	−12.9
Population	745,750	610,200	516,800	491,400	−18.2	−15.3	−4.9	−34.1
Employed	330,620	257,140	194,220	167,120	−22.2	−24.5	−14.0	−49.5
Unemployed	20,910	27,480	47,500	62,660	+31.4	+72.9	+31.9	+2000
Employment	400,940	346,094	261,374	230,617	−13.7	−24.5	−11.8	−42.5

Figure 2.2b: The main components of change, 1961–85

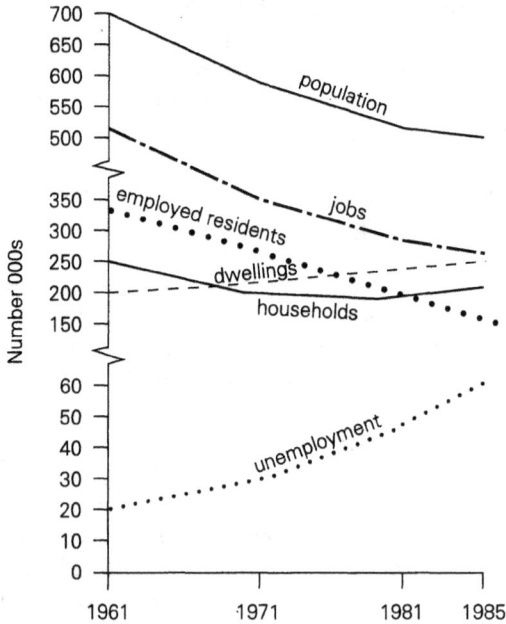

Source: Past Trends and Future Prospects (Urban Change in Liverpool 1961–2001) Liverpool City Council, February 1987

Figure 2.3:   Age group changes 1961–2000
(relative to 1961 levels = 100)

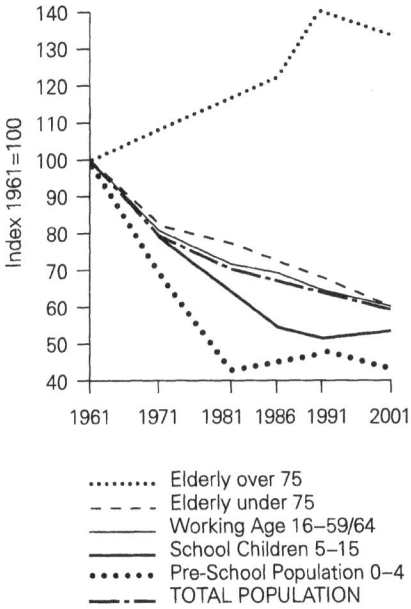

Figure 2.4:   Comparative population change,
1961–85, relative to 1961 population

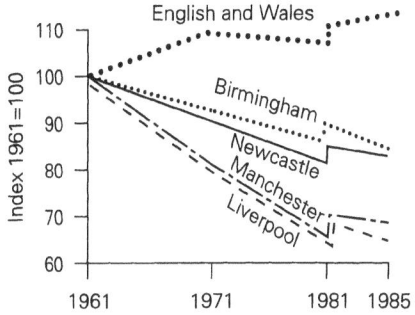

.... Elderly over 75
– – – – Elderly under 75
——— Working Age 16–59/64
——— School Children 5–15
••••• Pre-School Population 0–4
—.— TOTAL POPULATION

Figure 2.5:   Household, population and employment change (1961=100)

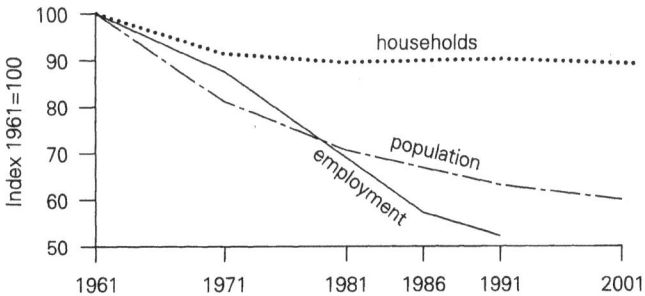

Source: Past Trends and Future Prospects (Urban Change in Liverpool 1961–2001) Liverpool
City Council, February 1987

Figure 2.6:   The relationship between population decline and severity of problems in selected functional urban regions

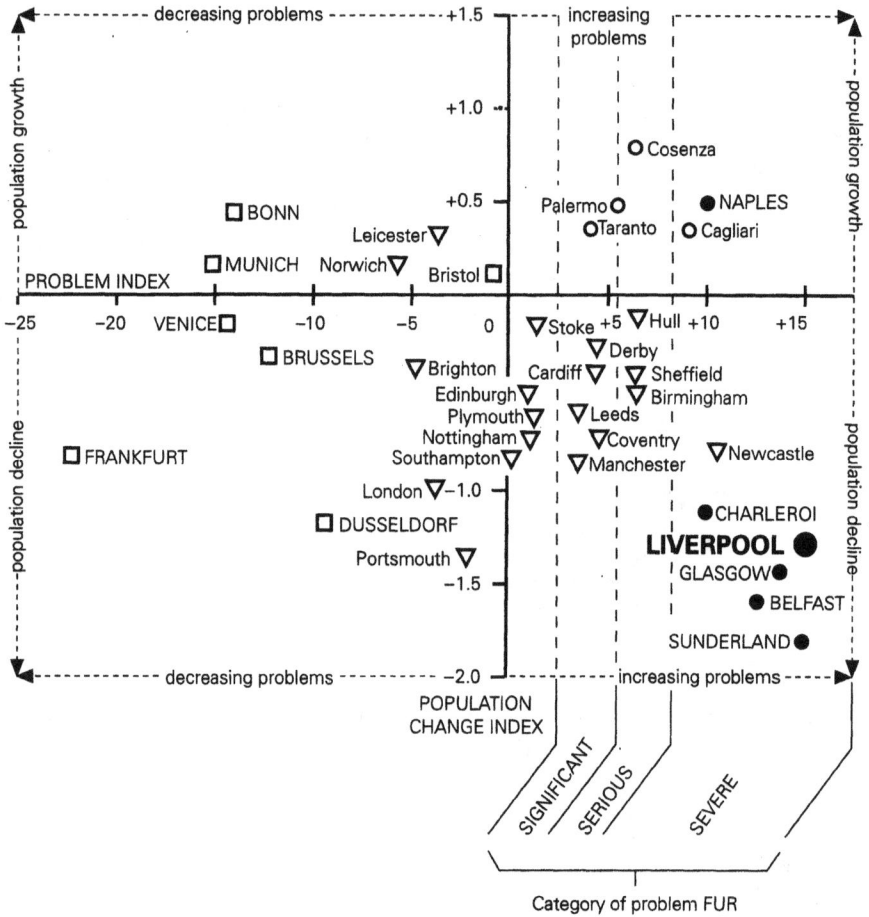

Category of problem FUR

☐ THE SIX CITIES WITH THE LOWEST PROBLEM SCORES
● THE SIX CITIES WITH THE HIGHEST PROBLEM SCORES
○ The southern Italian growing cities with 'problems'
▽ United Kingdom cities

Source: Past Trends and Future Prospects (Urban Change in Liverpool 1961–2001) Liverpool City Council, February 1987

Having considered the political, economic and social elements of the environment in which it operated, it is now important to say something of the more recent history of the Further Education service itself.

The Liverpool Further Education Service to August 1986

In 1983, Her Majesty's Inspectors and the District Audit Service undertook complementary studies of the Further Education Colleges in Liverpool. Adopting both quantitative and qualitative methods of investigation they produced individual reports on the Colleges surveyed. In September 1984, the Liverpool Education Authority produced a summary of the findings.[4] Set out below is an outline of these.

Reports of Her Majesty's Inspectorate

1 It was felt that the Education Authority should review the roles of its Colleges, their departmental structures, the re-allocation of accommodation and the replacement of physical resources *vis-à-vis* the changing needs of the City;

2 Academic staff levels in some work areas were notably generous leading to low Student:Staff ratios;

3 Accommodation was under-utilized whilst in parts there were shortages, such as student communal facilities. Split-site working militated against the unity of Colleges and could pose particular resource difficulties;

4 A modest programme of capital investment was needed for all Colleges in order to provide updated machinery and services;

5 The excellent curriculum review and development work identified in some areas needed to be extended;

6 College policies needed to be developed for the cross-curricular teaching of such subjects as General Studies, Mathematics and Computing;

7 High loss rates of students needed to be investigated.

8 There was a clear requirement for the improvement of the database relating to student enrolment patterns, student progression, drop-out and success rates (both for the Colleges and the Education Authority);

9 The presentation of examination results needed to be developed in a meaningful way;

10 The teaching methods and the resources associated with areas of high student loss needed to be reviewed;

11 The Authority and the Colleges should consider planned staff development policies — particularly in relation to new areas of teaching;

12 The Authority should consider the role of the Careers Service in Further Education; the Colleges should establish policies for careers guidance and student counselling.

Reports of the District Audit service

As Maclure and Lister[5] have pointed out, from its inception in 1983, when it was set up by the Government to secure greater value for council spending, the Audit Commission has had a firm commitment to scrutinize education, which accounts for the largest proportion of local government expenditure.

In 1983–84, the District Audit service studied a sample number of the Liverpool Colleges. Its findings were summarized by the Liverpool Authority in the same 1984 report which contained the abstract of HM Inspectorate (HMI) findings. Listed below are some of the twenty-one headings on the views of the District Audit service.

1 The major finding in every case was the under-utilization of the lecturing staff as shown by the teacher contact ratios;

2 There was a surfeit of teachers compared with the number of students available to teach;

3 There were instances in which systematic additional teaching duties (SAID), overtime and substitution pay continued to be paid even when the lecturer was under-employed on his full-time contract;

4 There appeared to be some confusion over the minimum class sizes required. Some classes were said to be small because of safety requirements, physical limitations on space, or in response to the requirements of the Manpower Services Commission (MSC). These factors did not seem to limit class sizes in other local authorities;

5 The number of teaching hours provided each week, or the number of weeks for which courses were programmed, appeared over-generous in some cases (particularly GCE 'A' level courses);

6 Courses were duplicated between Colleges and there were instances where two Colleges were providing identical courses below strength when the combined number of students would justify one course only. To avoid this duplication, some form of clearing house for student applications was required;

7 There appeared to have been a reluctance to make surplus lecturers redundant. It was suggested, therefore, that greater mobility of lecturers between Colleges was required;

8 Remission levels were quite high compared with other Colleges in the area. The basis for granting remission and the methods of monitoring it required review;

9 There were delays in submitting bills for fees, recoupments and MSC grants which involved the City Council in additional interest costs;

10 There was a lack of effective marketing. No budgetary provision

was made for advertising, and greater efforts should have been made to sell the available facilities outside the City limits;

11 Cleaning costs were higher than the national average. Staffing was based on a standard of 270 square feet per hour, which was 25 per cent lower than the standards applied elsewhere;

12 The form and content of attendance registers was variable and in many instances inadequate;

13 Control of library books seemed poor in the Colleges visited. Stock-taking was performed rarely and obsolete stock was disposed of at irregular intervals;

14 There was a lack of management information available, particularly in respect of actual student hours and lecturing hours. The information given to governors should have been greatly improved;

15 It was suggested that the ratios the District Audit calculated, based on actuals, should be reported annually to the governors and to the Director of Education.

The Reorganization of the Further Education Service, 1984–86

It is clear that some of these findings go beyond a call for good housekeeping, for example:

1 'The Education Authority should review the role of its Colleges, their departmental structure, the re-allocation of accommodation and the replacement of physical resources *vis-à-vis* the changing needs of the city'. (HMI);

2 'Accommodation was under-utilised whilst in parts shortages were being experienced'. (HMI);

3 'Courses were duplicated between Colleges and there were instances where two Colleges were providing identical courses below strength when the combined number of students would justify one course only'. (District Audit service);

4 'There appeared to have been a reluctance to make surplus lecturers redundant. It was suggested, therefore, that greater mobility of lecturers between Colleges was required'. (District Audit service).

Set out earlier in this book are details of the context within which the Colleges were now operating — the features of which were economic decline, a falling population, changes in demand and a substantial fall in the numbers of 16- to 19-year-olds. However, one recorder of the City's history[6] has pointed out that: 'The ability to think and act in a bold and comprehensive way has often been characteristic of Liverpool.' This now proved to be the case for Further Education.

Firstly, through its Education Authority, the City Council decided that the eight existing Colleges of Further Education should cease to operate on

31st August 1986 and that four new establishments would succeed them. The details were as follows:

1   A new *City College* would be formed from the Central Liverpool College of Further Education and the Colquitt Technical and Nautical Catering College;
2   *Millbrook College* would be formed from the amalgamation of the Millbank College of Commerce and the North East Liverpool Technical College;
3   The Mabel Fletcher Technical College and the Old Swan Technical College would be combined to form the new *Sandown College*, and
4   *South Mersey College* would be formed from the Riversdale College of Technology and the Childwall Hall College of Further Education.

At the same time, it was resolved that the location, viability and future development of the whole of the City's further education provision should be closely examined.

Breaking with its established policy of restricting appointments for new posts to Liverpool-serving teachers (known to the Authority and the trades unions concerned as 'the ring-fence agreement'), the posts of Principal at each of the four new Colleges were nationally advertised. Appointments to these posts were made by May 1985.

At the beginning of the 1985/86 Academic Year, the Colleges had been requested to provide details of courses and enrolments for the major areas of study (previous academic year) and to indicate broad trends (next few years). Also, through the mechanism of its Business and Technician Education Council (BTEC) Consultative and Co-ordinating Committee, and its subject subgroups, the Education Authority had attempted to monitor the development of some major vocational courses for a number of years. The reports of HMI and the District Audit service now available to it, together with the views of its own officers had appraised the Authority of the unprecedented scale and pace of change in the patterns of further education both locally and nationally. It was therefore clear that, alongside its own economic and social problems, fundamental alterations in the patterns and levels of participation were under way and were gathering momentum to an extent that demanded radical change. The establishment of four new Colleges was a major response to this but was only a single response. A major structural reorganization of Further Education was required together with a planned redistribution of resources. The analysis of market needs and the innovation of the curriculum required substantial, continuing attention. An accompanying strong focus on staff retraining and staff development would also be necessary.

Although the new Colleges would not begin to operate until 1st September 1986, the four Principals were appointed Principals-Designate with effect from 1st September 1985. They were set the task of proposing a model for the reorganization of Further Education, working in collaboration with Location of Courses/Groups and Officers of the Local Education Authority.

They were required to consult widely with Her Majesty's Inspectorate, the staff of the Colleges, students and other appropriate sources of advice and information.

It is beyond the scope of this book to discuss the planning process in detail. It is necessary, however, to discover how the pattern of provision allocated to South Mersey College was established. What follows, therefore, is an outline of the decisions taken with regard to the location, viability and future development of Further Education courses.

The criteria upon which the Principals-Designate, LEA Officers and others (hereafter called the 'Planning Group') were asked to work were as follows:

1   The Colleges should be, broadly speaking, of equal size — equating approximately to Burnham Group 7 (see p. 22);
2   Each will have a defined range of specialist areas of activity and a broadly based pattern of other provision encompassing general/ liberal, pre-vocational and adult and community educational programmes;
3   Each will have areas of work so allocated that full consideration had to be given to the future potential of the Colleges in local, national and other contexts.

A great deal of the work of the Planning Group was devoted to the proposed locations for the specialist areas of vocational study. Some of these specialist areas had to be deemed to be fixed, either because of the nature of the established facilities, because of the high capital cost of moving the facilities, or both. Marine engineering and catering provision provide the best examples of these specialist areas. Other curriculum areas were deemed to be quite mobile, whilst a third broad category included a number of areas perceived to fall between these two extremes and for which a negotiated consensus upon their ultimate location had to be achieved.

The Group was asked to consult widely and report upon its work by the beginning of November 1985. It was also required to act as a feedback device to the Authority on reactions to its proposals. Whilst it did this, its approach to reorganization was to lay to one side any obstacles to change which it did not consider educationally or financially valid, since the Authority believed that, given their head, the strong advocacy of sectional interests and appeals for preservation of the *status quo* could make more tangible impact than could calls for radical change necessitated by alterations in the boundary conditions affecting the City's Further Education system.

The details of *A recommendation for the reorganization of Further Education in Liverpool* (Figure 2.7) represent the considered judgment of the Planning Group. It was put forward as the firm and sole recommendation from the several alternatives examined. It was thought to approach most closely the objectives of broad parity of size and a balanced programme of general and specialist areas of work for each College.

Figure 2.7: A recommendation for the reorganization of Further Education in Liverpool

	Burnham Unit Totals 1984/85	
CITY		
Adult, Community)	382	
and General Education)	647	1029
Pre-Vocational Studies)		
Hairdressing and Beauty		305
Printing and Photography	349	
Art and Design	262	
Clothing and Theatre Wardrobe	669	1280
Interior Design, Furniture,)		
Timber Trades, Painting and Decorating)		
Catering, Hotel Services,)		
Bakery, Food Technology)		725
	Total:	3339
MILLBROOK		
Adult, Community)	503	
and General Education)	500	1003
Pre-Vocational Studies)		
Prison Education		68
Applied Science		664
Mechanical and Production Engineering	228	
'General' Engineering	100	
Welding and Fabrication	124	452
Business Studies	450	
Public Administration	31	
Office and Secretarial	750	1231
	Total:	3148
SANDOWN		
Adult, Community)	522	
and General Education)	186	
Pre-Vocational Studies)	180	888
Music and Drama		436
Health and Community Care		804
Electrical Engineering		427
Radio and Electronics		946
	Total:	3501
SOUTH MERSEY		
Adult, Community)	475	
and General Education)		
Pre-Vocational Studies)	588	1063
Construction and Civil Engineering		1072
Motor Vehicle Engineering		510
Navigation Studies	582	
Marine Engineering	426	1008
	Total:	3653

Explanatory Note: A minimum of 3750 Burnham Units placed a College in the Group 7 Category. Burnham Units were calculated as follows: *Category 3 Student Curricular Hours ÷ 300* and *Category 4 and 5 Student Curricular Hours ÷ 600. Category 3 Courses* = Higher Diploma/Certificate. *Category 4* = GCE 'A' Level; BTEC Diploma. *Category 5* = below Category 4, e.g. BTEC 1st Courses.

Despite what has been said earlier about certain areas of work being deemed to be fixed in location, the proposed model involved substantial transfers of technological and other work. The Group therefore recommended that a costing exercise of some refinement be carried out in relation to the proposal and, notwithstanding the fact that the availability of finance for capital projects was extremely limited, the necessary level of funding be made available by the Education Authority, subject to approval by the City Council and its Finance and Strategy Committee.

Bearing in mind the comments of HM Inspectorate and the District Audit service, the Group believed that their recommendations came closest to the educational ideal in that they appeared to ensure that key performance indicators such as quality and cost effectiveness were given proper attention whilst at the same time they provided a sound basis for the future development of further education in the City.

To demonstrate the scale of the reorganization, the list below gives specific details of the proposed relocation of course provision, including teaching and educational support staff, consumables and equipment.

Course Designation	Relocation Details (from the constituent institutions of the first named college)
Art and Design	Sandown College to City College
Clothing and Theatre Wardrobe	Sandown College to City College
Mechanical and Production Engineering	Sandown College to Millbrook College
Plant Maintenance	Sandown College to South Mersey College
Electronic and Radio Engineering	South Mersey College to Sandown College
Construction	City College to South Mersey College
Electrical Engineering	Millbrook College to Sandown College
Applied Science	Sandown College to Millbrook College

The year 1985–6, which was used for planning, was also used to discuss with the trade unions involved details of the proposed reorganization. A number of meetings were also held by each Principal Designate with those groups of staff allocated for transfer to his particular College. Whilst some teaching staff welcomed the proposed reorganization, seeing it a way of safeguarding the further education service, other staff maintained their neutrality to the proposals and others were opposed, indifferent, not to say angry. With regard to this last group, whilst the social scientist would have perceived within it some of the constructs associated with resistance to change, it has to be said that many of the fears and concerns were grounded in the political and financial crises in the City. These were now drawing the attention of the national communications media, many of whose comments were adverse.

Despite these preoccupations, however, the City Council moved swiftly and decisively to reorganize its Colleges, Firstly, it authorized the costing exercise requested by the Planning Group. This demonstrated that at least £750,000 would be required to complete the relocations listed on p. 23. Despite its grave financial situation, Council signalled that £660,000 would be made available. The proposed movements were carried out with this sum being totally expended on the two main features of the reorganization — the movement of Clothing and Theatre Wardrobe provision from Sandown College to City College, and the relocation of Electronic and Radio Engineering from South Mersey College to Sandown College. All the other features of the reorganization, including the movement of Construction courses from City College to South Mersey College, would have to be financed from the revenue estimates of the receiving College. This situation was accepted and the relocations were substantially carried out by 1 September 1986.

The Council also reaffirmed its policy of no redundancies for those already within its employment but offered premature retirement compensation (PRC) terms to those teachers wishing to retire. This resulted in a substantial reduction in teaching staff numbers (as will be demonstrated in Chapter 4 when the staffing profile of the South Mersey College is examined in some detail).

South Mersey College and Its Constituent Institutions

As a result of the reorganization, the South Mersey College was established on 1 September 1986 through the amalgamation of two of the City's eight Colleges of Further Education: the Riversdale College of Technology and the Childwall Hall College of Further Education.

The Riversdale College of Technology (opened in September 1952 as the Riversdale Technical College) was established in South Liverpool on a pleasant thirty acre site in Riversdale Road between Aigburth Road and the River Mersey. With its excellent playing fields extending down towards the Otterspool Promenade, it was the Liverpool Education Committee's first post-war project in the sphere of technical education.

The new College enabled the Education Committee to bring together a group of part-time day and evening classes, previously centred in the Toxteth Technical Institute (evening only provision) and also in temporary extensions at Garston (part-time provision for mechanical, electrical engineering and radio apprentices) and at Speke (similar provision for building crafts and motor vehicle work).

The College immediately experienced a heavy demand and with the introduction of full-time courses, a diploma course for sea-going engineers (1952) and a 'sandwich' ordinary national diploma (OND) engineering course (1953), it became clear that building extensions were already necessary. The first extension, for automobile engineering, was completed in 1960. A much larger extension became available in 1963. This provided accommodation for engineering and radio courses and for deck officer cadets attending pre-Sea and mid-Apprenticeship release courses. By the 1964–65 Academic Session, another major building extension, for Marine Engineering and Navigation was under construction. There was steady growth in all aspects of the College's activities for at least the next decade.

At the time of the Further Education reorganization in 1985, the College had six departments — Construction, Electronic and Radio Engineering, General and Automobile Engineering, Marine Engineering, Navigation and lastly — Scientific, General and Communication Studies which, largely, performed a servicing role for the other five Departments (in General and Communication Studies, Physical Education, Mathematics, Science and Computing).

The Childwall Hall College of Further Education

The Education Act of 1944 made provision for the establishment of County Colleges as an integrated part of the national system of education. The Act prescribed that, after a date to be appointed by the Minister of Education, it would be compulsory for young people between the ages of 15 and 18 years who were not otherwise receiving full-time education to attend at a County College for one day per week for the forty-four weeks in each year or for an annual equivalent period.

Subsequently, it did not prove practicable for the Minister to designate a date after which attendance at County Colleges would be compulsory. However, many local authorities, with the help of industrial and commercial organizations, began to develop, on a voluntary basis, establishments of further education at which young people of County College age attended on a part-time day basis for the continuation of their general education and training.

Soon after the end of the war, the Liverpool Education Authority received requests from several employers for part-time day continuation classes for their employees. Two Centres for this provision — at the Anfield and Garston Technical Institutes — were established in 1946. In 1947, a third

Centre was opened in Holly Bank, an old family mansion in Bankfield Road, West Derby. In the following Session (1949/50), at Anfield, full-time commercial courses in shorthand, typewriting, commerce and bookkeeping, with a balance of general education, were begun experimentally for the benefit of Secondary Modern school-leavers.

Over the next few years, the steady growth in the demand for these courses convinced the Authority that further advance could not be achieved without some measure of concentration. The Liverpool Corporation, through the generosity of the Marquess of Salisbury, had received the gift of Childwall Hall and the four and a half acres of land surrounding it. The Corporation was also able to purchase some fifty acres of parkland immediately adjacent to the site. The concept of transferring the Day Continuation Classes to the Hall was approved by the Authority and work began on the site in March, 1951. The premises were completed in the summer of 1954 and with the exception of those conducted at Sandown Hall, the Day Continuation Classes were concentrated at Childwall in August of that year. The new Childwall Hall County College (subsequently the Childwall Hall College of Further Education) was officially opened on 28th February 1955.

That it maintained, over the next three decades, essentially the same character (grounded in general education subjects and commercial skills courses) can be gathered from the fact that in the 1985–86 Session it offered:

full-time GCE 'O' and 'A' level courses;
a new 'Access to Higher Education' course for mature students;
full-time commercial courses;
the new Certificate of Pre-Vocational Education;
MSC sponsored courses for school-leavers;
and part-time courses for the unemployed.

In conclusion then, from the foregoing analysis, the following points emerge:

1   From the picture of grave, general decline it was clear that the stability and continuity of the City's further education service was threatened;
2   Extracts from the reports of Her Majesty's Inspectors and the District Audit Service indicated that for whatever reasons the service was failing its stakeholders — students, client organizations and the local community;
3   To fit the service more closely to the needs of a changing environment, the service was to be reorganized. (The reorganization process was described, and the new colleges of the service were listed);
4   The history of two of the former colleges was outlined. (These were to be constituent colleges of the new South Mersey College and their influence on its corporate culture will be apparent as we proceed).

Notes

1   LIVERPOOL CITY COUNCIL (1987) *Past Trends And Future Prospects, Urban Change in Liverpool 1961–2001*, Liverpool: City Planning Officer, pp. 2–4.
2   LIVERPOOL CITY COUNCIL (undated) *Social And Economic Change in Liverpool*, Liverpool: Public Relations and Information Unit, pp. 2–3.
3   Reported in LIVERPOOL CITY COUNCIL (1987) *Past Trends And Future Prospects, Urban Change in Liverpool 1961–2001*, reference 1 q.v., p. 31.
4   LIVERPOOL EDUCATION AUTHORITY (1984) *Further Education Management Audit Studies: 1984–5, H.M.I. And District Audit Studies — An Overview of the College Surveys*, pp. 5–7; pp. 7–16.
5   MACLURE, S. and LISTER, D. (1985) 'Demanding value for money', London: The *Times Educational Supplement*, 14, June.
6   HUGHES, Q. (1964) 'Seaport', *Architecture and Townscape in Liverpool*, London: Lund Humphries, p. ix.

Chapter 3

The Context of Further Education Provision

Environmental Turbulence

In Chapter 2 the organizational environment of a further education college was described as comprising all elements outside the boundary of the organization which have the potential to affect it. The role of the manager is to ensure that the structure and function of the organization change in a creative alignment with changing boundary conditions. In this manner, the threats posed by environmental change can be met and overcome, whilst advantage can be taken of any opportunities offered by change.

As Stoner and Freeman[1] have pointed out, when an organization operates in a stable and predictable external environment, its managers need pay only moderate attention to boundary conditions. Along with other management theorists, however, these writers indicate that, over time, environments tend to become more 'turbulent'.

Igor Ansoff,[2] a notable authority on strategic management, has described the organizational predicament as turbulence increases. Events are less predictable, changes are more frequent and experience is less relevant to current decision-making. Organizations need more time and greater knowledge of the environment in order to respond successfully. Greater resources will need to be devoted to environmental monitoring, forecasting mechanisms and strategy development.

This chapter describes major factors in the development of the environment of the Liverpool Further Education Colleges. These factors, which emerged during the four-year period of the research, indicate an increasing tendency to turbulence. They have to be taken into account so that the scale of South Mersey College's adaptation to its changing environment can be fully discerned.

The Local Education Authority was identified in Chapter 2 as an element in the College's 'task' or 'direct action' environment, thus exerting a direct influence on its actions. Following its reorganization of further education, the Liverpool Authority made a clear and comprehensive intervention in its operations. This will now be described.

Liverpool's Further Education Colleges: The Federal System

From 1984/85, having noted the comments of the District Audit Service and HMI, the Authority determined that the new Colleges would operate in an integrated manner, minimizing the risks of conflict and waste. Following the approach taken in the reorganization itself, 'federal' planning and integration became an established, continuous process.

One of the early mechanisms for collaboration came about as a result of the Government's White Paper, *Training for Jobs*[3] which was published in 1985. It diverted to the Manpower Services Commission (MSC)* an element of Rate Support Grant, which would otherwise have come to the Local Authorities. It was to be released on the conclusion and implementation of a contract for the delivery of non-advanced further education (NAFE). A Handbook of Guidance, devised by a working group comprising representatives of the Local Education Authorities (LEA), the MSC, the Department of Employment, and the Department of Education and Science (DES) was also issued to the Local Authorities in 1985.

Senior managers of the four Liverpool Colleges co-operated with each other and with the nominated LEA officer in the required planning process. They also participated in the subsequent discussions, leading up to the contractual arrangements, between the LEA and the nominated NAFE officer in the Area Office of the Training Agency. If the actual reorganization can be seen as the genesis of Liverpool's federal system of further education, the NAFE planning and consultation process was the second substantial, consolidating step.

The next significant development was the formation of the Professional Management Forum (PMF) and its associated Working Groups. The PMF was established upon the Authority's appointment of a new Senior Assistant Director of Further and Higher Education in the Autumn Term of 1987. The terms of reference of the PMF were as follows:

- To consider issues common to the Further Education Colleges and to make recommendations on these, as appropriate, to the Director of Education;
- To decide upon appropriate courses of action, in the common interest, on all matters delegated to it by the Council's FE Sub-Committee

* later to become the Training Agency.

or Director of Education and to exercise authority for implementing such decisions;
- To respond, as appropriate, on behalf of the Colleges' federal system, to local, regional and national demands for comment and assistance;
- To work collaboratively in order to develop and support the LEA's management information systems, curriculum and staff development projects and other further education affairs;
- To provide a framework within which the FE Service could operate effectively;
- To determine the scope and direction of programmes and initiatives;
- To create such working parties and sub-groups as were necessary for the effective and efficient discharge of its terms of reference;
- To receive the reports and recommendations of its working parties and sub-groups and to act on these, as appropriate.

The membership of the PMF was constituted as follows:

- The Principals and Vice Principals of the four FE Colleges;
- The Assistant Education Officers of the Authority;
- The FE Advisers of the Authority;
- The Chief Assistant (Administration) of the Authority's FE Section;
- The Authority's Principal Administrative Officer (FE);
- The Head of the Authority's Careers Department;
- The Senior Assistant Director (Further and Higher Education), who would act as Chair;
- The Senior Assistant (Administration) of the FE Section, who would act as Secretary.

(Additionally, the PMF had power to invite and co-opt as necessary). The meetings of the PMF were to take place monthly during each Academic Session (and this requirement was carefully observed).

Four Working Parties were established, reporting to the Professional Management Forum (PMF), to cover the areas of:

- The LEA's Non-Advanced Further Education (NAFE) Development Plan and Programme;
- The Publicity and Marketing of NAFE provision;
- The initiation and support of Curriculum innovation and development;
- Finance and Administration, including appropriate information systems.

The structure depicted below was initially established to cover the LEA's NAFE Development Plan and Programme but its activities were then extended to cover all the provision of the four Colleges.

Figure 3.1:   The professional management forum (PMF) and its working groups

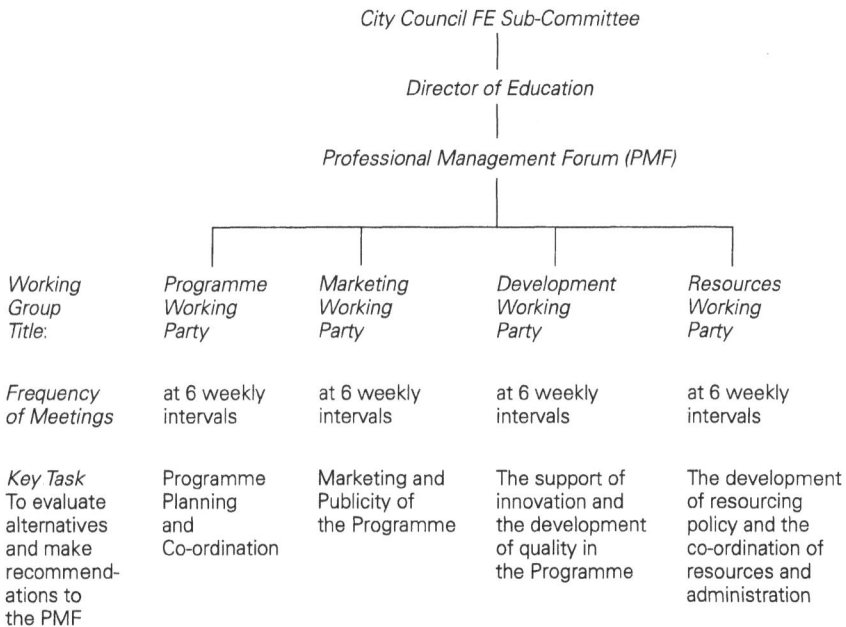

City Council FE Sub-Committee
|
Director of Education
|
Professional Management Forum (PMF)
|

Working Group Title:	Programme Working Party	Marketing Working Party	Development Working Party	Resources Working Party
Frequency of Meetings	at 6 weekly intervals	at 6 weekly intervals	at 6 weekly intervals	at 6 weekly intervals
Key Task To evaluate alternatives and make recommend-ations to the PMF	Programme Planning and Co-ordination	Marketing and Publicity of the Programme	The support of innovation and the development of quality in the Programme	The development of resourcing policy and the co-ordination of resources and administration

The terms of reference of these Working Groups, together with details of their membership are included in Appendices 1 to 4 (See pp. 194–198.). It will be seen from these that South Mersey College was represented in each of these (in effect, at the Vice Principal level).

Whilst it is not an objective of this book to describe all the detail of Liverpool's 'federal system' of further education, it is important to establish beyond doubt that it was a highly significant operational feature of the role of College managers. Some further detail is therefore necessary.

The collective activities of the four Colleges expanded significantly as a result of the Education Reform Act (1988). More will be said about the Act, but at this point, it would be useful to quote from Murray-Smith[4] who described the Act's influence on the contractual arrangements for the delivery of non-advanced further education (NAFE) as follows:

This Act has given LEAs the responsibility to plan all post-compulsory education and to produce a strategic plan for this work. This planning requirement clearly undermined the existing agreements between LEAs and the Training Agency as it no longer gave Authorities the responsibility to plan at course level and as a consequence the Training Agency to monitor or contract at course level. However

31

the TA does retain, for the time being anyway, the RSG (Rate Support Grant) element mentioned previously.

He goes on to explain how, in order to meet the planning requirements of the Education Reform Act, Liverpool LEA established a series of Programme Planning Groups, which would inform the Authority of developments in specific subject areas and also take part in the important task of setting and agreeing target student numbers for their programme areas, thus influencing the size and nature of the budgets of the four Colleges.

The list below indicates the classification of subject areas used for the establishment of these Programme Planning Groups.

Three other points should be noted:

1　These classifications were used by the LEA in allocating student numbers to Colleges within the LEA's programme planning for further education;

2　The arithmetic weightings set out to the right of each Programme Area were used to distribute funding to the Colleges based on the student number allocations;

3　These programme area groupings were consistent with the Training Agency's Training Occupation Categories (TOC) so that a high level of consistency with the Training Agency's requirements for Work Related Further Education (WRFE, previously referred to as NAFE) could be maintained.

	Programme Area	*Weighting*
1	Administrative and Clerical	1.15
2	Craft, Creative and Performing Arts	1.25
3	Caring, Social Work, Welfare, Health, Paramedical, Science and Horticulture	1.10
4	Service Industries	1.40
5	Construction	1.35
6	Engineering	1.40
7	General Education	1.00
8	Special Needs	2.00
9	Adult Basic Education	1.20
10	Community Education	1.10

In addition to these programme area groups a number of groups were to be formed to advise the area groups. The following table indicates the areas covered by these Cross-Sector Groups.

It would be possible to continue to describe the 'federal system' at some length, but it is beyond the scope of this book to do so. Perhaps enough has been said to establish the fact that the system was more than a loose federation of common interest. It was an extensive, purposive, decision-making apparatus which reached into every aspect of the College's activities and demanded a large proportion of Senior Management time. Appendix 5 is an extract from the Principal's diary and it indicates that between 18 April and 20 October 1988 he made no fewer than forty-nine visits to the LEA Offices in Sir Thomas Street and other addresses in Central Liverpool for discussions on federal issues. To these must be added the visits to the other Colleges for the same purpose, in order to obtain a complete picture of the demands on his management time. The pattern thus indicated was typical of the month by month external commitments imposed by the federal system. Moreover, following the news of the Education Reform Act (1988), this pattern intensified.

CROSS-SECTOR (ADVISORY) GROUPS
1   Information Technology
2   Enterprise (Marketing. PICKUP)
3   Equal Opportunities (Race, Gender, Special Needs)
4   Basic Education
5   Youth Training Scheme (YTS)
6   Pre-vocational Schemes
7   Open and Flexible Learning

In addition to programme planning, the determination and allocation of the federal and the Colleges' budgets and the establishment of management information systems, the Colleges collaborated very closely on numerous matters including staff development; quality control and institutional effectiveness; the planning and delivery of joint courses; the College calendar; shared use of accommodation and staffing; bids for external funding (for example European Social Fund: DES Capital Programme: Urban Programme; the Work-related FE Development Fund): the Post-16 Educational Consortia; the Certificate of Pre-Vocational Education (CPVE); the Technical and Vocational Initiative (TVEI): the Labour Market Information project (LMI) and the National Record of Vocational Achievement (NROVA) project.

None of these activities was spasmodic. They were part of a planned, continuous programme which took up a great deal of the time and energies of the relatively small senior management teams (eight per College, including the Chief Administration Officer) and other managers in the system. Though there was some streamlining of the existing committees in the federal system, towards the end of the 1980s, new issues and new developments constantly increased the pressure for the formation of committees and working groups. By the time the 1980s ended, the federal system comprised at least forty committees and working parties reporting directly and indirectly to the Professional Management Forum (PMF).

It is not the purpose of this book to pass judgment on the structure and functions of the federal system. It has to be borne in mind that the Colleges reaped a number of benefits of the federal system for the costs it entailed. Appendix 6, which relates to a programme of staff development concerned with the Single European Act (1992), gives some indication of the level of integration achieved by the federal system. Staff development was one area of very many in which a high level of planning and implementation was achieved.

The development of the federation was only one of a number of environmental forces affecting the work of the College management after the reorganization of 1985/86. Some of these other main environmental developments are now described.

The Education Reform Act

On 7th August 1987, the Department of Education and Science issued a Green Consultative Paper[5] indicating that the Government intended to include, in a forthcoming Education Bill, provisions on maintained further education. Comments were invited on the Paper. They were to be with the Department by 9th October 1987. An outline of the proposals is set out below:

1 It was the Government's view that the maintained FE Sector had a key part to play in equipping young people with the skills, knowledge and qualities needed for adult and working life, and in producing the highly trained, adaptable work force on whom continuing prosperity depended. (para. 1.4).

2 It recognized the achievements of the maintained FE Sector and the extent to which it had already adapted to meet new needs among both students and employers. But it believed that there was still scope for further reform, particularly in the way colleges were managed. (para. 1.6).

3 The Government therefore proposed to include in the Education Bill, which it intended to bring before Parliament that Autumn, provisions to place a duty on LEAs to delegate extensive financial powers to their FE colleges and reform the composition and role of FE college governing bodies so as to make them more independent and effective.

In order to provide a sound legal basis for these reforms, the Government proposed, within the Bill 'to clarify the law of further education' (para. 1.7) Part 2 of the consultative document outlined the proposals for financial delegation. Extracts from this Section are set out below:

1 The Government believes that LEA provided schools and colleges should be given as much freedom as possible to manage their own affairs and decide their own priorities for spending the resources allocated to them. (para. 2.1)

2 The Government therefore proposes that each LEA should be under a duty to devise and submit to the Secretary of State a scheme for delegating to its FE colleges extensive financial powers and responsibilities within a continuing framework of strategic planning by the LEA. (para. 2.3)

3 It will therefore be a key element in delegation schemes that each LEA should review each year what changes should be made to the existing pattern of provision so as to keep it in line with changing student and employer needs, and should work out what each college should contribute. (para. 2.4)

4 The Government intends that once each college's annual budget has been set, the governing body should be given maximum freedom to determine how it should be spent. In particular, it considers that:
   i   Governing bodies should be free to vire across all current expenditure headings ...
   ii Governing bodies should not be obliged either to make use of LEA common services and common purchasing arrangements — although it is to be expected that governing bodies would decide to make their own arrangements only where they could thereby obtain a better deal ...
   iii Governing bodies should have as much freedom to carry forward from one financial year to the next surpluses and deficits as prudent management allows ...
   iv Colleges should be able to retain a sufficient proportion of income earned through, for example, full-cost courses to ensure that there is an incentive to maximise such income. (para. 2.6)

5 The Government intends that as an integral part of delegation, governing bodies should be given greater powers over the appointment and dismissal of teaching and non-teaching staff. (para. 2.8)

6 Financial delegation would not affect the basic framework and provision of agreements, national or local, currently in force on pay and conditions for college staff. But subject to such agreements, and to the overall constraints of their budgets ... governing bodies would be free to determine the numbers and grading of

teaching and non-teaching staff posts without reference to the LEA. (para. 2.9)

7   In order to ensure proper accountability, the Government proposes that all delegation schemes should include a requirement on governing bodies to supply the LEA with such information as it needs to be able to monitor the college's progress. The report of the Joint Efficiency Study of NAFE provides guidance on data. . . . Such information would be taken into account when assessing each college's performance for the purpose of setting the following year's budget. (para. 2.14)

8   All colleges with more than 200 FTE students (as measured by the latest FESR data) would be included in FE delegation schemes. (para. 2.18)

Part 3 of the consultation paper dealt with College Governing Bodies. Here are some of its main proposals:

1   The Government attaches great significance to the role of governing bodies. . . . But to be fully effective they need to be independent, their membership needs to be properly balanced and they need to be assured a worthwhile and clearly defined part to play in determining the conduct and direction of the institution. (para. 3.1)

2   [The] governing bodies of all LEA maintained colleges with more than 200 FTE students should number between 20 and 25 members. . . . at least half the members should represent business, industrial, professional and other employment interests, including trade unionists and practitioners in areas relevant to the work of the college. (para. 3.3)

3   A typical governing body might be composed of:
    12   representatives of business, industrial, professional and other employment interests including not more than 2 from trade unions
    4   representatives of the LEA
    2   representatives of parents
    2   members drawn from neighbouring educational institutions
    2   representatives of the staff (teaching and non-teaching)
    1   representative of the students
    1   Principal
    24   Total. (para. 3.6)

4   [The] primary responsibilities of the new governing bodies would
    be:
    i   Responsibility for the general direction of the college.
    ii   Responsibility for the efficient management of the college with
         the sort of financial delegation regime sketched in part 2.
    iii Responsibility for the selection and dismissal of staff within
         the framework outlined in paragraphs 2.8–2.11 of the con-
         sultation document.

Part 4 of the paper dealt briefly with the Law of Further Education. It
made the point that while the necessary legal provisions would be incorporated in the Education Bill, which the Government would introduce in
Parliament in the Autumn ... 'at the same time the apparently unsatisfactory
state of the existing legal basis of further education will need to be put right'.
(para. 4.1)

Because of the many changes which had taken place since the approval
of LEA schemes in the years following the 1944 Education Act, a Working
Group had concluded in 1981 that much FE provision was almost certainly
ultra vires. The duty currently laid on local authorities relating to FE provision would be retained, but the Government proposed that the provisions of
the 1944 Act relating to FE schemes should be repealed, together with the
obsolete provisions relating to county colleges.

Implications of the Act for South Mersey College

The proposals of the Green Paper went on to the Statute Book[6] as the
Education Reform Act 1988. The amount of planning and preparatory work
the Colleges then had to undertake in conjunction with the Authority meant
that the 'federal' pressures on management were significantly increased.
Among the issues requiring sustained contact and collaboration were these:

* The Authority's scheme of planning and delegation related to the
  Act;
* the revised Instrument and Articles of Government of the College(s);
* procedures for the determination of College Budgets in the light of
  LEA strategic plans;
* procedures for reserving funds for capital expenditure and major
  structural maintenance;
* the costs of specified LEA administration and advisory services;
* the main powers of Governing bodies in relation to delegated
  budgets;
* competitive tendering requirements and the discretion of the Colleges as regards the use of LEA provided common services.

Managing Colleges Efficiently: The Joint Efficiency Study

The Steering Group which produced this study commenced work in 1985 and reported in July 1987. Its main participants were representatives of the Government (Department of Education and Science) and the Local Authorities (The Association of County Councils and the Association of Metropolitan Authorities).

A document fundamentally related to the report was the Audit Commission's *Obtaining Better Value from Further Education.*

The brief for the Joint Efficiency Study was as follows:

- To evaluate the past and current efficiency of the FE Service, within the limitations of the data available;
- to consider the validity of current performance indicators and measures of efficiency and to suggest values that might be appropriate for the future;
- to recommend means of improving the efficiency of the service and its evaluation with a programme for implementation.

As to indicators of efficiency, the report emphasized the need for objectives to be defined, against which the performance of the establishment could be compared. Units of measurement of input and output should be established uniformly employed by all agencies. Indicators should take account of qualitative as well as quantifiable values. All non-teaching costs should be evaluated as a major contribution to the measurement of efficiency, including staff, equipment, supplies, services and premises.

The general adoption of the Student:Staff Ratio (SSR) as a measure of efficiency was acknowledged and its continued application as a significant indicator was anticipated. It was recommended that agreed targets should be set for the efficiency indicators and used in the allocation of resources to and within colleges.

The report concluded that there was room for improvement of the current SSR over the whole range by the 1991/92 Annual Monitoring Survey of the DES. (The 1985/86 survey has shown a range of SSR outcomes, from below 9.1:1 to above 14:1, with some Art and Design Faculties as high as 17:1). It was suggested that those colleges currently operating at 9:1 should be able to increase that value to 10.4:1 whilst those in the upper 25 per cent should be able to increase from >11.2:1 to > 12.0:1 in the same time scale. The average value was expected to improve from 10.3:1 to 11.4:1 with no detriment to the quality of the service.

The implications for SSR and staffing were that, assuming an SSR target of 11.4:1, the staffing requirement in 1991/92 would be 49,000 FTE lecturers compared to the 60,000 in post in 1986. The report considered the range of data required by the colleges, LEAs, the DES and other external agencies in evaluating the attainment of performance targets and efficiency, making the following observations and recommendations:

1   Data required should be consistent in detail across the range of requesting agencies and should be useful to the college for its own management processes;
2   Reasons for data being required should be explicable and results should be published promptly in a form useful to colleges and LEAs.

The group acknowledged that the effective collection and processing of the increased amount of data required was unlikely to be possible without computerized systems which would take time to purchase and establish. It was recommended that all colleges should be operating suitable computerized management information systems within five years and that Education Departments and the Manpower Services Commission should contribute to their establishment.

The report acknowledged the potential costs of such developments in equipment, software and staff training, but highlighted the grants made available and the long-term benefits that would accrue. (Caution was advised to ensure that the demands of new management information systems did not impose additional administrative and clerical duties on teaching staff.)

The Education Reform Act of 1988 and the requirements of the Joint Efficiency Study constituted major environmental changes for FE Colleges. These changes did not end there, however, and one other major change will now be outlined.

The National Council for Vocational Qualifications

The Council was set up by the Government in 1986. Government's view was that economic growth and competitiveness depended upon the development of a well-trained and properly qualified national workforce. The Council was therefore to act as an 'engine of change' for the reform of the system of vocational qualifications in England, Wales and Northern Ireland. According to the Council's own literature.[7]

The new system covers all sectors of employment and all types of occupation, from basic to senior professional. Its purpose is to improve people's performance at work, as well as their personal progress, through National Vocational Qualifications (NVQs) which are based on the standards of competence needed in employment — and which are widely understood and prized by employees and employers alike.

Since in 1986 there were over 1.75 million awards offered each year by some 300 different examining bodies, there was a clear need for an integrated, coherent national system, which the Council (NCVQ) was set up to devise and operate.

NCVQ was not to be an examining body. Nor would it validate awards. Organizations such as the Business and Technician Education Council (BTEC), the Royal Society of Arts (RSA), the City and Guilds of London Institute (CGLI) and the numerous professional bodies would continue to operate. If their schemes satisfied NVQ criteria, the NCVQ would give accreditation to these organizations.

NVQs: The Criteria

The name and style NVQ would be accorded by the Council to vocational qualifications accredited and awarded by those bodies approved by Council. The criteria for NVQs can be deduced from the following statement:[8]

> The standards for NVQs are set by employers, trades unions and professions acting together on behalf of their employment sectors in lead bodies. These standards are based on the real needs of occupations in each sector. They specify the necessary skills, knowledge and understanding, as well as the performance that has to be assessed to ensure that holders of NVQs can actually do the required jobs.

The NCVQ would seek to ensure that a vocational qualification was a standard of competence — skills, knowledge, understanding and ability in application — needed to facilitate entry into, or progression in employment and/or further education. Learning achievements within and outside education and training institutions, such as work-based learning were to be recognized. There were a minimum of constraints on access to vocational qualifications, and there were to be clear relationships between vocational qualifications with awards given at the following testable levels: 'basic', 'standard', 'advanced' and 'higher', with an eventual fifth level linked to professional qualifications. The levels would relate to the attainment of competences and not to time periods.

By September 1989 there were over one hundred lead bodies in different sectors of employment at work setting standards under the sponsorship of the Training Agency. NCVQ aimed to develop a system by which individuals could gain an NVQ by accumulating credits for achievement in parts of the qualification over time. The lead bodies would determine which existing qualifications should be approved and what development work was required. As a Liverpool Education paper[9] pointed out, there were from the onset a number of projects under way linked to the recognition of work-based learning. NCVQ would enter discussions with the Secondary Examinations Council regarding linkages between academic levels, such as GCSE and GCE 'A' levels, and vocational qualifications.

In conclusion then, this chapter has more specifically described the environmental influences on the Liverpool further education colleges showing how these were developing increasing 'turbulence'. Factors in this included the intervention of the Local Education Authority, as an element in the 'direct-action' environment, through the establishment and operation of the 'federal system'. In their analysis of organizational environments, Stoner and Freeman[10] have indicated that 'outer layer' or indirect action elements, such as the politics of a society, affect the climate in which an organization operates and *have the potential to become direct-action elements* (author's emphasis).

Through its White Paper, *Training for Jobs* (DES, 1985); the Education Reform Act (DES, 1988); the Joint Efficiency Study of 1987 and the establishment of the National Council for Vocational Qualifications (NCVQ) in 1986, the Government became a direct environmental influence upon the further education service in no uncertain manner.

Notes

1 STONER J.A.F. and FREEMAN, R.E. (1989) *Management*, 4th Edition, Englewood Cliffs, New Jersey: Prentice-Hall International, Inc., p. 69.
2 ANSOFF, H.I. (1981) *Strategic Management*, New York, New York: Halsted Press.
3 DEPARTMENT OF EMPLOYMENT/DEPARTMENT OF EDUCATION AND SCIENCE (1984) *Training for Jobs*, Cmnd. 9135, London: HMSO.
4 MURRAY-SMITH, D. (1990) 'Organisation for planning agreements', Paper read at Seminar on the Strategic Plan for Further Education, City College, Canning Place, Liverpool, 19 January.
5 DEPARTMENT OF EDUCATION AND SCIENCE (1987) *Maintained Further Education: Financing, Governance and Law*, August, London: DES.
6 DEPARTMENT OF EDUCATION AND SCIENCE (1988) *Education Reform Act, 1988*, Chapter 40, London: HMSO.
7 NATIONAL COUNCIL FOR VOCATIONAL QUALIFICATIONS (1989) *Towards A Qualified Society*, September, London: NCVQ.
8 Ibid.
9 LIVERPOOL EDUCATION AUTHORITY (1987) *National Council for Vocational Qualifications* (Educ/278/1987), Paper prepared for Further Education Sub-Committee, 24 September, 1987, p. 2.
10 STONER, J.A.F. and FREEMAN, R.E. (1989) Op. cit., p. 70.

Chapter 4

The Formation of South Mersey College

Strategic Analysis

Strategic decisions are those decisions which determine the scope of an organization's activities, and as Johnson and Scholes[1] have indicated, strategy is really to do with the matching of the activities of an organization to the environment in which it operates.

As has been outlined earlier, the environment in which the new FE Colleges would operate was in no sense stable and contained many threatening features, including a declining population (the reduction being most marked among its younger segments), increasing unemployment, a declining industrial base and a reducing resource base, mainly as a result of changes in national Government policies for local authority funding.

It was the primary task of the senior management of South Mersey College to devise a strategic response which would assist the creative alignment of the College with its environment en route to survival and hopefully, growth. At its most basic, the process of objective setting consists of 'strategic analysis' and 'strategic choice' derived from the answers to these questions:

- Where are we now?
- Where are we going?
- How will we get there?
- When will we get there?
- How will we know when we've arrived?

The answer to the first question was fundamentally provided by the performance indicators of the two constituent institutions immediately prior to their amalgamation. Figure 4.1 gives a detailed picture of the Burnham Unit totals achieved by each Department of the Riversdale College of Technology for the ten year period immediately prior to the FE reorganization.

*Figure 4.1:   Riversdale College of Technology: Departmental unit totals (Burnham FE) —
1974/5 to 1983/4*

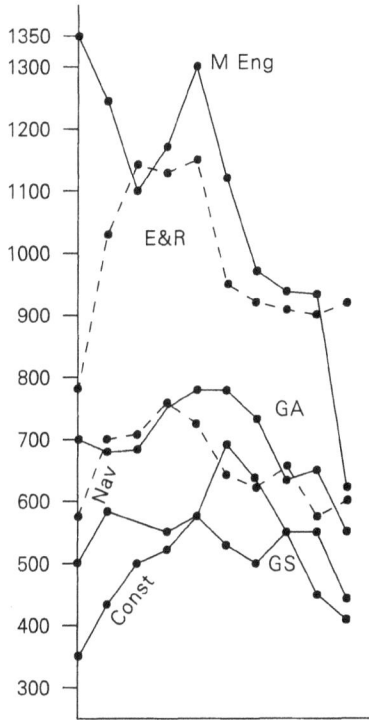

Legend

M Eng — Marine Engineering
E&R — Electronic and Radio
GA — General and Automobile Engineering
Nav — Navigation
GS — General Studies
Const — Construction

Figure 4.2 depicts the student curricular hours attained by Childwall College
in the seven years leading up to the reorganization. In both cases, a picture
of grave, general decline emerges which needs no elaboration.

A fixed and important factor in the strategic analysis preceding the formulation of a strategy for diversification and growth was the policy decision
of the City Council that the College's provision would be based upon:

1   the specialist areas of activity allocated to it in the FE
    reorganization: —

Figure 4.2: *Childwall Hall College of Further Education: Student curricular hours (thousands)*
— 1978/9 to 1984/5

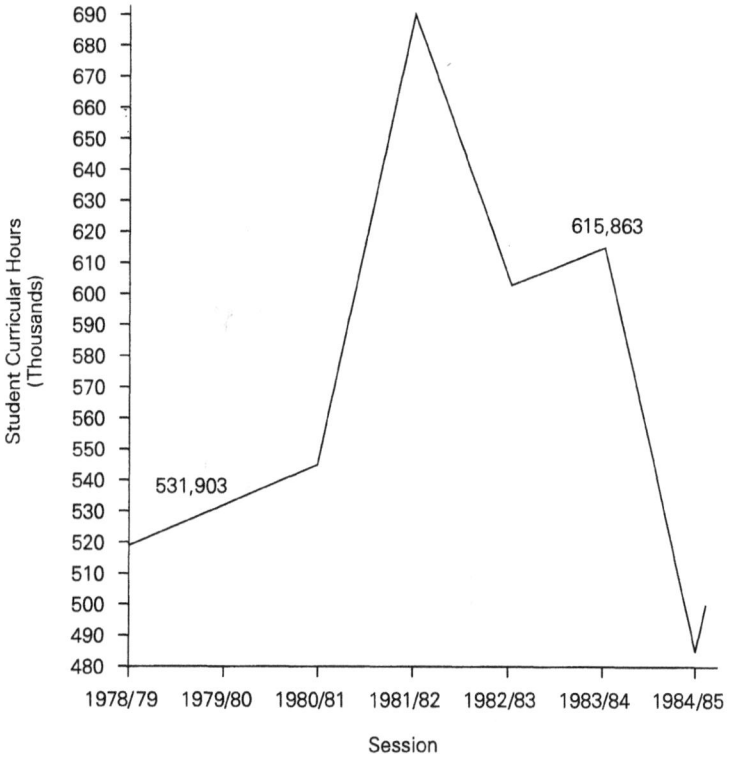

Construction and Civil Engineering;
Motor Vehicle Engineering;
Navigation Studies;
Marine Engineering;
2 the development of a broadly based pattern of community provision
encompassing general/liberal, pre-vocational and adult education
programmes.

Management realised that in order to provide a framework for action it was
necessary to refine and deepen these aims. The Principal recognized that
many of the constraints that had hindered change, and would continue to do
so, stemmed from the environment itself (government legislation, economic
and demographic forces, the emergence of powerful private sector competitors and so on) and from the particular circumstances of Liverpool itself,
resulting in lack of finance for the promotion of courses and for the renewal

of existing equipment and the provision of new equipment, particularly relating to information technology.

At the same time, he understood there was a growing theoretical real-
ization[2] that the strategy of an organization was fundamentally influenced by
its culture — the set of key values, beliefs, understandings and norms of
behaviour shared by the members of an organization.

In the work of Miles and Snow[3] for example, organizations in which the
prevailing beliefs are essentially conservative, where low-risk strategies, secure markets and well-tried solutions are valued, have been classified as
'defender'-type organizations. Those organizations in which the dominant beliefs had more to do with innovation and breaking new ground, in which management was more predisposed to higher-risk strategies and the quest for
new opportunities have been classified as 'prospector'-type organizations. In
'defender'-type organizations the value-systems derive from historical stability and consensus; in 'prospector'-type the organizations derive from growth
and change and, if necessary, from dissension rather than consensus.

During the year in which he had been Principal Designate there had
been an extended opportunity for the Principal of the new College to observe
and assess the types of culture which prevailed in the constituent Colleges —
Riversdale and Childwall.

Using these classifications, and no doubt because it was justly proud of
its former eminence as a maritime training establishment Riversdale might
well be perceived as a 'defender' type organization. Since the early 1950s, the
College had gained a world-wide reputation for its output of competent and
highly-skilled deck officers and marine engineers. However, the rise of containerization and airfreight had now reduced the world's shipping fleets to a
fraction of their former scale, resulting in marked diminution of the College's
former main client-base. The main stories of organizational history concerned
the visits of the shipping companies before each Academic Session with their
open cheque-books and requests for the maximum number of places for their
officer-cadets. Stories were also told of the cleanliness and order of the College
campus in former days, where these naval cadets marched in echelon to
classrooms and workshops, with a fixed weekly 'fatigues' period given over
to cleaning and tidying the campus.

Many of the cultural symbols were still in place — the large anchor
outside the teaching block reserved for maritime studies; a boatshop with a
motor-vessel located outside it; the manner in which many of the teaching
staff referred to each other by their former naval ranks; the way in which on
occasions a staff work-room was referred to as a cabin.

An observer could perceive that, for many of the teaching staff, the
unwritten informal norms that bound them together as organizational members were rooted in the College's naval tradition. This tradition provides an
explanation why the College's own frame of reference appeared to be well
beyond the City of Liverpool and why Riversdale was perceived by many as
being somewhat outside the City's further education service. The Principal

had also had the advantage of being in residence at the College for two years after taking up his assignment as Principal Designate in 1985. Through the network of social contacts he built up via retail, church and other organizations he was able to assess the perception of the College by a significant number of residents in its immediate catchment area. Uniformly, the College was respected for its reputation as a naval training establishment, but beyond this, or perhaps because of this, it was not clearly seen as being a facility for the community.

It was also important to note that the content of most current courses was provided by external (validating) organizations: the Business and Technician Education Council; the Department of Transport; GCE Examining Boards, etc. In consequence it appeared that many members of the teaching staff had no direct personal experience of the process of course development or of appropriate models or constructs for this activity.

Another significant factor deriving from the culture, emanated from the past professional experience of many of the teachers. As naval officers they had operated in a milieu whose concept of command and leadership was grounded on the principle of strict obedience to orders and unquestioned deference to the wisdom of superiors. By contrast, the new environmental pressures on the College were such that, in the words of the Principal Designate, it now needed 'not so much good officers as a few creative anarchists'. Nevertheless, observation made crystal clear the undoubted strengths available at Riversdale in the technical/vocational field. Harnessed to clear objectives and market opportunities these could constitute a powerful competitive weapon.

The staff at the former Childwall College had impressed HM Inspectors and other external assessors with the care and concern for the community, particularly its disadvantaged sections, which they had exhibited in their development of the curriculum. Her Majesty's Inspectors had advised the Principal Designate that if this community ethos could be wedded to the technological skills of Riversdale, the new College would be well placed to take advantage of changing patterns of demand. At the same time Her Majesty's Inspectors had expressed the view that there was no long-term future for Childwall's provision at its present site, not least because of its chronic roofing problems. Moreover, access to the College buildings was by way of a long unlit drive, which was an inhibitor of evening classes, particularly for women students.

Childwall could be classified as a 'prospector-type' organization (American studies, media studies and access to higher education courses were Childwall innovations which would subsequently assist the new College to make its mark). At the same time, however, the culture was in some respects rather inward-looking. The staff, for example, could not visualize moving from the site, which was near the boundaries of the City and therefore somewhat physically detached from the other Colleges of Further Education. The culture appeared to the Principal Designate to incorporate the features of the sociological concept of the 'isolated mass'. There was strong cohesion among group members, a clear sense of organizational identity, some mistrust of outside influences and a reinforcement of group members' behaviour, one to another, in this regard. As will be seen later this culture was to manifest itself most markedly when it was decided to concentrate all the College's provision on the Riversdale campus.

However, deriving from his year-long observation of the Riversdale and Childwall cultures, the Principal Designate had a clear, abiding, positive impression. It was that, if the technical and vocational strengths of the former could be annealed onto the community ethos of the latter making use of the excellent staff on both sites, it would produce a powerful synergistic effect which would offer the new College good prospects for survival and growth.

Strategic Choice

Following the processes of observation and analysis, management now had to guide the College's approach to an appropriate organization structure, to policy objectives and their implementation, and to the co-ordination of effort.

The question now was what conceptual framework was to be employed to undertake such tasks. If a particular leadership style was to be adopted, could it be supported by any interpretive theory? This is not to suggest that change resulted from any organizational grand design. For even where substantial strategic change is needed, it is often the case that the action required is outside the scope of the cultural recipe and the constraints of the cultural web. Strategies which are elegant analytically are sterile without an understanding of the processes actually at work. Mintzberg's historical studies of organizations[4] over many decades have demonstrated that global change is infrequent. Rather do organizations change incrementally. This was to be the case at South Mersey College. What follows is a commentary on the concepts which structured management's thinking during this process.

Open Systems Theory

Firstly, management believed that the view of an organization provided by a static organization chart and reflected in the structural dimensions of organizations was crucially incomplete and did not provide a comprehensive enough picture for co-ordination and control. A more satisfactory conceptualization could be derived from systems theory and particularly, from the open-system approach to organization analysis.

As Katz and Kahn[5] have described it, the open-system approach contrasts with common-sense approaches which tend to accept popular names and stereotypes as basic organizational properties and to identify the purpose of an organization in terms of the goals of its founders and leaders.

The open-system approach, on the other hand, begins by identifying and mapping the repeated cycles of input, transformation, output and renewed input which comprise the organizational pattern. This approach to organizations represents the adaptation of work in biology and in the physical sciences by von Bertalanffy and others. In its simplest form, an open system involves an input, a transformation process and an output. As Robertson and Cooper[6] indicate, a closed system, by contrast, does not involve inputs and outputs and is independent of external forces. Organizations which are part of the social and economic fabric of the environment in which they exist should clearly be represented as open systems. Figure 4.3 represents the open-system view of a further education college.

Figure 4.3: A view of a College of Further Education as an open system

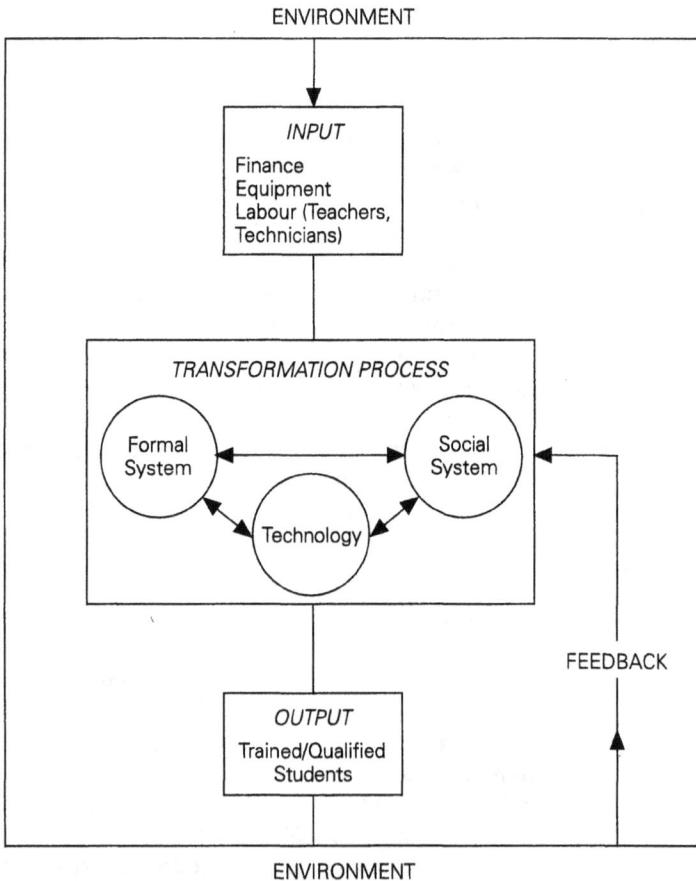

ENVIRONMENT

INPUT
Finance
Equipment
Labour (Teachers, Technicians)

TRANSFORMATION PROCESS

Formal System

Social System

Technology

FEEDBACK

OUTPUT
Trained/Qualified Students

ENVIRONMENT

Central to the concept of open systems is the notion of feedback which furnishes information to the organization about the environment. By monitoring changes in the environment and with consequential adjustments in its own structure and functions, the organization maintains itself or achieves homeostasis or 'steady state'. Reverting to biological processes, the steady state is seen in clear form in the homeostatic processes for the regulation of the body temperature: external conditions of humidity and temperature may vary, but the temperature of the body remains the same.

The College management was aware that organizational psychologists and sociologists had made use of systems concepts to study organizations at various levels of analysis. It found the approach appealing, intuitively and intellectually, not only because it made proposals about the properties of systems and the processes involved in system survival, growth and decay, but also because of its emphasis upon the importance of feedback. Management felt the feedback principle valuable, because it highlighted the relationship between environmental analysis and judicious use of resources, and because it provided important insights for the processes of curriculum development. Illustrations of how management made use of these concepts will be provided in later chapters.

Another body of concepts utilized by management derived from the work of Burns and Stalker[7] and that of Lawrence and Lorsch.[8] In collaboration with psychologist Stalker, sociologist Burns studied the attempt to introduce electronics development work into traditional Scottish firms with a view to entry into that industry as the markets for their own well-established products diminished. The difficulties which the firms faced in adjusting to the new situation of continuously changing technology and markets led Burns to describe two ideal types of management organization which are the extreme points of a continuum along which most organizations can be placed. Pugh, Hickson and Hinings[9] describe the Burns and Stalker typology as follows:

The mechanistic type of organisation is adapted to relatively stable conditions. In it the problems and tasks of management are broken down into specialisms·within which each individual carries out his assigned, precisely defined task. There is a clear hierarchy of control, and the responsibility for overall knowledge and co-ordination rests exclusively at the top of the hierarchy. Vertical communication and interaction (i.e. between superiors and subordinates) is emphasised, and there is an insistence on loyalty to the concern and obedience to superiors.

The *organismic* (also called organic) type of organization is adapted to unstable conditions when new and unfamiliar problems continually arise which cannot be broken down and distributed among the existing specialist roles. There is therefore a continual adjustment and redefinition of individual tasks, and the contributive rather than restrictive nature of specialist knowledge is emphasized. Interactions and communication (information and advice rather than orders) may occur at any level as required by the process, and a much higher degree of commitment to the aims of the organization as a whole is generated. In this system, organization charts laying down the exact functions and responsibilities of each individual are not found, *'and indeed their use may be explicitly rejected as hampering the efficient functioning of the organisation'*. (emphasis added)

Pugh, Hickson and Hinings add the researchers' view that: 'Pathological systems are attempts by mechanistic organisations to cope with new problems of change, innovation and uncertainty while sticking to the formal bureaucratic structure.' The management of South Mersey College believed that because the boundary conditions acting upon it were so novel, an hierarchically differentiated structure could constrain growth and development. Ways had to be found to liberate as much creative energy as possible. Strategies had to be devised to develop toleration of the ambiguities being produced by changing demand, shifts in Government policy and continuing uncertainty about resources.

Another cluster of concepts, assisting management to order its own thinking, related to the contribution of the social sciences to the study of personality, motivation and organizational behaviour. Management was aware of the influential content theory of motivation provided by the hierarchy of pre-potent needs formulated by Maslow.[10] He had perceived five categories of need and proposed that they were organized into a hierarchy. When the needs lower down the hierarchy (for example, physiological needs; safety and security needs) were satisfied, those needs at a higher level such as self esteem and self-actualisation emerged to play a prominent role in behaviour. Maslow's 'needs hierarchy' was an attempt to emphasize the positive side of human nature, since it stressed that despite their goal to satisfy lower order needs, humans would, whenever possible, strive to achieve their potential and attain the satisfaction to be derived from using their abilities and attributes to the full.

The College management was aware that attempts to explain motivation in terms of human needs could only be of value in organizational contexts, if the job factors involved in the satisfaction of such needs could be identified. They were aware of the 'two-factor' (or 'motivation-hygiene') theory of Herzberg,[11] who proposed that two different types of factors contributed to satisfaction and dissatisfaction at work. Factors associated with good feelings about the job (the motivators) were mostly derived from the job itself. The second set of factors (the hygiene factors) were mostly external to the job and involved aspects of the physical or psychological environment. Herzberg was primarily concerned with ways in which satisfaction and motivation could be improved by restructuring or enriching jobs so that they provided workers with rewarding experiences.

Herzberg held that it was not possible to motivate people solely by improving the hygiene factors. Betterment of working conditions or monetary rewards would perhaps decrease dissatisfaction but would not improve motivation. True motivation emanated from factors associated with the job itself and relied on opportunities for achievement, recognition and responsibility.

Again, management was aware that motivation theories, such as Maslow's hierarchy, focus on the content of motivation, whereas an alternative approach had involved an examination of the cognitive processes entailed. One significant process approach utilized ideas about the expectations people have about the consequences of their behaviour (Lawler).[12] In essence, this theory suggests that the amount of effort people are prepared to invest in a task depends on three factors:

1 Expectancy — whether the effort involved will result in better performance;
2 Instrumentality — whether the performance will result in beneficial outcomes, such as rewards;
3 Valence — whether the possible outcomes are attractive for the individual concerned.

According to Robertson and Cooper[13] theories involving the concepts of expectancy, instrumentality and valence (called either expectancy theory or expectancy/valence theory) form the basis of much current research on motivation and work behaviour (vide Steers and Porter).[14] The theory emphasizes that the attractiveness of specific outcomes or rewards is a very individualistic issue. What is attractive to one person may be irrelevant for another. So that although expectancy theory seeks to provide a general model of the factors involved in determining effort and performance for all employees, the individual differences between people is an integral part of the theory.

Nader and Lawler[15] have summarized some of the main implications for organizations:

1 Design pay and reward systems so that desirable performance is rewarded (do not reward mere membership by linking pay with years of service). The relationship between performance and reward is clear. Rewards such as upgradings resulting from good performance should be clear and explicit, rather than ambiguous and secret.
2 Design tasks, jobs and roles so that people have an opportunity to satisfy their own needs through their work, but do not assume everyone will want the same things. Some will look for enriched jobs with greater autonomy, feedback, etc. Others will not.
3 Individualize the organization. Expectancy theory proposes that people have different needs, valences, etc. Because of these individual differences it is important to allow people some opportunity to influence not only the type of work they do but many other aspects of organizational life.

The Marketing Concept

So far some knowledge of the theoretical insights into systems of organization and worker motivation which management found valuable has been elaborated. Among the other organizing concepts, pre-eminent was what has become known as the marketing philosophy or the marketing concept.

To some, the idea of education as a product to be marketed is something to be approached with diffidence. Others are repelled by the concept. It is perhaps fair to ask how those to whom we owe so much for their thinking about education — the Platos and the Lockes, the Rousseaus and the Froebels, the McMillans and the Montessorris, the Bubers and the Deweys — would have judged it.

Marketing, as commonly regarded, is a suspect process. Indeed, the suspicions may go back as far as Anarchus, who suggested that 'the market' [was] 'the place set aside where men may deceive each other.' As Gist[16] observes, it is not uncommon to find the word market used as a verb to suggest the action of dealing in or exposing for sale. This usage is undoubtedly one reason why many interpret marketing as synonymous with selling. Gist also avers that we probably remember the more offensive and inefficient encounters with salespeople more vividly than we recall the more pleasant and efficient ones. Such negative recall impels a mental stereotype which we tend to associate with all marketing activities.

J.K. Galbraith believes that marketing is synonymous with what he terms 'the organized market of the corporations'. Also, many regard marketing as a process less worthy than that of production. The manufacture of goods is referred to as production, so it is convenient to infer that non-manufacturing activities, such as the provision of services, are a form of non-production. Therefore, those engaged in manufacturing may be thought of as productive, while those in ancillary processes, such as marketing, are non-productive. It is a convenient, if illogical, dichotomy.

Here it is important to affirm that the term marketing, as understood by the management of South Mersey College, and as used throughout this book is the activity at the core of the marketing concept, which will now be explained. According to the marketing concept, when an idea for a product or service is conceived, the question of greatest importance is whether potential users share the same enthusiasm for the idea as those who have conceived it. Successful organizational enterprise rests, ultimately, upon market opportunity, and market opportunity is defined by user preferences. This priority of user preferences is the key element of the philosophy (Gist).[17]

In terms of organizational action, the concept rests on two fundamentals:

1   that the organization shall be oriented to the user in all phases of its operations and management;
2   that with this orientation the commercial organization should strive for an adequate return on its investment.

As a corollary of 2 the non-commercial organization should strive for the most productive use of scarce resources, i.e. for the most effective use of the social capital entrusted to it.

The marketing concept gained acceptance in Britain from the late 1950s when it was seen that science and technology were constantly generating ideas for faster and more cost-effective production. At the same time, it was becoming evident that the stability and permanence of the markets for many products was being undermined by changing economic and social forces. More and more markets were becoming 'dynamic', i.e. markets in which tastes and fashions were on the move. It thus became clear that these newer production techniques had the capacity to deliver either a higher standard of living or a mountain of waste, depending on whether the goods produced were in phase with the changing composition of user needs.

Organizations became preoccupied with 'market-induced flow', a process by which knowledge of the market was incorporated at the beginning rather than at the end of the production cycle — this knowledge having been acquired by the use of market research techniques.

Figure 4.4:   The marketing concept: User orientation

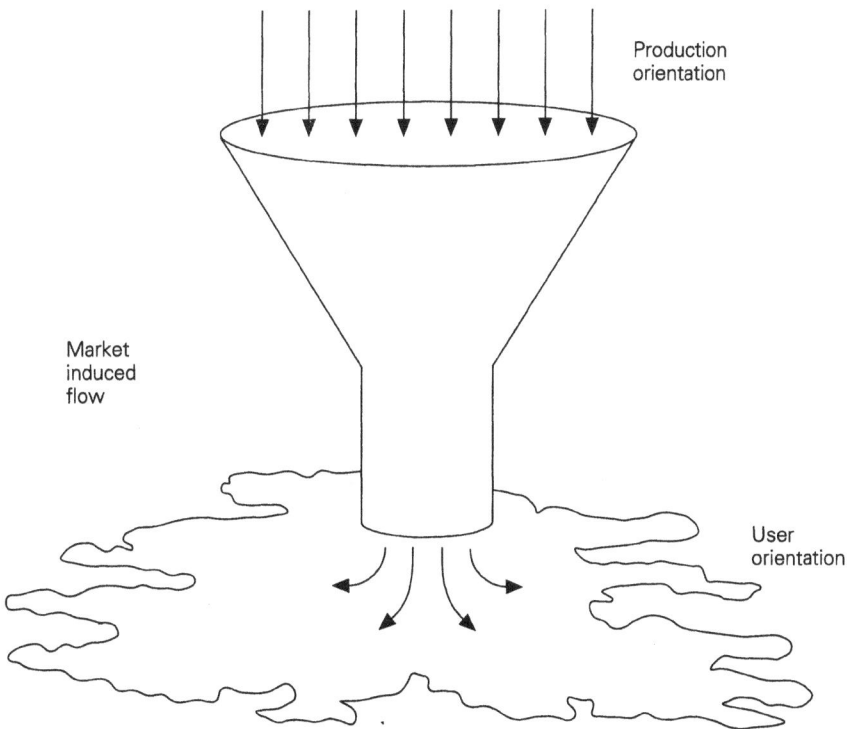

The organization paying little respect to consumer needs was said to be production oriented whilst the market or user-oriented firm was, and remained, extremely sensitive to the underlying reasons for any changes in the demand for its output. Delivery, in the production-oriented firm could be perceived as a process of force-pumping output into the top-end of a funnel (see Figure 4.4). In contrast, the user-oriented firm would allow a benevolent vacuum in the market to suction-draw its output into the market from the bottom end of the funnel. The vacuum would exist as a concomitant of the built-in acceptability which the output possessed. This acceptability would have been developed as a result of information gained from market research.

Early successes in applying the marketing concept were recorded for consumer products. The idea was rapidly taken up in the industrial goods field, being firmly established there by the mid nineteen-sixties. By the end of that decade the concept was being applied with marked success in the field of services, particularly in banking and insurance. In the early nineteen seventies, Professor Philip Kotler[18] alluded to the fact that in the United States, applications of the concept were appearing in institutional contexts — in hospitals, libraries, museums, welfare agencies, schools, churches, etc. From this he concluded that all organizations face marketing-like tasks: they all have products and customers. They all face the task of managing exchange processes. They are all engaged in 'furthering', i.e. advancing the cause of something. Kotler used the term 'metamarketing' to describe the processes involved in attempting to develop and maintain exchange relations involving products, services, institutions, places or causes.

So the management of South Mersey College believed that this concept should be central to its planning for survival and growth and that the notion of feedback, common to the idea of the College as an open system and to the marketing concept could operate as a powerful determinant of plans and programmes.

Course Development Strategy

There was a third area where the significance of feedback was acknowledged, the sphere of course development. The need for the development of new courses in both the vocational and the community fields was transparently clear. As has been remarked earlier, since the content of most current courses was provided by external (validating) organizations: Business and Technician Education Council; Department of Transport; GCE Examining Boards, etc., many members of the teaching staff had no direct, personal experience of course development (although a notable exception was the Access to Higher Educational course group at the Childwall College).

Thus it was important that the future course planning should utilise an adequate, defensible process model. The Principal of the College, formerly an HMI, informed colleagues that in advising the Department of Education and Science on course proposals from Further and Higher Education establishments, he had found the Tilley 'Technology of Training' model[19] a useful aid in structuring his own thinking.

Tilley proposes that from 'an analysis of the overall system' (p. 56) job descriptions should be derived, the job description attempting to answer two questions:

1   What does the worker have to do?
2   What are the acceptable criteria of the worker's success in doing so?

Once the performance expected at the end of training has been specified objectively, it is necessary to identify different classes of terminal behaviour which require different types of training for their accomplishment. 'Task analysis' is the term used to describe this process.

Tilley's view is that just as training will be ineffective if it fails to focus on the critical elements of the tasks to be learned, so it would also lose in effectiveness if it fails to take account of the knowledge and skills which students possess when they commence training. The Principal of South Mersey College had extended this requirement in his adaptation of the model so as to read 'or that they should possess, by way of prior experience or qualifications'. So an important element in this decision-tree approach was based upon student entry capabilities. The *task analysis* requires the logical accompaniment of *skills analysis*, so as to determine the knowledge and skill requirement underlying adequate performance of tasks. From this starting point, the content of courses and the development of appropriate methods of teaching and learning (including the sequencing of material to be learned, the provision of reinforcement, the provision of guidance and of opportunities for practice) could be examined and specified. The attainment of an effective technology of training is dependent upon the development of appropriate criteria-based tests of proficiency. These job-related criterion measures are an important determinant of the outcome of the course evaluation process. It may be thought that such an approach is unduly narrow and prescriptive, that it fails to allow for enrichment and that in general education, it is usually impossible to specify with any accuracy what jobs students would eventually be required to take up. Even so, the approach leads to a statement of educational objectives which emphasizes the student's ability to transfer or apply what he has learned to novel situations.

It is also true that Tilley's starting point, the analysis of the overall system, relates to the situation within an individual organization, rather than an industry or an economy. The Principal believed that the value of the model lay not in its specificity but in the framework it provided for the design and development of courses and that what was valuable in a micro sense was equally valuable in a macro sense. 'System' could be held to decribe the prevailing situation in a firm, an industry or an economic and social system without affecting the validity of the model. The utility of the approach to vocational provision was clear, for it:

1 emphasised a definition of learning objectives in behavioural terms and particularly attempted to define complex behaviour in terms of its simpler constituent elements;

2 attempted to define appropriate teaching and learning strategies in terms of interactions between student capabilities and the characteristics of subject matter;

3 assessed the effectiveness of courses in terms of the results they achieved.

Figure 4.5: A model for course and curriculum development (after Tilley's 'Technology of Training')

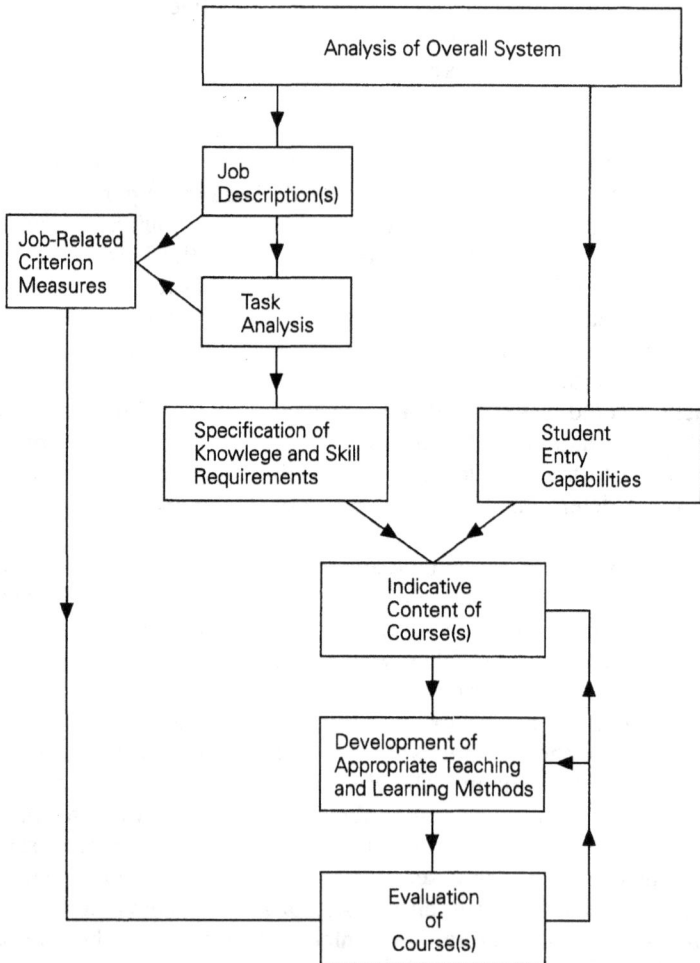

Figure 4.5 is representation of what Tilley had in mind. The Principal recommended its adoption based upon his own experience adding that the model had its genesis in the field of vocational training and that, into the foreseeable future, vocational training could constitute the greater part of the College's provision. With the advent of the Business and Technician Education Council (BTEC) which had also emphasized the importance of behavioural outcomes to course evaluation, the utility of Tilley's approach had been affirmed. The Principal's own experience suggested that the approach had great value in the development of all types of courses, vocational and non-vocational, because it structured thinking in a logical and disciplined manner.

Narrative

The foregoing analysis depicts management's initial approach to the development of the College. It was now necessary to make specific recommendations on how the personnel made available to it should best be organized to achieve that development.

The Advisory Formula in Teaching Staff Establishment

At its meeting on 3rd January 1986, the Education Committee of the Liverpool City Council considered and recommended the adoption of an advisory formula to guide the determination of teaching-manpower levels for its Colleges of Further Education. Consultations were undertaken with representatives of the teachers' union who were opposed to its adoption. Notwithstanding this, the Local Education Authority advised the Principals Designate of the reorganised FE Colleges that the formula was to be adopted for the calculation of the establishment of each of the four Colleges. The constitutent factors of the formula are, briefly, as follows:

1   *Student hour inputs.* It was considered that only actual hours of student attendance were to be used for the calculation of teaching staff levels.

2   *Average class sizes.* In order to arrive at the annual requirement of lecturer contact hours, the input of student hours had to be divided by a notional class size. The divisors to be adopted for the first year's operations of the new Colleges were six for Adult Basic Education and Special Needs classes and eleven for all other classes.

3   *Level of teaching posts (Burnham Proportions).* This calculation required that the student hour input was measured in terms of academic grades, in accordance with Appendix IIA of the Burnham Conditions of Service Document (the 'Blue Book') then in effect. The Authority had formally

adopted the midpoint of each discretionary band for the proportion of posts at each level, related to the teaching programme of the Colleges. The profile of staffing to be adopted was therefore as follows:

Category of Work	Type of work	Proportion of Posts
Level III	Study above Ordinary National Certificate but not necessarily leading to a University degree or equivalent qualification	$17\frac{1}{2}$ per cent Principal Lecturers $82\frac{1}{2}$ per cent Senior Lecturers
Level IV	Study of courses above the Ordinary Level of the General Certificate of Education or comparable level leading directly to the Ordinary National Certificate or courses or parts of courses of a comparable standard	$2\frac{1}{2}$ per cent Senior Lecturers $52\frac{1}{2}$ per cent Lecturers Grade II 45 per cent Lecturers Grade I
Level V	Courses other than those described above (and at a lower level)	$2\frac{1}{2}$ per cent Senior Lecturers 20 per cent Lecturers Grade II $77\frac{1}{2}$ per cent Lecturers Grade I
ABE/SN	Adult Basic Education and Special Needs Provision	as with Level V proportions

4 *Class contact hours for teaching staff.* The Local Education Authority had formally negotiated a set of class contact hours for each grade of teaching post. Based on a full teaching year of thirty-six weeks these were as follows:

Grade of Post	Weekly Contact Hours	Annual Contact Hours
Principal Lecturer	15	540
Senior Lecturer	16	576
Lecturer Grade II	18	648
Lecturer Grade I	21	756

5 *Part-time teaching staff levels.* A level of $17\frac{1}{2}$ per cent of the total establishment posts calculated by the Formula was to be adopted for part-time staffing.

6 *Remission.* The Formula was to provide for remission of class contact hours for full-time lecturers of up to 6 per cent of the annual programme, such remission to provide for tasks not normally performed as part of teachers' departmental/administrative duties, such as 'health and safety' activities.

7 *Base year for calculations.* These were to be based upon the student attendance hours achieved by the courses allocated to each reorganized College during the 1984/5 Session, this being the last Session for which complete data was available at the time of the establishment calculations.

The advisory formula calculation for the initial establishment of South Mersey College is set out in Figure 4.6. From this it can be seen that the rounded establishment for the College was 189 posts. To this figure the Local Education Authority added the equivalent of two Principal Lecturer posts to cover the ROTeC Unit and the College hostel Wardenships and two Lecturer Grade II posts for the proposed Trade Union Studies Unit. The purpose of the ROTeC Unit (Riversdale Open Technology Centre) will be outlined in later pages. The immediate point is that the Principal-Designate of the new College was elected to treat the ROTeC Principal Lecturer post as being within the establishment. External start-up funding for the post would eventually be withdrawn and provision for the post had to be made within the College's Revenue Estimates. The College's approved teaching establishment therefore comprised *192* posts (189 plus 3) to which the LEA approved management posts must be added:

1 Principal (Burnham FE Group 7);
2 Vice Principals (Burnham FE Group 7);
4 Heads of Department (Burnham FE Grade 6)

In full, therefore, the approved teaching establishment was as follows:

1	Principal
2	Vice Principals
4	Heads of Department
10	Principal Lecturers
44	Senior Lecturers
55	Lecturers Grade II
83	Lecturers Grade I

Total: 199 Posts

Organization Structure: Teaching Staff

During the months preceding the formation of the new Colleges, the Local Education Authority looked to each Principal Designate to recommend an

Figure 4.6: South Mersey College: Teaching staff establishment calculation, based on the proposed advisory formula

Category of Work	Attendance Hours	Class Size Divisor (Ave)	Annual Teaching Hours	X	Proportion of Posts	÷	Annual Contact Hours	FTE Staff PL	SL	LII	LI
III	345,659	11	31,424	X	17.5 per cent	÷	540	10.2			
				X	82.5 per cent	÷	576		45.0		
IV	566,529	11	51,503	X	2.5 per cent	÷	576		2.2		
				X	52.5 per cent	÷	648			41.7	
				X	45.0 per cent	÷	756				30.7
V	565,530	11	51,412	X	2.5 per cent	÷	576		2.2		
				X	20.0 per cent	÷	648			15.9	
				X	77.5 per cent	÷	756				52.7
ABE/SN	62,837	6	10,473	X	2.5 per cent	÷	576	0.5			
				X	20.0 per cent	÷	648			3.2	
				X	77.5 per cent	÷	756				10.8

	PL	SL	LII	LI
TOTAL	10.2	49.9	60.8	94.2
−17.5 per cent Part-Time Staff	1.8	8.7	10.7	16.5
TOTAL FTE Staff	8.4	41.2	50.1	77.7
+6 per cent Remission	0.5	2.5	3.0	4.7
Full-Time Posts	8.9	43.7	53.1	82.4

	PL	SL	LII	LI	TOTAL
Rounded Establishment	9	44	53	83	(189)
Staff in Post March 1986	13	84	56	91	(244)
	−4	−40	−3	−8	(−55)

organization structure for his approved teaching establishment. Following discussions with incumbent Heads of Department, members of the teaching staffs of the constituent Colleges and Trade Union representatives, the Principal-Designate of South Mersey College recommended a structure of four faculties, namely Automobile and General Engineering; Construction; General Studies; and Maritime Studies. The first of these was to be based on the existing provision of the Department of General and Automobile Engineering of the Riversdale College of Technology. The title was changed to Automobile and General Engineering.

The Faculty of Construction was formed from the Department of Construction at Riversdale and the related provision at the Central Liverpool College of Further Education which was to be transferred to South Mersey College. Details of the cognate areas involved are set out in Appendix 8.

The Faculty of General Studies was established through the amalgamation of the whole of the course provision of the Childwall Hall College of Further Education with that of the Department of Scientific, General and Communication Studies at Riversdale College.

The Faculty of Maritime Studies came together by combining Riversdale's Department of Navigation with its Department of Marine Engineering. (NB. From his own observation and by report, the Principal Designate had noted that the Marine Engineers and the teachers of Navigation studies tend to operate separately as general rule. Doubtless this was a continuation of shipboard culture where, allegedly, Engineers and Deck Officers tended to be psychologically distant from each other. He hoped that bringing the two specialisms together might be more in keeping with changed conditions).

The Faculty structures, showing their organization by cognate areas of provision, can be seen in Appendices 7 to 10. Set out below is the establishment profile for each Faculty, showing the distribution of the 192 teaching posts, calculated by the formula as outlined earlier.

Faculty of Automobile and General Engineering		*'Strength'*
Principal Lecturers	1	(1)
Senior Lecturers	8	(10)
Lecturers Grade II	6	(6)
Lecturers Grade I	12	(13)
TOTAL (Faculty)	27	(30)

Faculty of Construction		*'Strength'*
Principal Lecturers	3	(4)
Senior Lecturers	12	(13)
Lecturers Grade II	21	(11)
Lecturers Grade I	20	(22)
TOTAL (Faculty)	56	(50)

The Changing Culture of a College

Faculty of General Studies		'Strength'
Principal Lecturers	1	(2)
Senior Lecturers	11	(11)
Lecturers Grade II	17	(16)
Lecturers Grade I	41	(40)
TOTAL (Faculty)	70	(69)

Faculty of Maritime Studies		'Strength'
Principal Lecturers	4	(5)
Senior Lecturers	19	(24)
Lecturers Grade II	11	(12)
Lecturers Grade I	5	(6)
TOTAL (Faculty)	39	(47)
TOTAL (College)	192	196

A strict application of the advisory formula to the base year (1984/85) attendance hours of each Faculty in turn, would have resulted in an inequitable distribution of Senior posts because of the preponderance of lower category work (Levels 4 and 5) in the Faculty of General Studies. Yet, because of the number and variety of courses and the fact that it was the only Faculty required to operate over the two main campuses of the College, it posed great burdens in management terms.

By negotiation with the Deans Designate of all Faculties, the Principal Designate recommended to the Authority that extra management posts be allocated to the establishment of the Faculty of General studies, with consequential adjustments to other Faculties. This was approved and the Faculty establishments set out below were adopted.

Figure 4.7 sets out the establishment profile of South Mersey College (line 1). The number of teaching staff in post (former Colleges) immediately

Figure 4.7: *South Mersey College: Teaching staff profiles before and after reorganization*

	Principal Lecturers	Senior Lecturers	Lecturers Grade II	Lecturers Grade I
1 Establishment (Advisory Formula) (192)	10	44	55	83
2 Number in post to 31.8.85. (244)	13	84	56	91
3 Number in post plus approved vacancies at reorganization (1.9.85.) (196)	12	58	45	81

62

prior to reorganization is set out in Line 2. Line 3 is the total of lecturers in post on reorganization plus the vacancies the College was approved to fill (a total of 8, compromising two Senior Lecturers, two Lecturers Grade II and four Lecturers Grade I).

A number of points arise from the data set out in Figure 4.7:

1   Arising from the Premature Retirement Compensation (PRC) terms offered by the City Council, a significant number of teachers left its employment, bringing the number of staff in post much nearer the approved establishment figure (196 : 192);

2   There was still a significant imbalance when establishment was compared with strength in the supervisory posts (Principal Lecturer; Senior Lecturer). This was particularly noticeable in the case of Senior Lecturers (44 : 58). It was to constitute a difficulty in the new College when the Senior Management approached issues of career progression for younger staff, as we shall see later;

3   It must be remembered that the approved establishment was based upon the attained student attendance hours for the 1984/85 Session, the last period for which data were available. Any further decline, such as in Session 1985/86, would affect the balance between establishment and strength. Again, this was to prove a significant issue.

Three other points should be mentioned before concluding this Section. As happens with reorganizations, it is one thing to bring the number of people in post into line with the approved establishment, but frequently there is a mismatch between the types of posts then filled and the type of posts that College needs to fill. Re-deployment can be used to mitigate the problem but the strategy has its limits. It is difficult, if not impossible to re-deploy a marine engineer to a post in the humanities. Despite its need to make economies and the burden of financing the 'lump sum' entitlement of the large number of FE teachers leaving the service on PRC terms, it is greatly to the credit of the Liverpool City Council that it acted on this problem. It approved the filling of thirty vacancies by the FE Colleges and South Mersey College was allocated eight of these (two Senior Lecturers, two Lecturers Grade II and four Lecturers Grade I, as shown in Figure 4.7). These are included in the 'strength' number (actual number in post) set out to the right of the establishment calculations. At least two detailed points are worth noting here:

*   the significant undermanning of the Faculty of Construction;
*   the equally significant overmanning of the Faculty of Maritime Studies, particularly at the Senior Lecturer level.

In addition to the posts approved under the Establishment Formula, the City Council agreed that each College be approved to fill two Lecturer I posts (or their equivalent in terms of upgrading) in order to offset 'abated' posts (i.e. those posts used to perform extra-Faculty functions — curriculum development, health and safety, etc., on behalf of the College as a whole). Because of his concern about the short-term viability of the College, the Principal Designate decided that for some space of time such cross-College functions were to be carried out using approved remission from teaching duties (6 per cent of approved total full-time equivalent teaching posts as outlined on p. 59). The two Lecturer I posts would be set against the need for the College to absorb into its structure two Heads of Department who were not appointed to similar roles in the new Colleges. This is the final point concerning the structure. The organizational issues it raised will now be outlined.

The Liverpool City Council decided that the posts of Principal and Vice Principal (two per College) were to be nationally advertised and that posts of Heads of Department and below should be filled within the long-standing 'ring-fence' agreement Council had negotiated with trade unions. This meant that the Heads of Department posts were to be filled from the ranks of Liverpool serving teachers, who could apply for any post in any of the four new Colleges.

The South Mersey College was also asked to find roles for two Heads of Department of the former colleges in the FE service and to absorb them into the new College's establishment calculations at the earliest opportunity. The Principal Designate of South Mersey College decided that the posts, if not the grades, were to be calculated against the two Lecturer Grade I abated posts, which were *not* to be filled.

After interviews and further discussion, the Principal Designate offered one of the former Heads the post of Head of Academic Planning Services. This post-holder would be responsible for the compilation of reports, records and all statistical data on which the College's management information system would be based. The other Head was offered the post of Director of Marketing. It was intended that the responsibilities of this latter post would extend beyond promotion of the College's courses. It was also explained to the individuals involved that the two posts would be incorporated into the structure of the Senior Management team. Both of the Heads involved accepted the offers of these key posts.

After negotiation and discussion with the newly appointed Heads of Departments (to be called Deans of Faculty, since their Departments had come together from former Departments and were thus, in effect, Faculties) within each Faculty there were to be an Assistant Dean (Academic), an Assistant Dean (Resources) and also Section Heads, responsible for the management of cognate areas of provision within the Faculties. All of these posts were competition posts, filled after interviews with short-listed candidates. The management structure upon the formation of the College is set out in Figure 4.8. The structure for administrative, professional, technical and clerical staff was not yet determined (in September 1986) due to a dispute between the City Council and NALGO, the main trade union involved with APT & C issues.

Figure 4.8: South Mersey College: Management structure at 1 September 1986

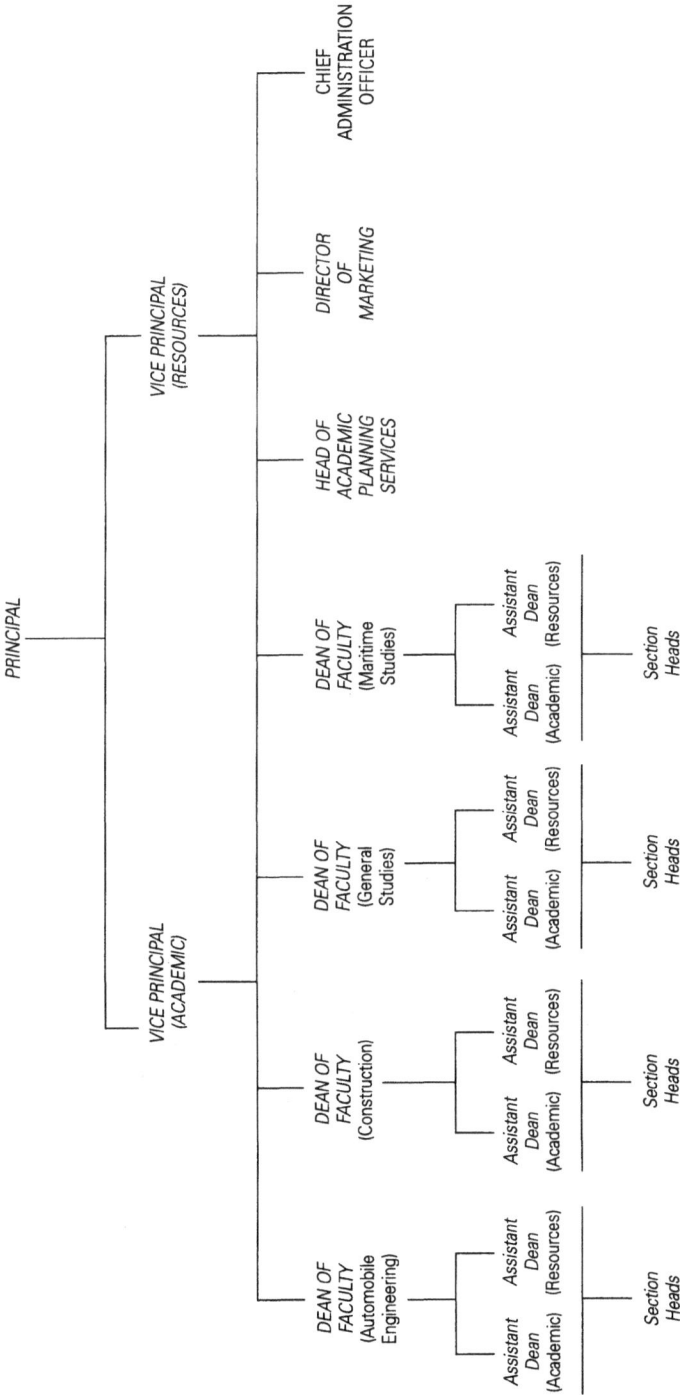

PRINCIPAL

VICE PRINCIPAL (ACADEMIC)

VICE PRINCIPAL (RESOURCES)

HEAD OF ACADEMIC PLANNING SERVICES

DIRECTOR OF MARKETING

CHIEF ADMINISTRATION OFFICER

DEAN OF FACULTY (Automobile Engineering)

DEAN OF FACULTY (Construction)

DEAN OF FACULTY (General Studies)

DEAN OF FACULTY (Maritime Studies)

Assistant Dean (Academic)

Assistant Dean (Resources)

Section Heads

It could be said, in summary, that there were three general concepts which conditioned management's thinking:

1 systems theory and the notion of the College as an open system;
2 the marketing concept, which argues that the organization shall be oriented to the user in all phases of its operations and management; and
3 a model of course and curriculum development which necessitated knowledge of the overall system and emphasized the importance of behavioural outcomes.[20]

It can be seen why management felt that these concepts were consistent with each other, for they all impress upon decision-makers the importance of the environment to organization. They all emphasize also, the importance of feedback, the notion that the organization's operations in relation to its environment should constantly be monitored and that any changes in the boundary conditions affecting the College should immediately be followed by consequential adjustments in the College's response to its environment.

There does, however, appear to be a mismatch between what theories of human motivation found of value and the organizational arrangements being made to motivate the College's teaching staff. For example, it has been stated (p. 50) that management acknowledged the view of Herzberg that true motivation relied on opportunities for achievement, recognition and responsibility. Similar beliefs were contained within expectancy/valence theory (p. 51) and these were also acknowledged by management.

Yet the manner in which the teaching staff were to be organized as described in the Narrative was along traditional lines, a mechanistic structure in which each individual carries out assigned, precisely defined tasks. Figure 4.8 is a clear representation of a hierarchically differentiated structure and seems at odds with the comments of Pugh, Hickson and Hinings that attempts to cope with problems of change, innovation and uncertainty while 'sticking to the formal bureaucratic structure' are 'pathological'. Yet management supposedly supported this view. Figure 4.9 depicts a matrix organization within a Faculty of Business Studies. The matrix has been introduced by some educational establishments with the objective of maintaining the required standards of quality and cost-effectiveness in conditions of change and uncertainty whilst at the same time increasing the motivation and commitment of Faculty members. Organizational analysts have pointed out that its features bear close resemblance to the product or brand management type of structure adopted by organizations with the marketing concept as the basis of their business policy. Would it not then seem logical for this thinking to have been applied at South Mersey College?

It would, after all, delegate responsibilities in a decided fashion, thereby enlarging the discretionary component of many jobs and enriching them, after the dicta of Maslow and Herzberg. Was the management lacking in conviction, therefore, in adopting the hierarchical structure?

Figure 4.9:   A matrix organization within a Faculty of Business Studies (from Frain)[20]

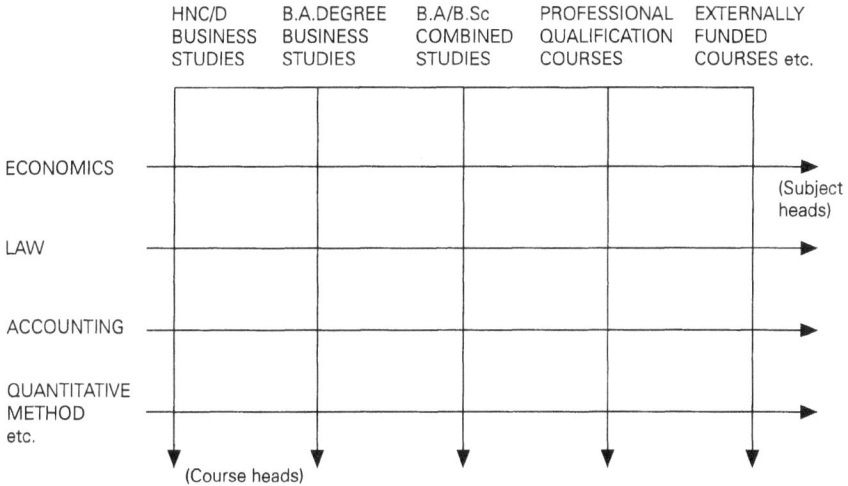

	HNC/D BUSINESS STUDIES	B.A.DEGREE BUSINESS STUDIES	B.A/B.Sc COMBINED STUDIES	PROFESSIONAL QUALIFICATION COURSES	EXTERNALLY FUNDED COURSES etc.
ECONOMICS						→(Subject heads)
LAW						→
ACCOUNTING						→
QUANTITATIVE METHOD etc.						→

(Course heads)

On the contrary, it declared that it was committed to revolutionary change but at an evolutionary pace. It had inherited a workforce which was, understandably uncertain and insecure; and at worst pessimistic about its future. Morale was low, largely as a result of the distribution of redundancy notices to 30,000 employees of the City Council. Underlying pragmatic optimism about the future of the College was difficult to discover. A number of the teachers believed that the new management had been appointed 'to wind down the FE service'. Here therefore was the organizational condition which affirmed Mintzberg's philosophy that any change would have to be incremental rather than global.

Management also recalled the tenet of an early organizational thinker, Mary Parker Follett[21] and her stress on 'the law of the situation'. Too much change too quickly in the shape of relatively novel organizational forms would be counter-productive in the prevailing organizational atmosphere, which was described by the Principal as one of 'Celtic gloom'.

There were other ways, for now, of attempting to develop participation and commitment. Some of these will be outlined in Chapter 5.

Notes

1 JOHNSON, G. and SCHOLES, K. (1989) *Exploring Corporate Strategy: Text and Cases*, Hemel Hempstead, Herts: Prentice Hall International (UK), Ltd., p. 6.
2 JOHNSON, G. and SCHOLES, K. (1989) Ibid., p. 38.
3 MILES, R. and SNOW, C. (1978) *Organizational Strategy, Structure and Process*, Maidenhead, Berks: McGraw Hill Book Co.

4 MINTZBERG, H. (1978) 'Patterns of strategy formation' in *Management Science*, May, pp. 934–48.

5 KATZ, D. and KAHN, R.L. (1970) 'Open-systems theory' in *The Sociology of Organizations*, GRUSKY, O. and MILLER, G.A. New York: The Free Press, pp. 149–158.

6 ROBERTSON, I.T. and COOPER, C.L. (1983) *Human Behaviour in Organizations*, Plymouth: Macdonald & Evans Ltd., p. 16.

7 BURNS, T. and STALKER, G.M. (1968) *The Management of Innovation*, 2nd Edition, London: Tavistock Publications.

8 LAWRENCE, P.R. and LORSCH, J.W. (1983) *Organization and Environment*, and other chapters in PUGH, D.S., HICKSON, D.J. and HININGS, C.R., *Writers on Organizations*, 3rd Edition, Harmondsworth, Middlesex: Penguin Books, Ltd., pp. 44–9.

9 PUGH, D.S., HICKSON, D.J. and HININGS, C.R. *Writers on Organizations*, 3rd Edition, Harmondsworth, Middlesex: Penguin Books, Ltd., pp. 32–3.

10 MASLOW, A.H. (1954) *Motivation and Personality*, New York, New York: Harper.

11 HERZBERG, F. (1968) 'One more time: How do you motivate employees?', *Harvard Business Review*, **46**, pp. 53–162, Cambridge, Massachusetts and HERZBERG, F., MAUSNER, B. and SNYDERMAN, B.B. (1959) *The Motivation to Work*, New York: John Wiley.

12 LAWLER, E.E. (1973) *Motivation in Work Organizations*, Belmont, California: Brooks/Cole .

13 ROBERTSON, I.T. and COOPER, C.L. (1983) *Human Behaviour in Organizations*, Plymouth, Devon: Macdonald & Evans Ltd., p. 83.

14 STEERS, R.M. and PORTER, L.W. (1979) *Motivation and Work Behaviour*, New York, New York: McGraw-Hill.

15 NADER, D.A. and LAWLER, E.E., III (1979) 'Motivation: A diagnostic approach', in STEERS, R.M. and PORTER, L.W., *Motivation and Work Behaviour*, New York, New York: McGraw-Hill.

16 GIST, R.R. (1971) *Marketing and Society: A Conceptual Introduction*, London: Holt Rinehart Winston, p. 5.

17 GIST, R.R. (1971) Ibid. p. 224.

18 KOTLER, P. (1971) 'Metamarketing: The furthering of organizations, persons, places and causes', *Marketing Forum* (UK Chartered Institute of Marketing, Cookham, Berks) July–August, pp. 13–23; and in *Marketing Management: Analysis, Planning and Control*, 2nd Edition, Englewood Cliffs, New Jersey Prentice Hall, 1972.

19 TILLEY, K. (1968) 'A technology of training' in Industrial Society: Social sciences in management', in PYM, D., *Industrial Society: Social Sciences in Management*, Harmondsworth, Middlesex: Penguin Books Ltd., pp. 111–33.

20 FRAIN, J. (1986) *Principles and Practice of Marketing*, London: Pitman Publishing Ltd., pp. 409.

21 FOLLETT, M.P. (1920) *The New State*, London: Longman; (1924) *Creative Experience* London: Longman and METCALF, H.C. and URWICK, L.F. (Eds) (1941) *Dynamic Administration*, London: Pitman.

Chapter 5

The 1986/87 Session

Strategic Analysis: The Cultural Recipe

In Chapter 4, data on the past performance of the constituent Colleges (in terms of Burnham Unit totals and Student Curricular hours) has provided a picture of decline. It was clear from these data that if the newly established College was to survive, its primary objectives had to be centred upon diversification and development.

As an organization established for the purpose of achieving these specific objectives, its best hope of achieving survival and, hopefully, growth was through the creative alignment of the College with its environment. In this process, management's view of the utility of open-system theory has also been described. This approach, which views the organization within its broader, external context, conceptualizing the organization as part of the social and economic fabric in which it exists, affecting it and being affected by it in turn, management found a powerful tool of strategic analysis.

Its value lay not only in its highlighting of the relationship between environmental analysis and judicious use of resources, and in its provision of important insights for the processes of curriculum development but also because of its influence in shaping corporate culture. In this regard, Mullins[1] speaks for many behavioural scientists when he declares that:

> The open system model provides a perspective for a managerial approach to organisational behaviour. It helps in the search for the most appropriate ways of influencing the behaviour of people within an organisational setting.

It will be evident from what has already been written that, in management's view, the College's culture was not aligned to its needs or environment. The cultural values in evidence reflected what worked and worked well in the past. Between desired cultural norms and values and actual norms and values impartial observation indicated that a culture gap had emerged.

As the book proceeds, the emergence of a new cultural recipe will be described. Before proceeding further, however, it might be helpful to exemplify what Emery and Trist[2] have described as the natural progress of all environments towards increasing complexity and uncertainty. Some of the macro-environmental influences which the College had to examine in re-shaping its curriculum offer were these:

Influences	*Examples*
Economic	Economic Prosperity (Employment levels);
Political	Government Policy on Education and Training;
Legal	Consumer Protection legislation; Health and Safety at Work Act;
Demographic	Size of the 16–19 cohort; effects of an ageing population;
Technological	Developments in Microelectronics, Waste Disposal, Alternative Energy Systems.

The effects of these influences and the adjustments called for by the College are self-evident, but it might be useful to provide a single elaboration of how such influences have led to what Ranson, Taylor and Brighouse[3] have described as the 'revolution in education and training'. It is worth quoting at length the views they expressed in 1986:

> The context of education and training has changed out of all recognition. The contraction in school rolls together with relatively stable participation rates have encouraged some LEAs to review the effectiveness of their traditional sixth form provision. The recession which has squeezed public expenditure, and education spending in particular, has only accelerated the reorganisation of provision. But the determining influence has been the structural transformation in employment. The post-manufacturing revolution in work, hailed since the 1960s, its lineages laid bare by Bell[4] in the 1970s, is now finally emerging, and in many parts of the country, at a considerable pace. It has led already to the rapid withdrawal of two age groups from the labour market: to a programme of early retirement and to the collapse of teenage employment for 16 and 17-year-olds. And, as unemployment is raising fundamental questions about the nature of work, social trends also show an ageing society, more fragmented patterns of family life often reflecting changing relations between men and women; a multi-cultural society striving for equality of opportunity; while a more politicised world emerges as conceptions about ways of resolving economic and social problems sharpen.

These writers go on to describe the impact of this transformed context upon the education service including the cry of the reformers for greater recognition of different kinds of achievement; a broadening of new (modular) organization of the curriculum; a move to non-didactic forms of teaching and to modes of assessment which credit prior achievement and enable progression.

Here then was a macro-environmental influence on which the College management was clear. The College's vocational provision was weighted towards the technologies (e.g. construction, automobile and civil engineering) — adding profoundly to the turbulence through which the College would have to steer to its objectives. Galbraith[5] had spoken of the 'age of discontinuity', in this regard whilst Alvin Toffler[6], in his notable social study *Future Shock* had been moved to speak of 'the roaring current of change, a current so powerful to-day that it overturns institutions, shifts our values and shrivels our roots'. Over-dramatic perhaps but accurate, for since the UK publication of Toffler's work in 1971 the pace of technological change had quickened even further. Moreover, the generic changes within the educational process as described by Ranson, *et al.* was making for vastly increased turbulence over time.

In this situation the development of South Mersey College was perceived as intrinsically a process of planning and managing change. The Principal of the College perceived his own role as that of a 'boundary spanner' — detecting and processing information about changes in the environment and representing the organization to the environment. He saw himself among the 'change-agents' and he believed it important for management to locate and support among the staff 'change-heroes' who, in assisting the College to adapt to its changed environment, would also act as catalysts in the emergence of a new culture recipe.

Strategic Analysis: Theoretical Constructs

Management was clear that if an internal culture could be developed which fitted the needs of the external environment and of a strategy for diversification and growth, then its highly committed staff would create a high performance organization.

At the same time, because revolutionary change could only be achieved at an evolutionary pace it would attempt to cope with problems of change, innovation and uncertainty with the hierarchical structures described in Chapter 4 — structures which, in such a context are generally regarded as 'pathological' (Burns and Stalker.[7]) This strategic choice was based upon the belief that too much change too quickly in the shape of such relatively novel forms as the 'matrix' approach (see Figure 4.9) might well be counterproductive.

Yet within this traditional framework clear signals for change had to be given and commitment secured. What follows is a commentary on the theoretical constructs management found helpful in this regard. Firstly, management perceived itself to be at least as much 'people-oriented' as 'task-oriented' and subscribed to the view of Elliot Jaques[8] that '[p]sycho-economic equilibrium is best achieved in the individual by a level of work corresponding to his capacity. . . .' It believed that many people could be given wider roles and that enriching jobs might be one way of testing McGregor's[9] postulate that 'the average human being learns, under proper conditions, not only to accept but to seek responsibility.'

It understood the mistrust that bureaucracies produce — a mistrust well-established before the advent of 'management-thinkers' and 'organizational analysis'. Bureaucracies produce, as Robert Louis Stevenson described them '. . . your sham impartialists, wolves in sheep's clothing, simpering honestly as they supress'.

There was to be a participative management style in which the College Academic Board would, hopefully, develop as the policy-making body. It would be encouraged to form appropriate sub-Committees to cover the functional areas of College managment and these in turn would be serviced by working groups whose activities would be problem-centred (in the Burns and Stalker tradition) and whose life would be limited, as problems were solved and new problems arose. Additionally, Faculties would be encouraged to establish Faculty Boards which in turn would be free to set up working groups as problems arose at the Faculty level.

Figure 5.1: *South Mersey College: Policy formulation and implementation*

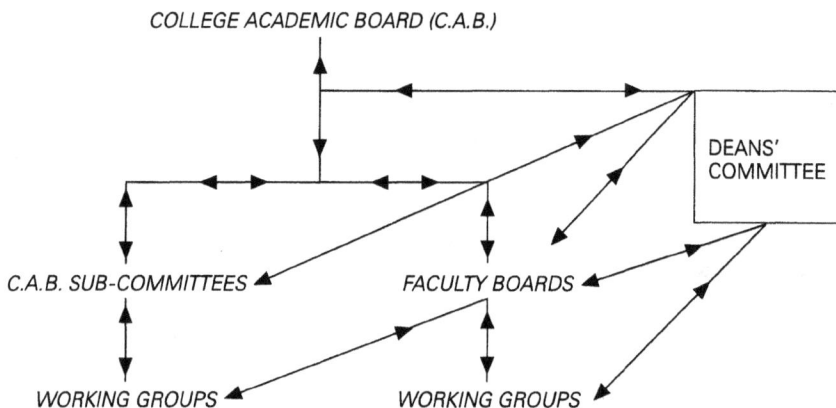

Figure 5.1 is a representation of the framework in which:

1. Communication was to be a two-way process at all levels in the framework.
2. The value of specialist contributions, whatever the hierarchical level of the specialist, would be emphasised.
3. The Deans' Committee (an executive group meeting fortnightly and chaired by the Principal) was to be seen in a staff relationship and

not a line relationship to the CAB framework: its role would be to offer advice, submit ideas and prompt decision-making through the interstices of the framework (as Figure 5.1 depicts).

College management shared the belief of Chester Barnard,[10] that while all organizations have a purpose this would not produce co-operative activity unless it was accepted by the members. That the work of the executive consisted of three tasks was another guide to action, these being:

1   the formulation of purpose and objectives;
2   the maintenance of organizational communication; and
3   the securing of essential services from individuals.

It was earnestly hoped that the framework shown in Figure 5.1 would enable these tasks to be accomplished. Its motives were not grounded in mock-democracy but in the genuine conviction that the surest way to retain any authority in the work-place was to share it, especially when it came to co-ordinating the efforts of professionals.

Also, management's view was that within a seemingly mechanistic structure it had to influence the development of opportunities for the personal and professional growth of its staff. Contributions to the development and operation of the College were to be energetically sought from all levels of its organization, and participation was to be strongly encouraged. Because it recognized that many members of staff had no experience in this regard, management could not, at the onset, be as neutral and non-directive as it would have wished to be. Nevertheless, it was determined to give a lead only when it was clearly responsible for doing so and only until such time as the Board and its Committees had matured in their roles.

Management's actions, to use Morgan's[11] typologies would be based on the notion of 'organizations as organisms' rather than of 'organisations as machines'. The ecology of the organization would derive from the creation of shared futures. It would be necessary, however, to assess periodically how well participation was developing. The formal structure might have a constraining influence, but so also might the fact that, understandably, the past experience of many staff was hardly appropriate to the demands of a rapidly changing context.

In this last respect, Gouldner's[12] categories of 'cosmopolitans' and 'locals' were pertinent. The cosmopolitans exhibited little loyalty to the organization itself but were much committed to their specialized skills, being extremely professional in their outlook. They thought of themselves primarily as engineers, accountants, etc. Locals, on the other hand, had great loyalty to the organization but little commitment to specialized skills. For organizational health there had to be an adequate presence of both categories. This in-built dilemma was regarded by Gouldner as a major cause for tension in organizations. The Management of South Mersey College perceived that it needed a few more cosmopolitans, i.e. members of staff with an adequate external frame of reference for the College to acquire a speedy enough signal of changes in its environment. At its inception, the College would indeed benefit from a few 'creative anarchists', in the Principal's phrase. Participation's progress would need to be monitored closely, for a lack of cosmopolitan thinking might well be a hazard on which it could founder.

The Politics of Cultural Change

It would be naive, of course, to believe that the members of an organization invariably constitute a monolithic group. The reality is that organizations consist of diverse groups and individuals, of multiple coalitions and alliances, with each striving to achieve its own goals and objectives. So any assumption that an organization exists apart from its members and that its goals are independent of the dominant groups or individuals within it is open to challenge.

In this regard, Mangham[13] writes forcefully:

> I am asserting nothing more nor less than that since the conduct of organisations, particularly large-scale organisations, implies a degree of choice about direction reasonable men are likely to differ about it. Reasonable men are likely to differ not only about ends but also about means and such differences are not readily reconciled since the choice of one course of action rather than another may affect the survival of the enterprise. Thus responsible men are obliged to fight for what they are convinced is right and, perhaps more significantly, against that which they are convinced is wrong.

Mangham's view is that where men share power, they differ about what must be done and where these differences are of some consequence, decisions and actions will be the result of a *political process* (emphasis added). What underpins the decision and produces the action is not determined by automatic machine-like interdependencies nor strongly influenced by principles of development nor automatic homeostatic systems, but is the direct result of the power and skill of the proponents and opponents of the action in question, and he concludes therefore that decisions and actions within organisations may be seen as the consequence of the pulling and hauling that is politics.

The basic model of Bowman and Asch[14] for the process of strategic management (see Figure 5.2) supports this standpoint. They contend that strategic charges come about through the interaction of the objective and subjective conditions depicted in the model. Objective conditions include the

Figure 5.2:   The process of strategic management (Bowman, C. and Asch, D.)

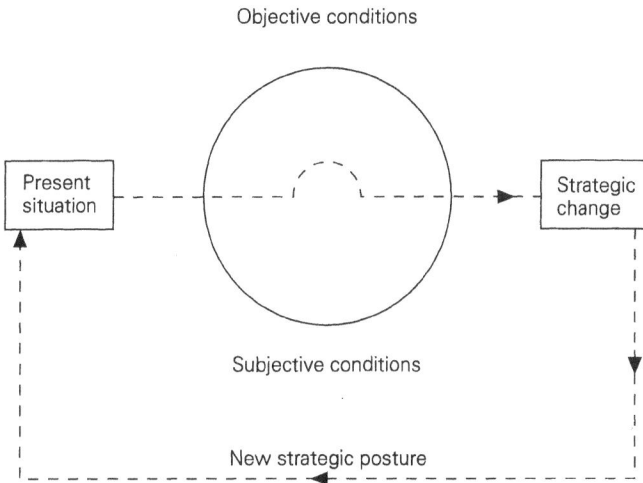

Objective conditions

Present situation

Strategic change

Subjective conditions

New strategic posture

present and future states of the organization's environment and the deployment of the organization's resources. Subjective conditions refer to 'the complex social, psychological and political variables that pervade the organisation'. The objective conditions are more amenable to systematic analysis than the subjective conditions. It is neither the objective conditions alone, nor the subjective conditions alone, which determine the shape of strategic change. Rather it is the interactions of both the objective and the subjective which produce the change. (NB. New strategic posture loop: The model is dynamic, implying that the process of strategic change is continuous. Today's strategic change forms tomorrow's present situation).

The management of the College believed that although it was acting as 'change-agent' in the process of diversifying and developing the College it had, at the same time, a robust enough appreciation of the politics of organizational change. An example of this issue might be helpful here.

Dearborn and Simon[15] tested the idea of alternative perception among a number of executives. They believed that even when executives are instructed to take a broad company-wide view of a problem, they perceive only those aspects of a situation that relate specifically to the attitudes and goals of their own departments. That is, when presented with a complex stimulus, the subject will account for it in terms with which he is familiar, and the more complex or ambiguous the stimulus, the more the perception is determined by what is already in the actor (as a product of his training which narrows and deepens his vision and results in a trained incapacity to perceive outside the particular perspective). Dearborn and Simon discovered that a group of executives asked to designate the most important problems facing a company depicted for them in a case study differed markedly in their perceptions of the problems. Eighty-three per cent of the sales executives, for example, mentioned sales as the most important problem, whereas only 29 per cent of the other executives ascribed any importance to it.

It could be argued that in education, the multiplicity of a college's publics, the diversification of control within the system and the variety of objectives which Local Education Authorities and colleges may pursue only serve to exacerbate this danger. Barnard[16] avers that while all organizations have a purpose, this does not produce co-operative activity unless it is accepted by the members. Hence his description of organizations as shifting multiple-goal coalitions and his view that '[t]he inculcation of belief in the real existence of a common purpose is an essential executive function.'

Some observers see educational institutions as no more than loose federations of groups of individuals pursuing their own objectives, who are often in conflict with each other, and who believe that departmental structures are a block to institutional change since they intensify the problem.

Taking note of these views, the Senior Management of South Mersey College maintained that, at the onset, the Faculty (i.e. departmental) structure was the one to be adopted, nonetheless for these reasons:

1   Any other structure would only aggravate the doubts and uncertainties which had produced such low staff morale;
2   'Whilst not many people within the system have talked hitherto of marketing, increasing numbers are recognizing the validity of "the responsive college", "student-centred curricula" and "flexible delivery systems". Marketing is taking place but more often than not unconsciously; this is reflected in the lack of clearly identified corporate marketing objectives for colleges, co-ordinated systems and procedures, and adequate resourcing specifically allocated to this function'. (Davies and Scribbins).[17] Understandably, given the background of the Senior Management they had faith in the contribution of the marketing approach to organizational change and believed there was much industrial and commercial evidence that this could be achieved with departmental structures. Policy and its implementation would stem from data-based intelligence on client needs and not from sectional interests;
3   In the matter of selective perception among executives, Dearborn and Simon had also remarked that whilst our particular set of symbols leads us to perceive the world in particular, occasionally idiosyncratic ways, it does not render us incapable of creating new perspectives.[18] Time, training and informed discussion were important.

Lupton[19] points out that the notion of hierarchy dies hard, as does the associated idea of managerial prerogative, 'ill though these notions seem to have served.' He goes on:

The manager's problem is therefore usually stated to be how to preserve managerial prerogatives from too much encroachment by
workers, while at the same time motivating those same workers to
commit themselves wholeheartedly to the aims of the organisation
defined by managers.

Lupton contends that his own attempts to assist managers to make organizational changes often rest on a diagnosis different from the one managers
usually make. His position, stated briefly, is that to become a manager does
not automatically confer wisdom greater than that found amongst people
who are not, and are never likely to become, managers. A manager might be
wise about some specialized matters but cannot be wise about all things all
the time; he or she is bound to be considerably less knowledgeable and less
wise about the jobs of some of his/her subordinates than they are. The management of South Mersey College claimed that it shared Lupton's belief in
'the competences of the underdog' and also recognized that because the pace
of organizational change was speeding up and increasing in complexity:

Increasingly, the packaged general solution to these problems will
have to be abandoned for a method of diagnosing just how flexible,
how adaptable, a particular organisation (or different parts of it)
needs to be, to cope with its environment and its technology of
manufacture or service. Which, once again, calls for detailed knowledge and the collaboration of everybody who knows anything that
is relevant and can contribute anything that is necessary.[20]

The competences of the managed were well enough understood and
would be enthusiastically sought and fostered but this did not alter management's conviction in the balanced benefit of adopting a departmental structure at the outset. This would not prevent the management aspiring to assist
the creation of what Handy[21] has called 'an organization of consent'. He
believes that such organizations:

1 recognize the right to disagree;
2 control by planning and not by checking;
3 manage by reciprocal trust ('trust and control displace each other');
4 manage by 'platoons' ('individuals find it easier to identify with smaller
   groups');
5 are personal rather than impersonal ('openness and frankness and
   sincerity are valued');
6 are ones in which the managerial role is exhausting ('To treat individuals as individuals, to welcome disagreement, to tolerate dissent
   ... all these ... require ... a great deal of energy'). Managers needed
   to husband their energy ('when energy fails we fall back on routines
   and general principles, we listen less and dictate more').

Leadership

Before concluding this section it might also be helpful to outline what conceptual views were held with regard to leadership styles. The Principal was well acquainted with the work of F.E. Fiedler,[22] Professor of Psychology and Director of the Organizational Research Group at the University of Washington. Fiedler's research programme into the nature of effective leadership had been carried out in a large range of organizations, including businesses, civil and military governmental agencies and voluntary organizations. The studies had concentrated on work groups rather than on organization 'in the round'.

Effectiveness is defined in a robust way: how well the group performs the primary task for which it exists, for example, output levels for production managers, students' standardized achievement-test grades for school principals.

Fiedler identifies two main leadership styles. 'Relationship-motivated leaders' obtain their main satisfaction from good personal relationships. They are very concerned with what group members feel. They encourage subordinates to participate and to offer ideas. 'Task-motivated leaders' are pre-eminently concerned with the successful completion of any task assigned to them. Their style is based upon clear orders and standardized procedures for subordinates.

The Fiedler 'contingency-model' is one of some elaboration and its precise description here would be somewhat out of place. What can be said, quite simply, is that both of the above styles can be effective in appropriate contexts. He takes a contingency approach to leadership and rejects the belief that there is a best style which is appropriate for all situations. As Pugh, Hickson and Hinnings summarize it, Fiedler's tenet is that: '[w]hat is effective leadership will be contingent on the nature of the task which the leader faces and the situation in which he operates.'

The Principal believed that the contingency approach provided a useful framework for the tasks of leadership in inducing organizational change. Beyond that he believed strongly in the salience of middle management to the accomplishment of change. Ford[23] had written that at the heart of successful change for an organization of whatever size, was the integration of two key factors:

> — an understanding of the content of change (the various necessary ingredients of enhanced performance) and the actual process by which change is to be brought about. The first is about 'managerial vision' and the second about managerial 'grip' — on the one hand developing a clear and inspirational view of the way ahead and, on the other, the ability to get done what has to be done.

Ford avers that both vision and grip must normally originate with the head of an organization. The job of the leader is, after all, to lead. The critical challenge, however, is to transfer them to other executive levels, from the 'bridge' to the middle managerial 'engine room', which is where 'things often tend to fall down'. The Principal of the College supported Ford's tenet that:

> The change must come and be developed from within the managerial heart of the organisation. It is the vision and grip of middle management which ultimately determines the success of the change and the results achieved,

so much so that he admitted to being more than a shade didactic about it. From his experience as an HMI he had perceived the harm done to colleges by the selective perception the Dearborn and Simon research had identified. When the Deans of Faculty were appointed he stated his view that the size of the Faculties they managed were, in effect, small colleges. Within broad policy, they would be given executive freedom to manage their small colleges, with accountability to the Principalship, the College Academic Board and its Committees, with the fundamental proviso that, if the College had a problem they all had a problem. There was to be no selective interpretation of problems, as perceived through the eyes of their own academic subjects and programmes of provision.

The Childwall Campus

In Chapter 4 some of the obstacles to cultural change were highlighted, including the future of the Childwall campus. The issue was one with significant strategic implications, hence its location in this chapter. To an informed observer, it also had pronounced theoretical interest for at least two reasons:

- the sociological concept of the 'isolated mass' and its repertoire of behaviours (mentioned earlier); and
- the proposition of Johnson and Scholes[24] that many public service organizations are frequently dominated by people with a strong professional view of their role which may not be in accord with the managerial view on how they can best be used as a resource.

As has also been previously mentioned (see Chapter 2), prior to the reorganization of Further Education in Liverpool, the HMI and the District Audit Service undertook complementary studies of the FE Service (1983). Among the observations of the Inspectorate was the point that accommodation was under-utilized whilst shortages were being experienced in other aspects, such as student communal facilities. HMI added, portentously, that split-site working militated against the unity of Colleges and could pose particular resource difficulties.

In the Session 1985–86, whilst serving as the Principal Designate of the projected new College, the Principal had made it clear to the staff at Childwall that he fully supported this view, especially because reorganization would leave serious under-utilization of the facilities at the large Riversdale site, leading inevitably to a high premises cost per full-time equivalent (FTE) student in the College as a whole.

Immediately following his appointment, HMI had also acquainted the new Principal with the serious roofing problems at the Childwall site, problems so endemic it had led them to conclude that the site had no viable long-term future. He was advised accordingly to plan for the closure of the site. This would clearly make good economic sense, since the saving in recurrent costs could be used for the betterment of provision at Riversdale, but it would also make good educational sense, for many of the staff at Childwall had expertise in curriculum development from which the technological provision at Riversdale would derive great benefit.

As an ex HMI, the Principal felt this view to be a reasonable one. He was particularly struck by the comment of the District and General Inspector that if the community ethos which directed the efforts of so many of the Childwall staff could be transferred to the Riversdale campus this would prove to be a key factor in the College's drive for diversification and development.

However, the move of the City Council, during the reorganization, towards the closure of the Childwall site, met with wholehearted opposition from virtually all the staff located there. Their main argument was loss of market, in that students in the Childwall catchment (the districts of Childwall, Netherley, Gateacre and Belle Vale) would not travel to Riversdale, which had no direct public transport links with their homes. Many of the Childwall students were unwaged and had no means of private transport.

The view of management was that the campuses were no more than four to five miles apart, that such problems could be overcome and that, in any event, thousands of Liverpool's disadvantaged lived within the catchment area of Riversdale (in the districts of Speke, Garston and Toxteth). Little was being done for them, and the College had a duty to remedy this situation, taking into account especially the excellent community facilities at Riversdale and the requirement to diversify provision there.

Discussions between the staff representatives, College management, officers of the Local Education Authority and elected representatives only intensified the resolve of the staff to oppose implacably the concentration of the College's work at Riversdale. It was pointed out to them that even if resistance to change was not ascribed to them and that their concern for the people in the Childwall catchment was taken at its face value, the staff had to realise the social consequences of their actions in that a sensitive social conscience or undue concern for a particular group of people might prove economically paralyzing to the College and prevent it from operating in a decisive and efficient way for the broader constituencies it had been set up to serve.

In the end, the Council decided not to proceed with the closure of the site for the time being. One of the main reasons for the decision was sympathy for the position of those students about to commence the second year of two year courses. Management, for its part, felt that a great educational and economic opportunity had been lost. It has to be noted here that, in accordance with the further education reorganization, the Council had agreed to reimburse any member of staff involved in additional travel costs as a result of the reorganization. It had honoured this commitment in full, but these arrangements had no attraction for the teachers of Childwall.

The Principal and his senior colleagues were to remember the stance taken by the Childwall staff, a stance which they felt went beyond what the social scientist would typify as resistance to change. In 1988, Bishop David Sheppard and Archbishop Derek Warlock were to publish their recollections of their respective ministries in Liverpool and their joint efforts in the cause of ecumenism. In their chapter on 'Coming to Liverpool', they wrote:

First impressions of Liverpool include a fierce sense of identity. Of late this has been all too easily equated with militancy, but even when translated to 'solidarity', it is still not as simple as that. It has to do with the most intense loyalties, which are themselves reflected in a strongly expressed possessiveness.

There is a strongly positive side to this sense of identity. Possessiveness is matched by a sense of belonging, responsibility for each other — generosity within the local community and dogged persistence if it comes to a strike for survival. Solidarity may find expression in the quickness, sharpness, wit and anger of a people united in vigorous response to an enemy.

There can be a negative side to this strong sense of identity too. At times it can lead almost to a kind of tribalism which is inward-looking, self-protective and exclusive: an automatic distrust of 'the other'; 'our group' to be defended right or wrong: a retreat into a fortress mentality which is closed to any argument or explanation if it seems to threaten tribal custom. Then the quick wit ceases to be good-humoured and develops an aggressively defensive tone, keeping strangers at arm's length.[25]

College management was to conclude that, despite its undoubted strengths, a part of the Childwall staff exhibited something of these tendencies. Moreover, these tendencies would still be in evidence when the City Council again proposed to close the site as part of its budgetary proposals for the 1989/90 financial year.

Although an opportunity had been lost, management held to the view that if it could begin to develop a high level of interaction between the

Childwall and the Riversdale campuses this, of itself, would contribute to changing the culture of the College.

It was therefore decided:

1   that within the General Studies Faculty some staff would be timetabled so that their teaching took place on both campuses;
2   that the new American Studies Resource Centre (see p. 85), the idea had emanated from Childwall, would be established, with transfer of the appropriate staff, at the Riversdale campus;
3   that the progress of newly established provision in media studies would be monitored with a view to its transfer from Childwall to Riversdale; and
4   that means had to be found to transfer, at minimum cost if possible, some technological courses from Riversdale to Childwall.

This concludes an outline of the key constructs of value to management in its first efforts to develop and diversify the College. There now follows a narrative history of the College's progress in its first Academic Session.

Narrative: The 1986/87 Academic Session

The College Academic Board and its Committees

The Board met on four occasions in the College's first Academic Session (18.12.1986; 19.1.1987; 8.4.1987 and 26.6.1987). The first items at the initial meeting were concerned with the role of the Board in the management of the College and a discussion on the Principal's papers concerning the Committees of the College Academic Board, the formation of Faculty Boards, and the rationale of Working Groups.

A teacher representative felt that the Board should be given time to consider the papers presented and that a special meeting should be set up to discuss the formation, numbers and terms of reference of the Committees and Working Parties of the Board. This was unanimously agreed and a special meeting took place on 19 January 1987. At the meeting a proposal from the College's Management Team on the structure of the Board's Committees and Working Groups was discussed. An extract from the proposal reads as follows:

The Management Team takes the view that the number of formal Committees of the CAB should be kept to a minimum to avoid the necessity of issues being referred between committees and to limit the commitment of staff time. For similar reasons, and in order that the Committees shall work speedily and effectively, it is also believed that their membership should not exceed ten persons. Thirdly, it is recognized that the Committees will need and wish to establish sub-committees or working parties in specific fields; it is believed that these should remain informal, with a limited membership, and in the case of working parties, may well be set up for a strictly finite period to achieve specific objectives. Three Committees are suggested, as set out below:

Figure 5.3:   *The College academic board and its committees*

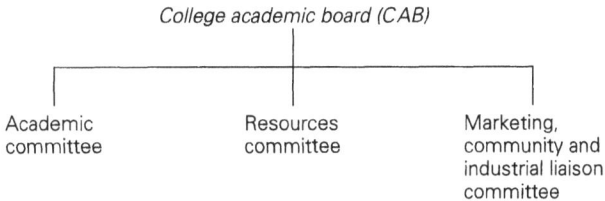

College academic board (CAB)

| Academic committee | Resources committee | Marketing, community and industrial liaison committee |

At the special meeting of the Board on Monday 19th January 1987 the report of the College Management Team was considered.

Members were of the opinion that Deans' nominees should, as far as possible, serve upon the (CAB) Committees as the Deans have a forum at their own fortnightly Deans' meetings. It was agreed that all Committees would be free to co-opt additional members for meetings or for individual items. (CAB Minutes Item 5(a)).

Subject to these comments it was resolved that:

... the structure set out, in the report of the College Management Team, for Committees to support the work of the College Academic Board be approved.

A content analysis of the minutes covering the four meetings of the Board in its first Session shows that strategic and broad managerial issues were brought to the Board for its consideration including:

The College Development Plan;
Multi-cultural and multi-racial provision;
The provision of Work-related non-advanced Further Education;
Grant-related In-Service Training (GRIST);
Special Needs provision;
Careers Education and Vocational Guidance;
The development of Open Learning;
Staff development for educational support staff;
The co-ordination of Learning Resources; and
College policy on Equal Opportunities.

In addition, the Board received termly reports from each Dean of Faculty, the Director of Marketing and the Head of Academic Planning Services as well as similar reports from its own Committees.

Minutes of the Committees of the Board are also available which demonstrate that following their establishment they met with adequate frequency during the remainder of the 1986/87 Session and discussed strategic issues at that level of complexity appropriate to the discharge of support to the Academic Board as a body responsible for the development and implementation of College policy. Documentary evidence is also available attesting to the early formation of Faculty Boards.

Reports from the Faculties: 1986/87 Session

Automobile and General Engineering

This Faculty began its operations by undertaking an extensive programme of industrial liaison. Among other things this resulted in some noteworthy benefactions (of equipment and vehicles). A Road Transport Industry Training Board (RTITB) Skills Testing Centre was established at the College and the Board's Regional Apprentice Competition was held there.

New courses were established in Auto-Engineering Crafts (full-time) and Auto-Electronics for Mature Students (evening). Business and Technician Council approvals were obtained for First Awards in General Engineering and Automobile Engineering and for a National Certificate in Automobile Engineering. The Faculty also began to provide for Special Needs students with a seven-week Summer Course for students from a nearby Training Centre. They did generally well in Examinations, with National and Regional awards appearing in the results. This Faculty perceived a clear need for the continuous technological up-dating of its teaching staff and during the Session it released members for courses in Computer-Aided Design, Computer-Aided Manufacture and Diesel Fuel Injection.

Construction

The establishment of this Faculty necessitated the transfer of large quantities of equipment, materials and other resources and teaching and support staff from the former Central College of Further Education at Clarence Street, Liverpool 3. Because of the dire shortage of money, the City Council had been unable to make any capital allocation to the College for it to undertake this transfer. The enthusiastic cooperation of teaching and support staff made it possible to complete the move at a reasonable cost (borne by the College's revenue allocation) and with no adverse effects on course provision. The efforts of the staff were commended by the Construction Industry Training Board (CITB) and by Her Majesty's Inspectors (HMI).

In addition to its rate-borne provision, a large number of income-earning courses were successfully operated for the Manpower Services Commission, the CITB, and other agencies. This resulted in a total income to the Authority of £193,000. Students of the Faculty obtained five national prizes and, with the object of raising its visibility in the catchment, the Faculty hosted the Annual Brickwork Competition for Merseyside Colleges.

General Studies

In support of the College's diversification and development programme, the Faculty undertook a highly significant amount of growth activity during the Session. New courses included basic and refresher provision in English and Mathematics. Drama and Video classes were developed for Special Needs students. Pre- and Active retirement courses, Media Studies courses and courses in Psychology were offered for the first time, as were a wide range of evening classes and a number of seminars on AIDS.

Of great importance was the establishment by the College of the Merseyside Trades Union Education Unit. This was achieved with the enthusiastic support of the Liverpool City Council and the Regional Education Officer of the TUC. By July 1987, the Unit had generated no less than 30,000 hours of Burnham Category III (Advanced) tuition.

The new College had acquired a well-established Access to Higher Education course (from the Childwall Hall College of Further Education) and this began to develop markedly. In the 1986–87 Session 100 students enrolled on the course. In September 1987, forty-seven of these joined University and Polytechnic courses.

Extensive curriculum development activity resulted in the addition of new options to the Access to Higher Education course, as well as a whole series of opportunities at the GCSE and GCE 'A' levels. Preliminary work began to establish an Open Learning Workshop at Childwall. The energetic development of Enterprise Education resulted in the establishment of 'Start Your Own Business' courses at both the Riversdale and Childwall campuses. The number of Reading Clubs organized by the Faculty was also increased.

A Certificate in Pre-Vocational Education (CPVE) course was initiated and in June 1987, the College's two-year Adult Literacy and Basic Skills Unit (ALBSU) project, which over its duration attracted external funding in excess of £80,000.00, commenced operations at an outreach centre in Speke.

On its formation, the College had made a bid to house the American Studies Resource Centre (North) — one of only two in the country. In March 1987, the College was advised by the British Association for American Studies (BAAS) that the Cultural Affairs Office in the US Embassy in London had agreed that the Centre be located at the College, within the General Studies Faculty. The decision was accompanied by first-year support funding of $10,000. The College was asked to make arrangements for an official inauguration ceremony at an early date.

Maritime Studies

Because of the grave condition of the shipping industry, this Faculty was faced with serious and sustained decline in its traditional role for the training of deck officers and marine engineers. Despite the departure of a large number of teaching staff, under the Premature Retirement Compensation (PRC) Scheme which accompanied reorganization, the Faculty was formed with fifty-one teaching staff against an establishment of thirty-nine, as determined by the Authority's Advisory Formula.

Nine of these staff were transferred to other Faculties during the Session, two were to leave the College in July 1987 under a further round of PRC offers by the Authority and three were seconded to other institutions (one to Burton Manor College, two to Liverpool Polytechnic). This reduced the teaching complement to thirty-seven. In addition, five of the fourteen technicians in post were transferred to other Faculties.

The Faculty was asked to vacate substantial Engineering Workshop areas (B106, B108 and A118) which were transferred to the Faculty of Construction. A programme to vacate a further workshop (A116) was also begun. The Faculty vacated two Staff Workrooms (G120 and G124) to provide for a College Crèche, and a third Staff Workroom (E210) in order for the College to create an Open Learning Workshop at Riversdale.

Despite these necessary retrenchments, the Faculty pursued a creditable number of market opportunities. One hundred and sixty-five courses were mounted during the Session, with a total enrolment of 3209 students. Income to the Authority from Faculty short courses amounted to £78,507, with the total of fees and other income reaching £244,713. Students attending the Faculty's traditional courses came from as far afield as Saudi Arabia, Iran, West Indies, Nigeria, Ethiopia, Pakistan, Libya, West Germany and the Gilbert and Ellice Islands.

Courses in Electronic Navigation Systems and Radio Telephony for Yachtsmen were introduced together with a Rummage and Safety course for H.M. Customs and Excise, which promised continuous and extended support.

The Faculty's links with the Royal Yachting Association (RYA) continued successfully both through its course provision and its work as an examination centre. An important income-earning link was established with the North Wales Institute of Higher Education. Under contract to the Institute, staff from the Faculty conducted a five-week workshop at Nigeria Polytechnic. Again, this connection offered prospects of extension and there was a firm intention to actively pursue similar opportunities.

Prior to the FE reorganization the ROTeC facility (Riversdale Open Technology Centre) had been established with start-up funding from the Manpower Services Commission (MSC). The Senior Management of the new College regarded this Facility, located within the Faculty of Maritime Studies and serviced by its staff, as one of the potential growth points for the College. Its status had been confirmed and a policy established that it should operate on trading account lines on termination of MSC funding, covering its expenditure with income. During the 1986/87 Session, ROTeC attracted support from a number of public and private sector organizations and the College received a number of commendations from clients for the quality of ROTeC's services.

The Faculty also obtained supplementary income from gifts of equipment, the leasing of craft, the provision of examination facilities and the sale of surplus equipment.

Equal Opportunities

The College began to develop an open-door policy to encourage all sections of the community, including ethnic minority groups, to use the facilities of the College, including its buildings and grounds. In this context, two noteworthy events took place in the 1986/87 Session:

- On Sunday, 28th June, the All-Britain Fleadh (Irish Traditional Music and Song Championships) were held at the Riversdale Campus. Seven hundred competitors took part in these Championships which were attended by 2000 spectators from all parts of Britain.
- From 17th to 21st July, a four-day Gathering of Britain's Moslem Students' Society took place at Riversdale. In the College hostels and in a forty tent village on the playing fields, 1550 men, women and children were in residence. During the event there were 400 extra visitors.

The organizers for both events signified their wish to return to the College.

Management felt that the publicity and goodwill generated by these events did a great deal to emphasize the commitment of the College to become a significant multi-cultural, multi-racial institution. An extract from the Principal's report to the Governing Body for the Session reads as follows:

Whilst the staff of the constituent Colleges have lengthy experience in assimilating into the student body people from many lands and many cultures, 1986/87 saw a collective will emerge not only to devise and publish an anti-racist/equal opportunities policy, but also to implement it. Steps are in hand to produce statistical profiles of staff and student populations, together with student retention rates; to continuously review publicity and marketing material; to review curricula; to provide appropriate staff development and not least, to mount a programme of close and continuing links with community groups.

Resources

In the Financial Year 1986/87 the College operated on the basis of separate budgets from the former Riversdale College (£5,680,700) and the Childwall Hall College (£1,276,100). These expenditures were offset to some extent by the income generated by the City Council through 'pooling' arrangements, payments from other Local Education Authorities, the Rate Support Grant, fees income from the Manpower Services Commission (subsequently the Training Agency) and from other clients. The cost of the College to the Liverpool ratepayers was, therefore, considerably less than the initial figures suggest. The cost was quite considerable, even so, given the City's financial position.

That said, the College's management felt it necessary to inform the Governing Body that in all budget categories, but particularly in educational equipment, books, stationery and telephone expenditure, there were severe resource problems. The shortage of computing equipment and workshop/laboratory equipment was particularly noticeable. The extended lack of capital investment (i.e. in the constituent Colleges and subsequently in the new College) coupled with a severely curtailed revenue budget led to criticisms from validating bodies, (such as the Construction Industry Training Board and the Business and Technician Advisory Council), from Her Majesty's Inspectorate, from customer organizations and from the staff and students of the College. Governors were warned of the threat to the continuance of some courses, particularly those in the technologies.

By the end of the 1986/87 Academic Session, management was able to feel it had helped to establish the new College and to introduce into its own conceptual thinking certain theoretical principles which it believed to be wholly appropriate to, and equitable for, the development and diversification of the College. Among these principles were:

- the efficacy of 'open-system' theory as a perspective for a managerial approach to organizational behaviour and for changing the cultural recipe;
- the importance of macro-environmental influences and the need for attention to these in shaping corporate culture, particularly as the College was now operating in an environment of increasing turbulence;
- the need for managers to operate in a boundary-spanning role between the College and its environment, to also act as change-agents and to make every effort to locate and support 'change-heroes' within the staffing profile;
- to establish that while the initial organization structure was hierarchical, the Academic Board and its sub-Committees were the mechanisms for policy formulation, particularly with regard to the development of the curriculum and the allocation of resources;

and to ensure that:

- communication was to be perceived as a two-way process;
- the value of specialist contributions to decision-making was to be emphasized, no matter from what hierarchical level these emanated;
- diversification and development were to take place within a process of strategic management which demonstrated an adequate awareness of the politics of organizational change;
- management saw the inculcation of the belief in the existence of a common purpose as one of its most salient roles;
- despite the need, in the short run, for management to take the lead in both strategic and tactical issues, the objective was for the College to become an 'organization of consent' in which the right to disagree was fully recognized;
- the leadership style to be adopted was dependent on factors of task and situation;
- the salience of middle management as 'change-agents' was acknowledged and encouraged.

Figure 5.4 depicts the analytical process which management hoped would characterize the College's approach to devising and revising its strategy, as circumstances dictated. Central to this approach was the belief that organizations can learn from their experience and can learn to learn: that, in Morgan's[26] phrase, such learning would be 'double-loop', as opposed to 'single-loop' learning (see Figure 5.5).

The Principal felt able to report to the Governing Body, on 8th October 1987 that:

Despite the problems, which included burst pipes, break-ins and thefts of equipment, 1986/87 was a year in which South Mersey College demonstrated that it can diversify and it can be successful.

The management also felt that the concept of 'achieving revolutionary change at an evolutionary pace' had proved well-founded for the staff had at first been reluctant to participate in the decision-making process (via the College Academic Board and its Committees). They were used to hierarchical approaches to decisions and views had been expressed that there were 'too many Committees'. Already, however, this reaction was beginning to disappear.

All in all, it had been a succesful first Session but management was clear, perusing the following statistics:

Year	Fte Students	Fte Staff	Student: Staff Ratio
1986–7	1601	208.74	7.67

Figure 5.4: A model of strategy formulation

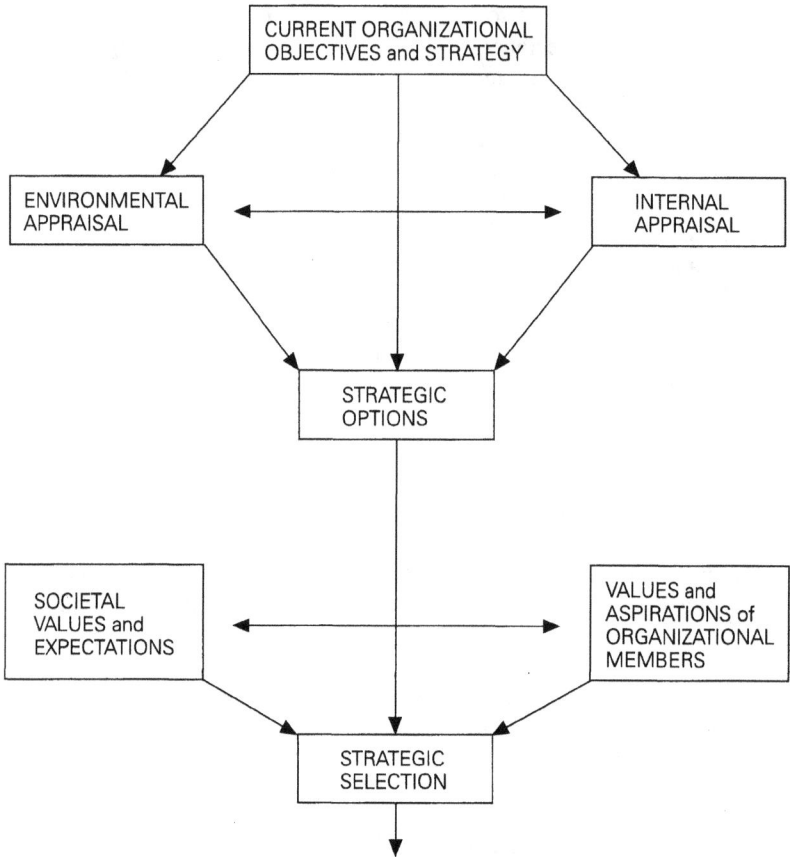

that there was a great deal of work to be done in order to achieve 'steady state' in the face of changing markets and a changing environment.

Figure 5.5: Single and double-loop learning

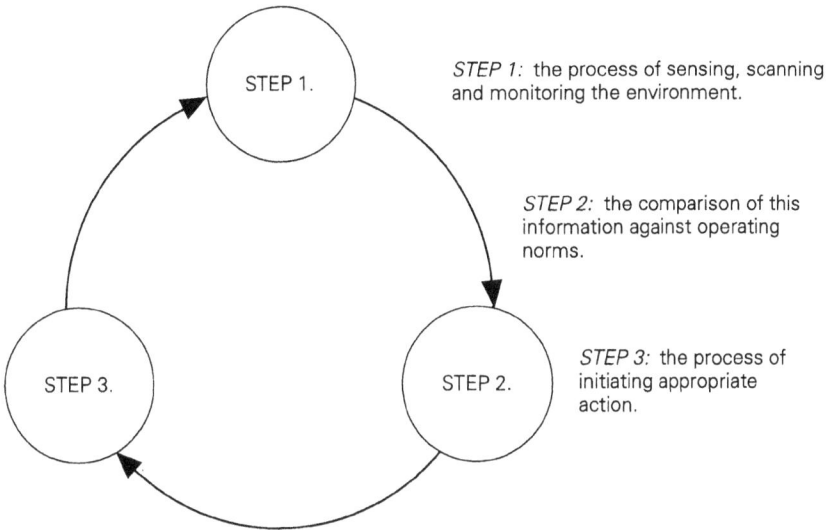

STEP 1.

STEP 1: the process of sensing, scanning and monitoring the environment.

STEP 2: the comparison of this information against operating norms.

STEP 3.

STEP 2.

STEP 3: the process of initiating appropriate action.

Single-loop learning rests in an ability to detect and correct error in relation to a given set of operating norms.

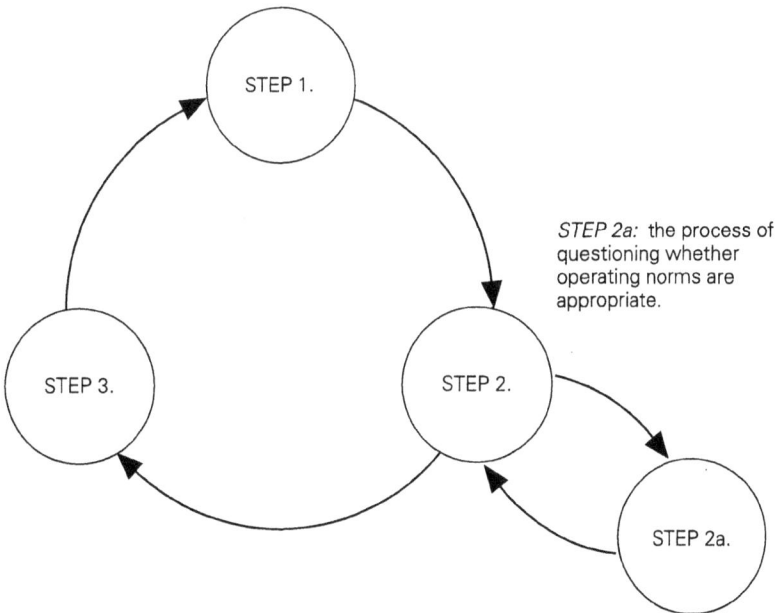

STEP 1.

STEP 2a: the process of questioning whether operating norms are appropriate.

STEP 3.

STEP 2.

STEP 2a.

Double-loop learning depends on being able to take a 'double look' at the situation by questioning the relevance of operating norms.

Notes

1 MULLINS, L.J. (1989) *Management and Organizational Behaviour*, 2nd Edition, London: Pitman Publishing, p. 19.
2 EMERY, F. and TRIST, E. (1965) 'The causal texture of organizational environments', *Human Relations*, **18**, August, pp. 124–51.
3 RANSON, S., TAYLOR, B. and BRIGHOUSE, T. (1986) *The Revolution in Education and Training*, Harlow, Essex: Longman Group (UK) Ltd., p. 2.
4 BELL, D. (1976) *The Coming of Post-Industrial Society*, Harmondsworth, Middlesex: Penguin Books Ltd.
5 GALBRAITH, J.K. (1977) *The Age of Uncertainty*, London: British Broadcasting Corporation, Andre Deutsch, p. 7.
6 TOFFLER, A. (1971) *Future Shock*, London: Pan Books, p. 11.
7 BURNS, T. and STALKER, G.M. (1968) *The Management of Innovation*, 2nd Edition, London: Tavistock Publications.
8 JAQUES, E. (1956) *The Measurement of Responsibility*, London: Tavistock Publications and (1982) *Free Enterprise, Fair Employment*, London: Heinemann.
9 McGREGOR, D. (1960) *The Human Side of Enterprise*, New York, New York: McGraw-Hill.
10 BARNARD, C.I. (1983) *The Functions of the Executive*, and (1948) *Organization and Management*, Cambridge, Massachusetts: Harvard University Press.
11 MORGAN, G. (1986) *Images of Organization*, London: Sage Publications Inc., pp. 39–76.
12 GOULDNER, A.W. (1957) 'Cosmopolitans and locals: Towards an analysis of latent social roles', *Administrative Science Quarterly* **I**, pp. 281–306.
13 MANGHAM, I. (1979) *The Politics of Organizational Change*, London: Associated Business Press, pp. 16–17.
14 BOWMAN C. and ASCH, D. (1987) *Strategic Management*, London: Macmillan Education Ltd., p. 5.
15 DEARBORN, C. and SIMON, H. (1968) 'Selective perception: A note on departmental identification of executives', *Sociometry*, **21**, and reported in MANGHAM, I. (1979) (reference 13), p. 27.
16 BARNARD, C.I. (1983) Op. cit. (see reference 10).
17 DAVIES, P. and SCRIBBINS, K. (1985) *Marketing Further and Higher Education*, London: Longman, for Further Education Unit (FEU) and Further Education Staff College (FESC), p. vii.
18 DEARBORN, C. and SIMON, H. (1979) reported in MANGHAM, I. (reference 13), p. 28.
19 LUPTON, T. (1986) in MAYON-WHITE, B. (Ed.) *Planning and Managing Change*, London: Harper and Row, p. 57.
20 LUPTON, T. (1986) Ibid., p. 61.
21 HANDY, C.B. (1983) 'The organisations of consent' in BOYD-BARRETT, O., BUSH, T., GOODEY, J., McNAY, I. and PREEDY, M. (Eds) *Approaches to Post-School Management*, London: Harper and Row, Publishers, pp. 254–55.
22 FIEDLER, F.E. (1983) in PUGH, D.S., HICKSON, D.J. and HININGS, C.R. (Eds) *Writers on Organizations*, 3rd Edition, Harmondsworth, Middlesex: Penguin Books Ltd., pp. 187–92.
23 FORD, J. (1988) 'Managing change — Do you have the vision and the grip?', *North West Business Monthly* (July) p. 10.
24 JOHNSON, G. and SCHOLES, K. (1989) *Exploring Corporate Strategy: Text and Cases*, Hemel Hempstead: Prentice Hall International (UK) Ltd., p. 117.
25 SHEPPARD, D. and WARLOCK, D. (1988) *Better Together: Christian Partnership in a Hurt City*, London: Hodder & Stoughton, p. 42.
26 MORGAN, G. (1986) Op. cit., p. 88 (see reference 11).

Chapter 6

The 1987/88 Session

Strategic Analysis: The Changing Culture

As has been stated earlier, the cultural paradigms or recipes held relatively commonly throughout both Riversdale and Childwall, and taken for granted there, but discernible to the participant observer, had been perceived by management to be in need of change in the face of new threats and opportunities. Yet the new College had begun to develop and grow within a short space of time and the cultures had already begun to fuse into a common culture grounded in responsiveness and flexibility.

In earlier chapters, the reasons have been set out to explain why, given the College was to be avowedly responsive to change, it had adopted a formal organization structure at the outset. In fact, the structure was now being regularly reviewed in the light of external changes acting upon the College, and an early modification to the organization of the Faculty of General Studies was put in hand. Details of this are given in Appendix 11.

In a more general sense, Frean[1] has suggested that:

A good way of assessing an organization is properly structured is to find out how much time managers have to spend on primary tasks (keeping internal relations sweet). If the managers have to spend more than 20 per cent of their time on purely maintenance activities, a very careful review of the organization structure is likely to produce worthwhile improvements.

In a period following a reorganization and in the face of continuing change, it was inevitable that Faculty managers needed to devote some time to resolving conflict and building morale, but in the view of Senior Management, this was not taking up an excessive amount of the time that would otherwise be devoted to development tasks. As the Principal's reports to the Governors demonstrate, a considerable amount of development and expansion was in hand. Perhaps the fact that the sub-Committees of the College Academic Boards were now well established and were meeting frequently and that resources were being allocated to Faculties in close proportion to the volume of work undertaken assisted staff:management relationships. On the subject of developing a company ethos, Frean[2] remarks that:

> People in industry have to come to terms with the fact that although work can be difficult, demanding and unpleasant, it still has to be done for economic survival.

The recent upheavals of reorganization, the departure of a large number of teachers under premature retirement terms and the continuing financial problems of the City kept the notion of economic survival in clear focus and doubtless made a contribution to cultural change. Robert Blauner[3] suggests that:

> Alienation exists when workers are unable to control their immediate work processes, to develop a sense of purpose and function which connects their jobs to the overall organization of production, to belong to integrated industrial communities, and when they fail to become involved in the activity of work as a mode of personal self-expression.

In relation to this phase of the College's development, management would claim that its exhortations for the College to develop were accompanied by delegation as well as encouragement so that a number of staff benefited from the widening discretion. This was a powerful motivating factor, for these same individuals were making unstinted efforts to maintain and increase student numbers. They were also providing a significant number of worthwhile ideas for diversification, a point to which we shall return.

The Processes of Growth and Diversification

In his authoritative work on corporate strategy, Igor Ansoff[4] describes strategic change as a realignment of an organization's product-market co-ordinates. Figure 6.1 is an adaptation of his 'Product-mission matrix'.

Figure 6.1: A courses-markets matrix (After Ansoff, H.I.)

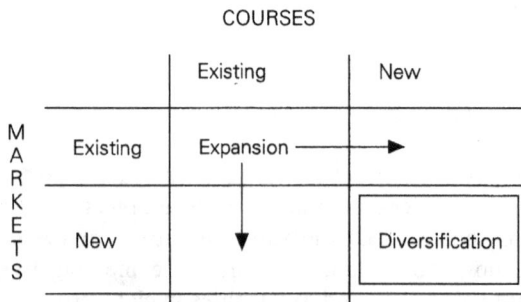

He makes the point that this realignment does not necessarily mean diversification, as shown in the growth vector matrix above. Growth is in two parts, expansion and diversification. The former, as shown in this adapted model can come from:

- increased penetration of existing markets with existing courses
- the development of new markets for existing courses
- the development of new courses for existing markets

It is thus fair to say that in most organizations, strategy does not remain static but evolves, however slowly, in response to changes in the environment. By its very definition, however, diversification is the more drastic and risky element in corporate strategy, since it involves a simultaneous departure from familiar products (i.e. courses) and familiar markets. An analysis of the Faculty reports set out later demonstrates that in the 1987/88 Session, both expansion and diversification were taking place at South Mersey College and, moreover, at a notable pace.

Moreover, the ideas for much of the diversification were emanating from the teaching staff, many of whom were at the main lecturer grades, examples here being the development of American Studies, Open Learning, Management training for small businesses, Media Studies and many of the Community Education courses.

It appeared that the College was fortunate in possessing staff whom Michael Argyle[5] would have described as being high in 'achievement motivation', those found to be most concerned with completion of a task (contrasted with 'affiliative motivation', which is more concerned with 'getting on well with the other group members'). In fact, management would aver that what Argyle[6] describes as 'group convergence towards shared norms' (often alluded to as an inhibitor of change) was, in truth, a powerful positive factor in the College's expansion and diversification. Nowhere was this more in evidence than at the Childwall campus. Some of the most important implications of the theory of Herzberg, Mausner and Snyderman[7] relate to the improvement of satisfaction and motivation by restructuring or enriching jobs so that they provide people with rewarding experiences. Expansion and diversification were increasing job enrichment, and hence the motivation of a number of individuals. Management believed its role in this process was based on two factors:

1 its readiness to share with staff its own authority to make change happen; and
2 its allocation of resources to those areas where growth and diversification were taking place.

Plant[8] suggests that resistance to change comes essentially in two forms — systemic and behavioural. 'Systemic resistance' arises from lack of appropriate knowledge, information, skills and managerial capacity. 'Behavioural resistance' describes resistance deriving from the reactions, perceptions and assumptions of individuals or groups in the organization.

> Levels of resistance will inevitably be higher if the levels of involvement and information are low. This is the essence of parallel implementation. The less I know about plans to change, the more I assume, the more suspicious I become, and the more I direct my energy into the counterproductive 'resister games'. . . . Once I feel manipulated, or uninvolved, I will inevitably tend to veer towards a negative view of the change and its effect on me.

Plant adds that the management of resistance demands attention to the systemic aspects such as information and communication flow which need to be considerably increased during the uncertainty of the change process. Management's view was that it did *not* pay sufficient attention to information and communication flow. Its efforts to communicate to College staff the broader aspects of the need for change it felt to be adequate enough. But more detailed and continuing communication were lacking, with insufficient attention to those weak signals which might indicate bigger problems to come. The reasons for management's feelings of its own inadequate performance in this regard will be made explicit.

Management would claim that its efforts to communicate at both the Faculty and the College meeting level, though somewhat simplistic, episodic and emotional even, were fitting and of value. It was aware of the 'paralysis by analysis' syndrome which, as Plant[9] points out, occurs especially in organizations which consist of highly intelligent, rational people with a great leaning towards the intellectual enjoyment of the analysis process for its own sake. He adds:

> The significant point here for the change manager is that he can inadvertently be seduced into reinforcing this process out of sheer intellectual curiosity and unwittingly find himself colluding in avoiding action. The seductiveness of the analysis game is that there is a very thin line between a good thorough analysis and avoiding action.

College management would state, therefore, that improvement was being effected but not to any organizational grand design. Such planning as was taking place was being done as part of the Education Authority's 3-year Plan and Annual programme carried out in accordance with the requirements of the Training Agency and its funding of Work-related Non-advanced Further Education (WRNAFE). Beyond that, and equally important however, was the creation of an organizational climate in which change (i.e. expansion and diversification) could take place. Here management saw its primary task as concerned with the process of co-ordinating the interface of the College and its environment. In this it was anxious to give a lead in making external contacts (which it perceived to be sorely needed) and in raising the visibility of the College in its catchment. Its attitudes are best summarized by Lupton and Tanner[10] who have written:

> We appreciate ... that experienced managers do in fact work intuitively with complex multi-variate models of their own organisations or the parts of them that they manage. They decide quickly on fairly simple courses of action with improvement in mind based on their intuitive diagnoses and these courses of action do often lead to the predicted improvements.

These authors plead, however, for an examination of the reasoning behind this intuitive, successful planning of change and make the point[11] that:

> If successful management pays, among other things, 'scrupulous attention to detail' then the management of change must rigorously adhere to that principle.

In Chapter 5 the belief of College management that the process of change should be strategically planned was set out in some detail (see, for example, Figure 5.5, Single and double-loop learning). Yet management would not yet claim that diversification and development were taking place as a result of comprehensive planning nor by paying the scrupulous attention to detail which Lupton and Tanner judge to be so important. Even so, it would affirm that, if not in a totally structured manner, it was managing change after the manner advocated by Plant,[12] and represented by Figure 6.2:

Figure 6.2: *Change: The six key activities for successful implementation, (adapted from Plant, R. (1987) Managing Change).*

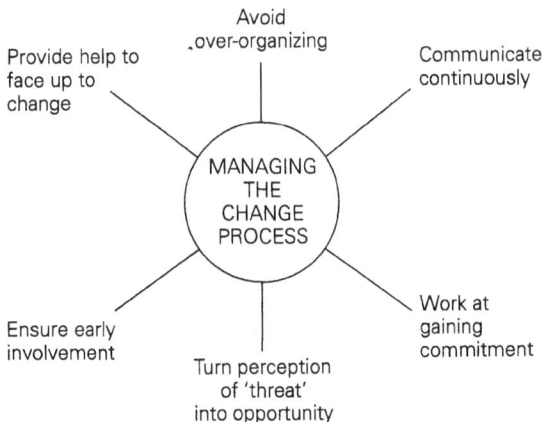

If the management of South Mersey College felt itself to be less effective than it would have wished to be in any of these activities it would be in communication. The reasons for this will subsequently become apparent. In the meantime, management felt that it was displaying a belief in what Lupton[13] has referred to as 'the competences of the underdog' (see Chapter 5). Its trust in this respect had been rewarded by the steady stream of ideas for expansion and diversification emanating from all levels of the teaching staff.

Organizational Communication

In his approach to communication, Francis[14] uses a concept from Gestalt psychology which suggests that an organization can be compared to a plumbing system with an interlinked pattern of pipes. Maximum effectiveness comes when the pipes are unblocked. Blockages affect the whole system and reduce overall effectiveness. Improving the system means the reduction and elimination of blockages. In his suggestions for improvement, he includes the advice that a strategy of change depends on intensive work to clear a few blockages and that management should not spread its energy too thinly. The management of the College would claim that while its efforts at communication were more spasmodic than the ideal, it was communicating (or clearing the blockages) along those channels it judged would lead to purposive change.

Francis suggests there are four purposes of communication:

Figure 6.3: The four purposes of communication (from Francis, D., *Unblocking Organizational Communication*)

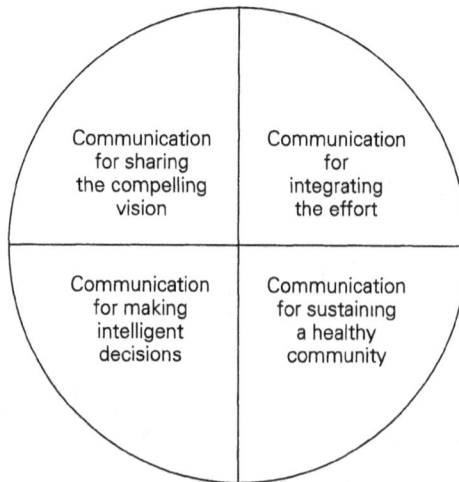

Some words of explanation for the terms used in each quadrant of the diagram might be helpful:

1 Sharing the compelling vision — Communication is the medium through which managers give direction and sustain dynamism. Organizational cultures tend to be passive. A 'compelling vision' is the corporate identity expressed in ways that stir commitment.

2 Integrating the effort — Much communication is concerned with integrating the efforts of different people to get complex things done. Integration is facilitated in three ways. Administrative devices integrate the work of specialists. Geographical closeness enables informal integration to take place. Lastly, integration is encouraged by effective downwards direction.

3 Sustaining a healthy community — A healthy community is populated by willing people who are generally satisfied, and devote themselves to improvement within the system. The power structure within the organization is accepted. People are valued for their own sake. Closeness and cooperation are present.

4 Making intelligent decisions — Accurate and speedy information is needed in order to take high quality decisions. This means that important information must be detected and processed quickly. The quality of managerial decisions is partly a function of the effectiveness of the communication system.

There are a number of points to be made apropos management's role at this stage in the development of the College:

1 Senior management would claim that, whatever the pressures, time was being found for 'sharing the compelling vision' — meetings were taking place with large groups, small groups and individuals by way of which a vision of the future was being conveyed to everyone in the organization. This was communication which Francis[15] would describe as bringing 'vision, hope, direction, value, importance and meaning in a language that can be understood';

2 Management would state that as far as the other quadrants in the Francis model were concerned, it was not yet communicating in a way which its education, instincts, business background and training would tell it was adequate. Integration was being 'encouraged by effective downwards direction' but not in an extended and sustained enough manner. The flow of accurate and speedy information needed to take high quality decisions was not yet well developed;

3 The failure to concentrate the work of the College on the Riversdale site had been, in management's view, a great opportunity lost for 'integrating the effort'. Apart from the travel costs and the demands on management time, the College was lacking that 'geographical closeness' of its staff which would enable informal integration to take place. Francis avers that in this situation 'cliques develop, defensive walls are erected and massive confusions occur.' It was clear to management that, at best, a psychological distance still separated a number of staff on the respective sites. A speedier rate of integration would also allow savings to be made in course provision — small groups could be combined wherever academically defensible.

In order to confront both the attitudinal and the resource issues, management intended to increase further the timetable commitment of Childwall staff on the Riversdale site and vice versa.

Francis[16] has developed his basic model (as set out in Figure 6.3) so as to clarify the components underlying the purposes of organizational communication. He argues that the four main purposes each have three components. These are now set out in Figure 6.4. Management's view of its own contribution at this time would be that its main communicative effort was directed to 'sharing the compelling vision', as has been said, and that its main characteristic in this regard was its 'sensitivity to the external environment'. This is not difficult to grasp given the leaning of management towards the 'marketing concept'. It might be helpful here to quote further from Francis;[17]

> Top managers are the only group who can direct the organization. In a real sense they are 'the brain of the firm'. Failure to perform this function means that the organization drifts, loses a sense of purpose and misses key opportunities. Top managers make fundamental decisions about the direction and identity of the enterprise.

He believes that this is easy to assert but much more difficult to practice. The most significant problem for senior management is the handling of complexity. 'So much data on the environment is available that managers can be swallowed by a quicksand of information.' He proposes two remedies, both of which are indispensable:

Figure 6.4: The twelve components of organizational communication (from Francis, D.,1987)

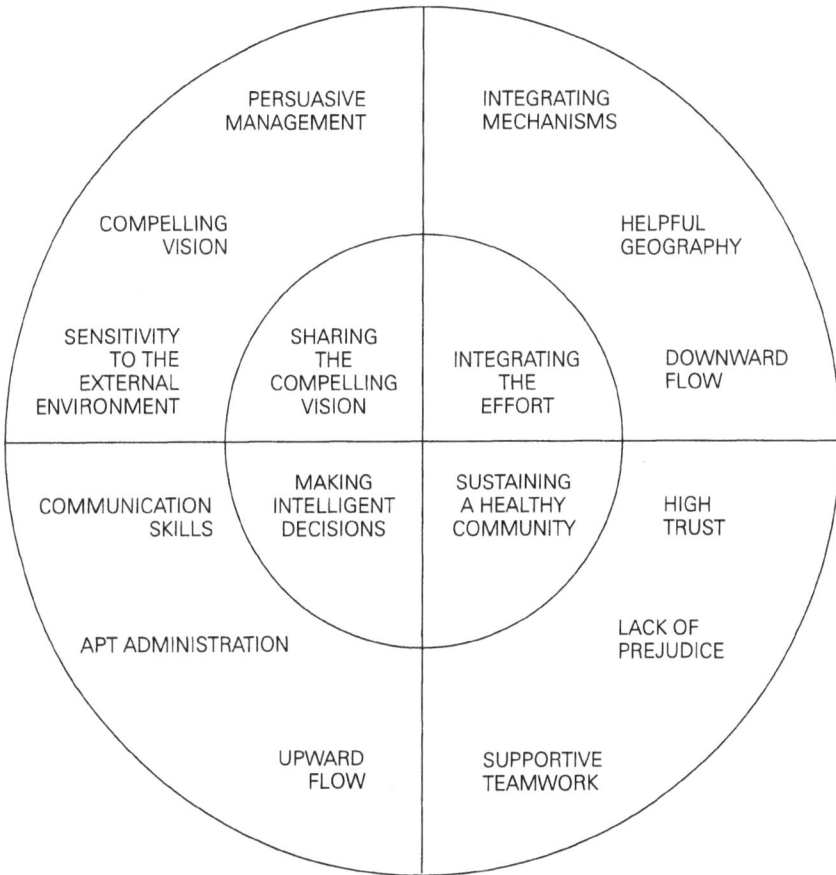

1 Management must use the principles of scientific method to structure the data it collects. Objectivity, structured observation, hypothesis, experimentation and research are the only tools with which to interpret hugely complex phenomena;
2 'Even with the most sophisticated rational systems, top managers must use their experience, instincts and hunches.' Some matters were too ephemeral or unpredictable for intellectual analysis. 'We must trust the wisdom and judgement of shrewd people'.

This second proposition, that communication with the environment can never be purely rational, has been advanced by Mintzberg[18] in an earlier work. Drawing on a paradigm from the business world, Mintzberg argues that intuitive (as well as rational) understanding of the environment enables management to identify the discontinuities, the signs that patterns are changing. The 'brain' of the organization must be capable of an intellectual leap so as to predict changes in the environment. The senior management of the College believed that perhaps its most important contribution to change and diversification was its recognition of the changing environment and its implications for the curriculum. For example, management believed that what Stankiewicz[19] has described as the obstacles to university-industry relations often held good for FE Colleges and the industrial and commercial organizations relevant to their work. Stankiewicz writes:

> If two parties who apparently stand to benefit from an exchange of goods or services do not engage in such an exchange, we can suspect that either they are unaware of the advantages they are foregoing or else regard the costs of the transactions required as too high compared with the expected gains. This general logic seems to apply to university-industry relations.
>
> The ignorance of the potential benefits of closer links between the universities and industry is certainly a significant factor inhibiting interactions between the two. Both academic research and industrial technology are evolving rapidly on a large number of fronts so it is not easy for the average scientist or engineer to keep abreast of the developments. Thus the academics tend to have a poor understanding of the needs of industry, and the industrial people poor insights into what the academic scientists have to offer.

At its own level, with its own potential clients, 'South Mersey' had to take note of this argument. This was after all management's view about the need for increased interaction between the College and its environment: so that the content of its courses became increasingly adapted to the developing scene, but also to ensure that valuable opportunities for income generation (through courses and consultancy services) were not lost.

In its communications to teaching staff, senior management repeatedly emphasized the importance of frequent and sustained external liaison and took the lead in developing these links. It was gratifying that a significant number of staff responded to this, for it was to become an important factor in the College's development.

Creativity

The point has been made earlier (p. 95), that the trust of management in the commitment of the teaching staff and its readiness to divert resources in support of such commitment was being rewarded with a steady stream of ideas for expansion and diversification. As a rule, this did not consist of the identification or discovery of ideas or processes which were absolutely new or unique (termed 'pure creativity', by writers on the subject). Rather it was comprised of ideas or processes which had become established (i.e. 'relative creativity') such as Open Learning, American Studies and new courses for the Community, but which were being adapted or introduced into the College's markets for the very first time. So that although the ideas were not unique, they were unique to the College.

Pauric McGowan,[20] in discussing why one organization may be more innovative than another, lists the factors which influence an organization's level of success as a creative and innovative operation. In addition to the efficient application of the innovation process and the effectiveness of screening the ideas for adoption, etc., he includes:

the environment within the organisation and whether or not it is conducive to such activity and attractive to the people who have the potential for it.

This statement encapsulates what the College management perceived its own responsibilities to be. The ready response to encouragement now being made manifest by a number of teachers is reflected in the observations of Bowman and Asch[21] who, in a section of their work on strategic management entitled 'Resistance to change reconsidered' write:

Much of the early literature on organisational change perpetuated the idea that employees inevitably resist attempts to get them to behave differently. There was little consideration of the idea that employees may respond positively to change or indeed, initiate it themselves. This sort of expectation that people will resist change, can become a self-fulfilling prophecy.

They point out that the dangers of automatically expecting resistance to change are now more widely appreciated and the idea that employees may welcome change has gained credence (Powell and Posner[22]). The management of South Mersey College believed that its main contribution to resurgence was in the creation of a context which was encouraging to ideas. A significant enough proportion of the teaching staff was responding to this context.

The Role of Publicity in Changing the Culture

Among the writings of management theoreticians, the internal culture has surfaced as being extremely important to competitive advantage. An internal culture fitted to the needs of the external environment and to a compelling visionary strategy is likely to create a high-performance organization.

To change corporate culture, managers can utilize such cultural artefacts as symbols and ceremonies. In this context a symbol is an object, act or event which conveys meaning to others, and a ceremony is an activity planned and conducted for the benefit of an audience. It can be used to dramatize new or emerging corporate values. It can reinforce valued accomplishments, create a bond among staff through their sharing the important event and, not least, it can be used to celebrate personal accomplishment.

Having articulated a vision for organizational change which generates commitment and is credible, a manager wishing to reinforce the vision must search for opportunities which will yield up the necessary cultural artefacts. This process is typically successful because managers are watched by employees, who attempt to read signals from what managers do and not merely what they say. As has been indicated in Chapter 5, the Principal had described his own perception of his role as a 'boundary-spanner', interpreting the environment to the College and vice versa. In addition, however, he was convinced that the College was in 'dire need of quick victories', not only for their value in absolute terms but also for their influence in shaping the internal culture.

The paragraphs which follow provide an illustration of the process at work. Firstly, however, some explanation is necessary. In the Principal's own work on Marketing[23], when describing the elements of marketing communications he sets out what he believes to be an acceptable consensus, namely that:

- Advertising consists of the purchase and use of space in newspapers, magazines and outdoor locations or the purchase and use of time on radio and television, by an identified sponsor, for the promotion of goods, services or ideas;

- Sales promotion usually complements the organization's advertising, personal selling efforts and publicity and includes those activities designed to encourage user-purchase at point-of-sale and dealer effectiveness, such as in-store displays, demonstrations and exhibitions;

- Publicity can usually be taken to mean the creation of a favourable atmosphere in which an organization can promote its products or services by means of free publicity, such as editorial features in newspapers and magazines or programmes on radio and television in which the organization and/or its personalities, products, processes and discoveries receive favourable mention.

Whilst an increasing number of commercial organizations employ relatively sophisticated techniques to determine the required funding for their marketing communications effort (relative to sales and profit objectives), in colleges and other public sector organizations the matter receives little if any attention. Up to the Education Reform Act (see Chapter 3) it was all too often the case that the advertising 'line' in a College's revenue budget was based on an historical figure to which had been applied an estimated rate of inflation for the financial year in question.

Not only did the funding so calculated bear little or no relation to the College's development plans, it was usually used, in the main, for staff recruitment and the production of the College prospectus. This last item's place in the marketing strategy for FE colleges usually went unchallenged and no effort was made to assess its effect pro rata to its cost.

The contribution of South Mersey College's senior management to change in this context was its emphasis to staff that the generation of free publicity by way of newspaper articles, air time, etc., was extremely important to the College. Every effort had to be made to cultivate the 'external face' of the College and to develop an institutional image of a 'go-ahead' dynamic establishment, sensitive to the needs of the community and the local economy. An example of the College's efforts in this regard may make the strategy clearer.

On Thursday, 3rd December 1987 the American Studies Resource Centre (North) was formally inaugurated. The Centre had been established at the College by a grant-in-aid from the US Government, through its Embassy in London, and with the support of the British Association for American Studies (BAAS). The Centre was officially opened by the Cultural Attaché of the Embassy in the presence of invited guests, including senior members of the Liverpool City Council and local industrialists. A programme of appropriate music was provided by members of the Royal Liverpool Philharmonic Orchestra (the College was cultivating a working relationship with the Orchestra which used College premises for its rehearsals from time to time). The College succeeded in obtaining sponsorship from the Save and Prosper Educational Trust for this event and this, in itself, was noteworthy, for management had stressed to staff the importance of 'plural funding'. Seeking benefactions for the College's work was an important part of this approach to funding and the Save and Prosper sponsorship of the Inauguration Ceremony was its first success. More were to follow.

The event contributed to 'the raising of the College's visibility in its catchment' and from this point on, the College energetically pursued every opportunity to obtain publicity for its courses, its students and staff and for any newsworthy aspects of its development. Management also felt the approach helped to improve staff morale at a time when this was much needed. (An extract from the commemorative brochure for the Inauguration Ceremony is included as an Appendix). Dickinson[24] makes the point that the current environment demands communication skills of all managers, whatever their sphere of operation. The College's management shared this judgment and were prepared to give a clear lead in this respect.

The Changing Culture: Concluding Observations

Two or three other points need to be made on how management viewed its own role in changing the culture. Hewton[25] believes that culture offers a unifying concept, insofar as it assumes certain similarities and a degree of consensus between members of a particular group. At the same time, it indicates the diversity which can be found between groups. With regard to subject disciplines and culture he adds that the problem raised by different disciplinary cultures is particularly apparent when attempts are made to bring subjects together to create interdisciplinary courses. Relevant case studies make the reader acutely aware of the different expectations and assumptions held by people from different disciplines. They point to the possibility of considerable variation in what different audiences will find acceptable as evidence (of the need for change), what will convince and what will lead to rethinking and change.

Within the new College, not only were there people from different disciplines, and hence cultures, there were people from different Colleges, namely Riversdale and Childwall, each with its own history and traditions, types of clientele and patterns of provision — so that cultural differences were even more marked. The need for organizational integration was paramount. This was another reason for the commitment of senior management to publicity and public relations. This could, through establishing a clear identity for the College in the public mind, also do so in the staff mind. The external face could be a powerful integrating force for the internal corpus.

Management was also able to perceive the probability of *role strain* at the cultural level. Peeke,[26] for example, has suggested that a major source of strain is a conflict of ideology. This can occur when the ideology of the professional (the lecturer) comes into conflict with the role expectations of administrators or other professionals. He adds that the strain between the demands of the administration and those of professional standards is an important one, concluding that 'The administrative system in further education ensures that there are ample opportunities for conflict here.'

Reference will be made to this in Chapter 9 in the context of the capacity of FE managers to manage. Peter Drucker has attempted a reinterpretation of the role of the contemporary manager in the light of economic and social change.[27] In addition to the economic role of the manager he makes the point that 'Management is generic and the central social function in our society rather than the isolated peculiarity of the business enterprise.'

It would have been difficult for anyone of reasonable sensitivity to manage an organization in Liverpool in the late 1980s and not to recognize that one had a social function to perform. Sheppard and Warlock[28] have written of the 'fierce sense of identity' which has to be included in first impressions of Liverpool. Initial wariness of outsiders is quickly replaced by warmth and generosity, however, when it is perceived that commitment to the service of the city and its people is genuine and sustained. The Principal and his colleagues hoped that in these vital, early days of the College, their commitment was being made manifest.

At the end of Chapter 5, statistical information for the 1986–87 Academic Session was set out. This is reproduced below, together with comparable statistics for the Session which is now to be described.

Academic Session	FTE Students	FTE Teaching Staff	Student: Staff ratio
1986–87	1601	208.74	7.67
1987–88	1742	209.88	8.30

The College's situation was improving and the following section provides a detailed illustration of this.

Narrative: The 1987/88 Academic Session

The details which follow are set out, as in Chapter 5, primarily in the form of reports from the Faculties. The material for the reports has been extracted from the Principal's own reports to the College Governing Body for its meetings in the Autumn Term (meeting of 30th October 1987); Spring Term (meeting of 12th February 1988); and Summer Term (meeting of 17th June 1988).

Automobile and general engineering

There was a healthy recruitment to the Faculty's full-time courses in Automobile Engineering (1st Year Diploma Course thirty-five students, 1st Year Craft course eighteen students) with a new full-time 3rd Year Certificate in this subject recruiting fifteen students. The demand for evening courses in auto-electronics increased significantly (forty students enrolled compared to twelve in 1986/87). Two new Youth Training Schemes (YTS) courses were formed (twenty; fifteen students) and a First Year BTEC course in Automobile Engineering achieved viable numbers (there were insufficient enrolments in the previous year). The Faculty also enrolled over 150 students on Schools Link courses.

The Road Transport Industry Training Board (RTITB) Skills Testing Service was extended to post-Foundation Course modules and the Faculty began to receive enquiries for skills testing in vehicle body work and paintwork. It also acquired a second-hand minibus to cater for its growing involvement in the field of Special Educational Needs. Its examination results for 1986/87 were in line with national averages.

In January 1988 a new first year YTS course in Mechanical Engineering Craft Studies commenced operations. At this time a Motor Cycle Repair and Maintenance course was also established at the Childwall Campus. Schools link-work was extended in the early months of 1988 as was RTITB skills testing provision.

Under the continuing phased reorganization of further education in the City, it had been agreed by the Local Education Authority that all courses for the vehicle body trades, encompassing provision in coach building, fibreglass work, metal repairs and body painting would be transferred from

Liverpool's City College to the Riversdale Campus of South Mersey College. During the summer months there was intense activity to ensure that all the relevant equipment and other facilities were re-located in time for a September 1988 start.

The provision of education and training for Special Needs students begun in the 1986/87 Session and due to the initiative and commitment of staff from this Faculty, had received much commendation across the City. The Authority's Coordinator of Special Needs Education brought this to the attention of College Management. This evaluation provided a significant opportunity for expansion and enhancement of the College's programme.

In January 1988, the Liverpool Health Authority agreed to provide £49,494 for development at the College. It was to be used for the provision of education and training facilities for young people with moderate and severe learning difficulties. The Health Authority also agreed to finance the appointment of two care assistants. The grant funded the establishment of a facility at Riversdale which included a fully-fitted kitchen, a 'bed-sit' livingroom, a DIY workshop, a room for craft training and an office (with typewriter and word processor). Two Ford Transit fifteen-seater minibuses and a supply of outdoor pursuits equipment were also acquired, and existing facilities for gardening were improved as a result of this subvention. Sufficient funds for building alterations were also available.

By January 1988, no fewer than ninety-six Special Needs students had been enrolled and a programme was operating which offered modules in literacy, numeracy, arts and crafts, computer studies, gardening, motor vehicle engineering, outdoor pursuits/PE, pottery and sailing.

The establishment of this Special Needs Unit was subsequently to prove one of the most important variables in changing the culture of the College, as will be explained in Chapter 7.

Construction

The total Autumn enrolment (1200 students) was broadly comparable to that in the 1986/87 Session, with a viable distribution to all courses. New developments included Open Learning provision for the National Examinations Board in Supervisory Studies (NEBSS); a full-time Quantities and Estimating course for the Manpower Services Commission (MSC); a national residential course for the Heating and Ventilating industry (designed to become the first of a series) and a pre-viewers course in Surveying, for the Liverpool City Council, which was related to the maintenance and upgrading of property.

Examination results for 1986/87 proved to be of a good overall standard, and the Faculty conducted a careful analysis of its monitoring survey, devised in support of the College's Equal Opportunities Policy. Although the Faculty benefited from the filling of vacant teaching posts and an increase in its technician complement (from three to nine and deployed, in the main, from the Faculty of Maritime Studies), it still had grave problems with lack of class-attendants and continued to employ a high proportion of part-time to full-time teachers (20:51).

By the Spring term, the Faculty's student recruitment was in excess of 1300, and it had begun to collaborate with the Automobile Engineering and General Studies Faculties to derive a new pattern of provision for the YTS Horticulture course. Moves were also made to increase provision for the unemployed in the field of construction crafts.

Development work to increase the Faculty's laboratory and workshop space continued and an additional Brickwork shop became available in November 1987. The metal arc welding facilities, the final move following FE reorganization, were completed in the Spring of 1988.

In the context of equal opportunities, the Faculty strove to increase its involvement with the ethnic minority areas of the City. Its increased participation in schools link-work and its investigation into the establishment of a multi-skills centre in the Toxteth district, were two aspects of this effort. Carpentry and joinery courses were offered for women, as well as other courses in construction crafts. Faculty policy was established that women were always to be accepted on courses of their choice.

By the Summer Term, the Faculty's enrolments had reached 1500 — a marginal increase on the previous Session. The full-time course in Quantities and Estimating (for the Manpower Services Commission) had become fully operational and a review of the Previewers/Surveyors course indicated that it was well regarded by representatives of the City Council. The Construction Industry Training Board (CITB) requested extra provision to be made for YTS courses in Brickwork, Plastering and Building Services (BTEC). Intensive efforts were made to promote an income-earning short course in Wastes Management (for overseas students) utilizing a world-wide range of contacts. This Faculty was also becoming involved in Skills Testing services, concentrating its initial efforts on the Heating and Ventilating Industry but expecting, subsequently, to extend into other craft skills including plumbing.

When the CITB Monitoring Team returned to the College to make a final post-reorganization inspection of the Building Services workshops, it pronounced itself extremely satisfied with the progress made. The Chairman of the group monitoring Heating and Ventilating provision stated that the College now had the best site-simulation facilities which he had seen. On a later visit, Her Majesty's Inspectors (HMI) reinforced these good impressions. (Here, it is worth re-stating that the College undertook all the physical moves and building adaptations entailed by its part in the FE reorganization entirely from its own revenue estimate resources. This makes its own commentary on the commitment and energies of the staff involved).

The income-earning capacity of the Construction Faculty increased steadily. Income from the Session was expected to reach £206,000 and with additional contracts being agreed for the 1988/89 Session, it was confidently expected that the figure would be exceeded in the ensuing year.

Financial constraints were such that the Faculty still needed to fill eight teaching posts and four educational support posts in order to achieve the staffing establishment agreed in 1986. Even so, the Faculty could demonstrate evidence of some solid achievements since reorganization, including the significant numbers attending 'taster' courses for girls (school link) and other initiatives in the equal opportunities field.

General studies

At the Childwall Campus, a former staff-room was converted for use as an Open Learning Workshop for Mathematics and English (note: this was to prove another cardinal factor in the subsequent growth and diversification of the College; early in the Autumn Term over 200 students were in weekly attendance).

The already successful Access to Higher Education course attracted 150 students (a 50 per cent increase on the previous year). Due to lack of full-time staffing resources, recruitment had to be curtailed at that figure. It was reported that during the Session, the notably developing Trades Union Education Unit would be offering 100 short courses for YTS trainees, whilst provision in Media Studies was also attracting increasing support (1986/87:30 students; 1987/88:113 students).

With regard to general academic provision the following data indicate the encouraging start made to the Session:

Course		*Enrolments (September)*		
		1985	1986	1987
		(Former Colleges)	*(South Mersey College)*	*(South Mersey College)*
GCE 'O' Level/GCSE	(Childwall)	213	237	339
GCE 'O' Level/GCSE	(Riversdale)	12	43	70
GCE 'A' Level	(Childwall)	78	100	126
GCE 'A' Level	(Riversdale)	—	—	12
	Total	303	380	547

Recruitment to the Business and Commercial courses was on a par with the 1986/87 Session, but the Start Your Own Business courses continued to grow. Enrolment to Adult and Community courses were also broadly comparable to the previous Session but there were some problem areas, (such as Active Retirement courses).

Because of the College's overall staffing position, at the beginning of the Session the Faculty employed no fewer than seventy part-time teachers. By early 1988, the Faculty had sound evidence to indicate that there would be a 39 per cent increase in student hours for the Session, the details being as follows:

	Student Hours 1986/87 *Session*	Student Hours 1987/88 *Session*
Childwall Campus	513,845	678,993
Riversdale Campus	43,239	81,543
Trades Union Education Unit	35,208	45,000
Total:	592,292	805,536

Increase of 1987/88 Session over 1986/87 Session: 39 per cent

A review carried out on 21st January 1988 indicated a notable improvement in the student:staff ratio (from 7.4:1 to approximately 10.0:1).

Moreover, it was felt that there was potential for expansion in all areas. Even in GCE 'A' Level where it was felt the market was in decline overall, the Faculty had maintained its numbers. Areas of particular promise were:

— Open Learning (especially for Basic Literacy and Numeracy);
— English as a Second Language/English as a Foreign Language;
— Access to Higher Education courses;
— Media Studies;
— GCSE for Mature Students;
— Trades Union Education;
— Community Education (with further expansion to take place on the Riversdale Campus, where there was little current provision);
— American Studies and European Studies;
— Business Studies (Secretarial and Office Skills).

The Faculty Board devised a strategy for further expansion within existing resources. From September 1988 wider provision would be offered at Riversdale including GCSE for Mature Students, ESL/EFL and Community Education. In addition to the well-established provision at Childwall, the new Session's programme there would include GCE 'A' Level provision and an expansion of Access courses.

As part of its Equal Opportunities strategy, the Faculty arranged several meetings with representatives of the black community in Liverpool. It also initiated a 'phone-in' for the general public on horticultural issues. Twenty-two enquiries were received on the first afternoon of this service and its success quickly guaranteed a viable course for the 1988/89 Session.

By the Summer Term, the growth and size of the Faculty were beginning to pose operational difficulties. Changes were therefore proposed in its organization structure, and these were approved by the College Academic Board (at its 20th May 1988 meeting) and by the College Governing Body (at its meeting of 17th June 1988). They were intended to cope with managerial problems of increasing size whilst at the same time maintaining the Faculty's response to its market.

Over 200 courses were now being offered by the Faculty and new areas of work were still being developed. A wide range of Summer Term courses had been offered and had met with a good response. The Faculty's Commercial courses were a pronounced success, those in Word Processing being among the most notable in the Region. Seventy-eight students had enrolled for commercial courses at the Riversdale Campus, many of whom had been past students of private institutions. Student evaluation of teaching standards for these courses had proved very complimentary and students attending the newly-devised drop-in Electronic Office facility had been particularly successful in obtaining employment.

For the 1988/89 Academic Session, the number of places on the Access to Higher Education course was to be increased from 150 to 180. No fewer than eighty-two current students were being offered places in Higher Education for the coming Session, with a significant number of these students receiving multiple offers. Noteworthy 'firsts' among these acceptances were for degrees in English and Nursing. Commendations on the standards of preparation for the College's students had recently been received from the University of Manchester and the Law Department of Liverpool Polytechnic.

Recent courses mounted by the Trades Union Education Unit had included a programme for NUT members relating to the reorganization of primary schools in Liverpool; a number of courses in 'handling the media' (based at the Riversdale TV Studio) and 'updating' courses for union officials with responsibility for advice and guidance on pension matters. In conjunction with the Faculty of Automobile Engineering, it was planned to provide a series of courses on 'Hazpak' regulations for drivers of heavy goods vehicles.

After the vetting of syllabuses, staffing and other resources, the College had been accepted as a member of the British Association of State Colleges in English Language Training (BASCELT). Among other things, the College would now be featured by the BASCELT organization, throughout the world, as one of its approved providers. An Urban Aid grant of £7,500 had been obtained for the Crèche facility at the Riversdale campus. It would be utilized for modifications to the Unit and equipment and supplies — these improvements to be completed by September 1988.

To inform the staffs of community organizations and employment agencies of the work of the Faculty and the College, a series of working lunches was arranged. For this promotional activity, a special information pack had been devised and more than 100 organizations contacted. At the first session (Friday, 20th May 1988), nineteen staff from local Job Centres were in attendance.

Maritime studies. Despite the discouraging 'climate', 650 students had been enrolled in the Autumn Term, and the projections were for a further 2500 students by the end of the Session (total 3150). This would broadly equal the 1986/87 enrolment (3209 students). New courses included a variety of income-earning courses for yachtsmen; an extended income-earning course for HM Customs and Excise and provision in the field of refrigeration and air conditioning. A significant increase in Open Learning enrolments was also expected.

In late 1987, with the support of the City Council, the College was in the process of acquiring a second lifeboat. This was for use with the well-supported Offshore Survival courses. It was expected that this would help to secure validation of these courses by the Offshore Petroleum Industry Training Board (OPITB) thus increasing their potential to generate income. In combination with the Southampton College of Maritime Studies, the Faculty prepared for BTEC approval a full-time course in Maritime Studies. This was to replace the Diploma in Technology course which had been introduced in 1986 by several Colleges but had been totally unsuccessful in attracting post-16-year-olds unsponsored entry into training for the Shipping Industry.

By early 1988, 115 courses had been mounted, with a total enrolment of 1400 students. In an effort to diversify and stem its decline, up to 30 per cent more courses had been offered in 1987/88 than in the previous Session. Two or three points are worth emphasizing:

1 The new income-earning course for HM Customs and Excise Officers was proving successful and more courses had been arranged;
2 New income-earning courses for yachtsmen and small boat owners were attracting a steady flow of applications and open-learning packages were being prepared for the same market;
3 The number of students attending the Faculty's ROTeC facility (Riversdale Open Technology Centre) was increasing steadily. ROTeC had been set up on trading account lines and by 31st March 1988 it would be equalizing its costs with income. One of the most significant developments was its entry into management training for small businesses, with the Merseyside Enterprise Board as its first client organization.

More generally, the Faculty stepped up its direct contacts with shipping companies and manning agencies and these confirmed the emerging shortage of junior officers in the industry. Enquiries for the Marine Diploma course were increasing steadily. The Faculty was also increasingly active in the Equal Opportunities field. Visits to the local Community Relations Council had taken place to discuss course provision for black students. Trade Unions and Job Centres had been contacted in order to promote greater participation by ethnic minorities in Offshore Survival courses. A quite extensive programme of staff development was being undertaken. This including training programmes in a number of fields, including Marketing and Resource Management.

By the end of the Session, 170 courses had been mounted, with a total enrolment of 2500 students. Faculty revenues were approaching £230,000, of which £135,000 was attributable to income-earning courses.

HM Customs and Excise Officers from all parts of the UK were now requesting a specially devised course. The Customs Service expected demand for it to continue for a further three years. Other new provision included plant maintenance for the Leisure and Recreation Industry, open-learning for the Royal Yachting Association and a GCSE course in Electronics.

Approval had been obtained from a number of validating bodies, such as BTEC, City and Guilds of London Institute, the Royal Society of Arts, for a number of courses to commence in the 1988/89 Session. The subject areas included maritime technology, transport studies, plant engineering and information technology. Approval from BTEC was awaited for a new Diploma and Higher Certificate/Diploma scheme in marine engineering. It was also hoped that final approval for a YTS course in marine engineering would not be long delayed. All the unsponsored Diploma and Higher Diploma students completing their studies in 1987/88 secured posts with shipping companies.

ROTeC continued to develop and was now providing several local and national programmes. Computer training was being provided for the staff of several organizations, and staff development programmes were being provided for colleagues in Liverpool colleges. All current customer organizations were considering extensions of their present programmes with ROTeC, and negotiations were in hand with a number of prospective clients. Liaison had been developed with the City Council's organization and methods section, which had a co-ordinating role for the training needs of the Council's staff. It was hoped that as computer applications developed within the local Authority, ROTeC would be a major provider in this sector.

The programme of business management training for the Merseyside Enterprise Board was well under way and had received favourable comments from both the Board and participating companies. There was every indication that a repeat contract would follow. This had been a stimulating challenge for the ROTeC Unit and one with prospects for considerable growth.

The Open College, a new national organization with an approach to skills training utilizing 'open-learning' techniques, had begun operations in the 1987/88 Session. As students worked through their Open College courses, support was available from a national network of approximately one hundred Open Access Centres. South Mersey College had been chosen to provide such a Centre through its ROTeC facility. In all Centres initial enrolments had been modest. It was notable, however, that the College was in the forefront of this initiative and it was hoped that certain related commercial proposals would enhance this work in the future.

Negotiations with the Royal Society of Arts (RSA), the City and Guilds of London Institute (CGLI) and the Scottish Vocational Education Council (SCOTVEC) linked with the establishment of a national qualification for practitioners in Open Learning had led to ROTeC being invited to pilot the accreditation scheme for the North West region. Given the recent growth of this method of learning, it was hoped that ROTeC would build upon its local success and become a significant regional, and perhaps national, provider.

Performance Indicators

Considerable changes in student numbers and reductions in staff over the first two years of the College's existence had improved the College's position as measured by such indicators of efficiency as the student:staff ratio (SSR). (see Figure 6.5) The development of the College had been largely in newly developed fields of activity. The main increase in student numbers was concentrated in trade union studies, 'second chance' (or access) courses for unemployed adults, general community provision, courses for women, education for students with special needs, media studies, and specialist provision for industry and commerce.

These areas of work had generated the equivalent of approximately 300 additional full-time students, enabling the General Studies Faculty to grow rapidly. About half the College's provision was now in the Community, Trades Union and General Education fields (approximately 860 full-time equivalent students). Figure 6.5 illustrates the consequential improvement in the student:staff ratio.

Figure 6.5:   Student and staff numbers and improvements in efficiency 1986–88

	Number of Students (fte)*	Number of Teaching Staff (fte)	Student: Staff Ratio (SSR)
1985–86 Former Colleges (Riversdale College of Technology, Childwall Hall College of FE)	1967	263	7.5
1986–87 South Mersey College (1st Year — new College)	1602	208	7.7
1987–88 South Mersey College	1837	206	9.0

Source: College Statistics and Annual Monitoring Survey (where completed)
* full-time equivalent

NB (i) An SSR below 9.0 was reckoned by the Audit Commission to be a 'cause for concern';
    (ii) The Joint Efficiency Study[29] recommended colleges attain an SSR (using the Annual Monitoring Survey (AMS) method of calculation) of 11.4:1 to be achieved by 1991/92; as compared with the 1985/86 figure of 10.3:1. The report is commonly referred to as JES, the Joint Efficiency Study, since it was a joint Department of Education and Science, Local Authority Association officers' report.

The 1987/88 revenue estimates had projected income at £1,541,800. By February 1988, the Governors were being advised that the anticipated income was £2,086,142. In addition, Manpower Services Commission's sponsorship of work related to non-advanced further education also brought revenue to the City Council. Significant efforts were now being made to sustain, and where possible, increase such income. This would meet a very significant proportion of the College's current net deficit whilst Rate Support was also triggered by increased numbers of students in further education.

In non-economic indicators of performance, although technological provision was, and would continue to be, of fundamental importance, there had been a quite dramatic change in the balance of the College's work as reflected by the pattern of enrolments since September 1986. Data indicated that about half of the College's provision was now in the newly developed areas of community education, access to higher education, media studies, trades union studies and similar courses.

When the development of special needs education and equal opportunities began to make their contribution, the changes in the College's profile would become more marked. The staff felt that the City Council's objective that South Mersey, no less than its other FE establishments, should become a community College in the fullest and best sense, was now well on the way to being realised. An important aspect of the College's operations in the community was its catchment. Detailed comments are set out in the section which follows.

The South City Post-16 Educational Consortium

In order to develop the initiatives taken by the structural reorganization of its secondary schools and its further education colleges, the Liverpool Education Committee resolved (in the 1985/86 Session) to establish four Area Consortia for post-16 education. Each consortium was to consist of representatives of one of the four further education colleges and of the community comprehensive schools and adult centres within a designated area. Membership was also to include representatives of the City Council, the Director of Education, student bodies, local voluntary projects and youth and community projects.

South Mersey College was to be in membership of the South City Consortium, which held its inaugural planning meeting at the Riversdale Campus of the College on 26th February 1986. Term meetings were then held from September 1986, following the formation of the new Colleges. Much of the business of these meetings had concentrated on collaborative course ventures and joint publicity activities.

By the Autumn of 1987, the College was gratified by the progress achieved. In the 1987/88 Session, for example, it was collaborating with eight schools in a Certificate of Pre-Vocational Education (CPVE) programme. Two days each week, 120 pupils were timetabled for College provision (average group size 16.13 pupils). Weekly meetings of staff from schools and the College were held at the Riversdale Campus to deal with pupil profiling, assessment, progression and other issues.

Beyond this programme, there was a steadily extending pattern of link-courses as the following statistics demonstrate:

College Faculty	Number of Pupils	Number of Schools
Automobile and General Engineering	140	7
Construction	30	2
General Studies	110	6
Maritime Studies	1084	13

Source: Principal's report to College Governing Body, 9 October 1987.

The College hoped to continue to develop this emerging pattern of Schools-College collaboration and was finding its membership of the South City Consortium of value in this regard.

In this Session, the exhortations of management for the development and growth of the College were accompanied by the widening of the delegation and the increase in the discretionary component of the jobs of junior managers and section heads. From observations of their response, these staff found this decidedly beneficial; not only did they produce worthwhile ideas for retention and expansion of existing provision, sound concepts for diversification were also forthcoming.

On the other hand, although it appreciated that the management of resistance to change demands attention to the systemic resistance which arises from lack of information and adequate communication flow, the senior management of the College felt that it was not paying adequate attention to this.

In the quest for survival and growth, there was no organizational grand design, apart from the planning implicit in the Local Education Authority's Three Year Plan and Annual Programme. As is indicated in the literature of management theory, change was taking place incrementally rather than globally. Yet, this left the organization free from the danger of 'paralysis by analysis', and management was working towards this incremental change with an intuitive, yet complex, multivariate model of its own. Above all, it was sharing a vision and integrating effort, though in this respect it would have wished to communicate more and was saddened that the geographical closeness which would have assisted integration, through concentration of provision on to a single campus, was being denied to it.

Sensitivity to the external environment was increasing. An internal environment conducive to creativity was also emerging. The role of publicity in shaping the internal culture was being utilized and emphasis was being laid on the symbols of cultural change. The inauguration ceremony at the American Studies Centre was extremely valuable in this respect.

The evidence of progress is provided by the reports from the Faculties. The details set out illustrate that there had been marked expansion in some areas of provision, notably General Studies, but the process of diversification was also proceeding significantly. In the latter respect, the institution of an open-learning workshop at Childwall was an important factor, as was the increased momentum in special needs education, in management training for small businesses, in the implementation of the Council's equal opportunities policy and the moves to develop General Education courses at Riversdale. The success of the Trades Union Education Unit, with its emphasis on workshop courses, was also a powerful element in the change process.

The College was developing its entrepreneurial outlook, as evidenced by the introduction of new income-earning programmes and the establishment of skills-testing facilities. Contacts with industrial and commercial organizations were being stepped up and schools link-work was being extended. It seemed that rather than be the passive recipient of the threats posed by environmental change, the College was taking positive steps to shape its own future.

The Session was not one of unalloyed success. The failure of the Diploma in Technology course to attract post-16 unsponsored entry into the Shipping Industry had been very disappointing. Resources problems persisted. Although there had been some improvement in the equipment position, the College recognized it was markedly failing to match the rate of introduction of new technologies in its customer organizations. Expansion was bringing with it an increasing reliance on part-time teachers and in some areas of its work the College clearly needed more educational support staff. Although external monitors had affirmed the progress made in the reorganization and improvement of its workshops, many of the College's buildings, including its residential hostels, were badly in need of repair and redecoration. This not only impaired the education environment for current students, it also set something of a brake on the College's response to market opportunities.

Nonetheless some advance in the College's fortunes was now in evidence. The outlook of the staff was generally positive and particularly so in some instances. The Faculty of Automobile and General Engineering, in an attempt to remedy some of its pressing equipment deficiencies, had acquired several thousand pounds' worth as gifts from industry. Many teachers recognized that while an improvement in the student: staff ratio was encouraging, action had to be taken to improve the student retention rate.

Notes

1 FREAN, D. (1977) *The Board and Management Development*, London: Business Books Ltd., pp. 16–17.
2 FREAN, D. (1977) Ibid., p. 9.
3 BLAUNER, R. (1974) 'Alienation and freedom', University of Chicago Press, in ARMSTRONG, P. and DAWSON, C. (1981) *People in Organisations*, Huntingdon, Cambs.: E.L.M. Publications, p. 342.
4 ANSOFF, H.I. (1975) *Corporate Strategy*, Harmondsworth, Middlesex: Penguin Books Ltd., p. 113. et seq.
5 ARGYLE, M. (1972) *The Psychology of Interpersonal Behaviour*, Harmondsworth, Middlesex: Penguin Books Ltd., p. 24.
6 ARGYLE, M. (1972) Ibid., p. 129.

7   HERZBERG, F., MAUSNER, B. and SNYDERMAN, B.B. (1959) *The Motivation to Work*, New York, New York: John Wiley, and HERZBERG, F. (1968) *Harvard Business Review*, **46**, pp. 53–162.

8   PLANT, R. (1987) *Managing Change*, Aldershot, Hants: Gower Publishing Co. Ltd., p. 19.

9   PLANT, R. (1987) Ibid., p. 20.

10 LUPTON, T. and TANNER, I. (1987) *Achieving Change: A Systematic Approach*, Aldershot, Hants.: Gower Publishing Co. Ltd., pp. vii–ix.

11 LUPTON, T. and TANNER, I. (1987) Ibid., p. 2.

12 PLANT, R. (1987) See reference 9. p. 32.

13 LUPTON, T. (1986) in MAYON-WHITE, B. (Ed.) *Planning and Managing Change*, London: Harper and Row, Publishers, p. 57.

14 FRANCIS, D. (1987) *Unblocking Organizational Communication*, Aldershot, Hants.: Gower Publishing Co. Ltd., p. xiii.

15 FRANCIS, D. (1987) Ibid., p. 6.

16 FRANCIS, D. (1987) Ibid., p. 19.

17 FRANCIS, D. (1987) Ibid., p. 26.

18 MINTZBERG, H. (1983) 'The mind of the strategist(s)' in SRIVASTA, S. and Associates *The Executive Mind*, San Francisco: Jossey-Bass Publishers.

19 STANKIEWICZ, R. (1986) *Academics and Entrepreneurs: Developing University-Industry Relations*, London: Frances Pinter (Publishers) Ltd., p. 25.

20 MCGOWAN, P. (1987) 'Creativity and innovation' in STEWART, D.M. (Ed.) *Handbook of Management Skills*, Aldershot, Hants.: Gower Publishing Co. Ltd., p. 491.

21 BOWMAN, C. and ASCH, D. (1987) *Strategic Management*, Basingstoke, Hants: Macmillan Education Ltd., p. 213.

22 POWELL, C. and POSNER, B.Z. (1978) *Resistance to Change Reconsidered: Implications for Managers, Human Resource Management*, **17**, Spring.

23 FRAIN, J. (1986) *Principles and Practice of Marketing*, London: Pitman Publishing Ltd., pp. 276–7.

24 DICKINSON, A. (1988) 'Communication by public relations' in HELLER, R. (Ed.) *The Complete Guide to Modern Management*, London: Harrap Ltd., p. 219.

25 HEWTON, E. (1987) 'Inside knowledge: Rethinking education change' in BOYD-BARRETT, O., BUSH, T., GOODEY, J., MCNAY, I. and PREEDY, M., (Eds) *Approaches to Post-school Management*, London: Harper & Row Ltd., pp. 257, 264–65.

26 PEEKE, G. (1987) 'Role strain in the further education college' in BOYD-BARRETT, *et al.*, ibid., p. 229.

27 DRUCKER, P. (1978) *Technology Management and Society*, reported in BOOT, R.L., COWLING, A.G. and STANWORTH, M.J.K. (1982) *Behavioural Sciences for Managers*, London: Edward Arnold (Publishers) Ltd., pp. 159–160.

28 SHEPPARD, D. and WARLOCK, D. (1988) *Better Together: Christian Partnership in a Hurt City*, London: Hodder & Stoughton, p. 42.

29 DEPARTMENT OF EDUCATION AND SCIENCE (1987) *Managing College Efficiently* (EDUC/280/1987), and *The Joint Efficiency Study* (JES), London: DES/Local Authority Association Officers report.

Chapter 7

The 1988/89 Session

The formation of South Mersey College was described in Chapter 4. Reference was made (p. 47) to Mintzberg' historical studies of organizations which over many decades have demonstrated that global change is infrequent. Organizations more generally change incrementally. In its own initial conceptual analysis the College management aligned itself with this view, believing there to be a critical rate of change — almost a 'confidence-level' of change and that it was as dangerous to be above this level as to be below it.

Thus at the onset, (Chapter 4, p. 66) it was felt that in the organizational atmosphere then prevailing too much change too quickly in the shape of relatively novel organizational forms would be counterproductive, calling for *too* great a toleration of ambiguity on the part of staff. A traditional hierarchical structure was adopted which would be carefully monitored, and adjusted if appropriate, in the light of experience.

In the Spring of 1989, the Management Team proposed a revised Academic Structure for the College. It was generally accepted that the structure established upon the creation of the College in 1986 had worked reasonably well in reducing the uncertainty consequent upon the reorganization of Further Education in Liverpool and in ensuring the continuation of growth of traditional provision. The structure has also supported the achievement of a considerable measure of diversification. New areas of provision, including Trades Union Studies, Media Studies and Special Needs education, had developed rapidly. Offshore Survival courses (until suspended), Adult and Community courses, Basic Education courses and Access to Higher Education courses had also grown markedly. Marine Engineering provision gave some indication of possibly re-establishing itself; Vehicle Body courses had been transferred to the College and a major workshop reorganization following the relocation of all Construction education in the City had largely been completed. Additionally, new forms of 'delivery', especially Open Learning, had been successfully pioneered and FTE student numbers had grown significantly.

However, within the College Management Team a consensus had

developed that the current academic structure required modification if it was to enable change to occur at the increasingly rapid pace necessitated by the Education Reform Act and other highly significant developments. (See Chapter 3 p. 34 ff.) This had been partially recognized in the minor modifications to the structure carried through in 1988 and designed to support a more speedy development of community provision on the Riversdale campus and to improve inter-Faculty and Cross-College operations. Even so, more radical change was now believed to be necessary, according to a Management Team report,[1] if the College was to achieve:

- significant improvements in the pace of implementing Equal Opportunities policies;
- a real tilt in provision towards student centred learning;
- the extension of Open Learning across all academic areas;
- an increase in the pace of reducing/eliminating declining areas of provision and assistance to the rise of new ones;
- improved financial and management information services to enable clearer and more cohesive planning and control to take place.

A variety of structures designed to facilitate change was examined. Whilst in due course it might be necessary to reduce or eliminate traditional Faculty or Departmental structures, the view was that it would be counter-productive to make such an adjustment at this stage. However, in the light of trends within Maritime Studies (despite increased marketing activity, no substantial progress was being made), and in order to respond to the changing composition of client needs, some reorganization of the Faculties was necessary. It was therefore proposed that:

1　The Faculty of Construction would remain substantially as it was, with the addition of Horticultural provision (transferred from the Faculty of General Studies). Its work was to be arranged within three or four Schools which were to be finally identified following further discussions within the Faculty;
2　The Faculty of Transport, a new Faculty, would be formed by the amalgamation of the current Maritime Studies and Automobile and General Engineering Faculties and arranged into two Schools;

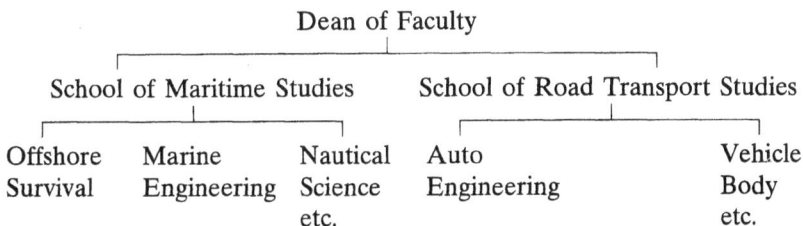

Dean of Faculty

School of Maritime Studies | School of Road Transport Studies

| Offshore Survival | Marine Engineering | Nautical Science etc. | Auto Engineering | Vehicle Body etc. |

3   The Faculty of Adult and Community Education would be based substantially on the existing Faculty of General Studies but without its provision in Trade Union Studies, Management and Supervisory Studies and Keyboard Skills. Its work would be arranged into three Schools:

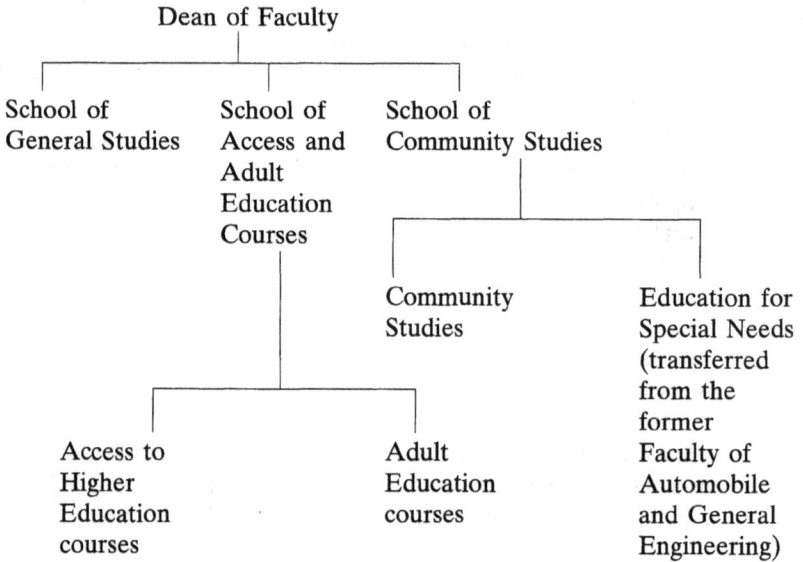

```
                      Dean of Faculty
                            |
   ┌────────────────────────┼────────────────────┐
School of              School of            School of
General Studies        Access and           Community Studies
                       Adult
                       Education                  |
                       Courses         ┌──────────┴──────────┐
                                    Community          Education for
                                    Studies            Special Needs
                                                       (transferred
                          |                            from the
               ┌──────────┴──────────┐                former
          Access to              Adult               Faculty of
          Higher                 Education           Automobile
          Education              courses             and General
          courses                                    Engineering)
```

4   The Faculty of Organization, Information and Communication Studies: this completely new Faculty would be structured as shown below. It was expected to make a significant contribution to the further growth and development of the College, as well as having a considerable role in staff development.

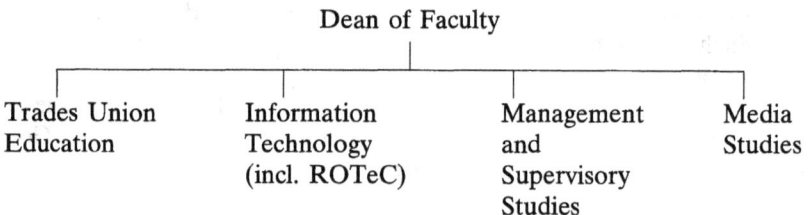

```
                         Dean of Faculty
                                |
   ┌────────────────┬───────────┼────────────────┬──────────┐
Trades Union    Information          Management          Media
Education       Technology           and                 Studies
                (incl. ROTeC)        Supervisory
                                     Studies
```

Supplementary Note: a strong consensus had emerged that a range of cross-College functions had to be strengthened and that this should entail the creation of new Units within the College. In order to achieve development in delivery methods and cross-College functions it was proposed to establish a College Academic Planning and Development Unit, with posts of Head of Unit and Coordinator in the identified areas.

It was also proposed to establish a Division of Resources Administration and College Services. This would provide and manage learning support and other Student and College services. Additionally, it would be the focus for the management information and control systems.

Although progress was made with the establishment of the management information system, progress on the establishment of the Units and some of the cross-College functions was curtailed when the Local Education Authority announced towards the end of the Session that it would be carrying out a Further Education Review. The indications were that this would mean a further reduction in the number of FE Colleges to be maintained by the Authority.

In order to demonstrate the organizational approach of College Management, a full diagrammatic representation of the proposed structure, including the new Units and the co-ordination of cross-College functions is shown in Appendix 13. The 1986 and 1988 Management Structures are shown in Appendices 14 and 15.

The City Council's current financial position and the College's own budgetary provision permitted no increase in expenditure. Indeed, given the circumstances which would apply after the Education Reform Act, it would be necessary to reduce expenditure. It was also believed that if the College was to achieve its aims some redirection of resources from academic to support staffing would be essential. Consequently, it was intended to achieve this structural change without additional expenditure and the pace of change would depend upon a number of factors, including the 'take-up' of any offers of pre-retirement compensation.

Quality Control and Institutional Effectiveness

The second factor of strategic significance derived from the fact that in late 1988 and early 1989, the Liverpool Education Authority produced a mission statement which placed emphasis on development of the quality of its further education service through the informed view of the needs of existing and potential users of the service. This 'user orientation' entitled the client to access and opportunity for progression, derived from a policy of equal opportunities for all. In order to implement the objectives of the mission statement, the Authority mounted a number of week-end conferences for the management teams of its four Colleges. Subsequently, each College was asked to produce a Position Statement of its aims for quality control and institutional effectiveness, indicating how these aims were to be achieved.

As has been indicated (in Chapter 4, Figure 4.4) the idea of 'user orientation' is a fundamental tenet of the marketing concept, which the management of South Mersey College believed should inform its approach to development and diversification. At one of the Authority conferences, the issues of 'Industry', 'Equity' and 'Client Centredness' were seen as the focal points for the development of each College's action plan for the implementation of the mission statement. The Position Statement devised and implemented by the management team at South Mersey College is incorporated in Appendix 16. Examples of ways in which the outlined Action Plan was carried through will follow.

The Closure of the Childwall Campus

In Chapter 4 (p. 46) the issue of provision at the Childwall Campus has been outlined. In Chapter 5 (p. 79 ff.) the reasons why College Management supported the view of HMI that the campus had no long term future were also explained. The main economic reasons were that despite the growth of the College there was still a serious under-utilization of accommodation and that the persistent roofing problems at Childwall were of such a scale that sufficient finance would never be made available to solve them. Moreover, Management estimated that quite aside from substantial savings in the time and energy of the teaching and administrative staff which would result in concentrating provision at Riversdale, the College budget would also gain from a £100,000 saving in recurrent costs (heating, lighting, cleaning, caretaking, etc.). Additionally, as has been explained in Chapters 4 and 5, management believed that a great step forward in changing the culture would be achieved by the coalescence of the community ethos prevailing at Childwall and the undoubted technical strengths and expertise available at Riversdale. For this reason, when the decision was taken that the Childwall Campus would remain open 'for the time being' (p. 81) management felt that a great educational, as well as economic, opportunity had been lost. In this regard, the measures taken since 1986 in timetabling a number of staff over both sites, moving some technological provision to Childwall and importing some curriculum development expertise into Riversdale from Childwall were only palliatives.

In June 1989, the College Principal submitted to the Liverpool Authority a summary of the educational advantages of concentrating provision at the Riversdale campus. This is now set out below.

1 More Liverpool residents could be assisted to obtain employment if the experience gained from the Access to Higher Education course at Childwall were applied to the technological faculties at Riversdale. People returning to education responded to a non-traditional, supportive type of provision which assisted them to gain confidence. Access to the technical areas would improve markedly if returners were assisted in mathematics and computing in the manner of the students at Childwall. Bringing the staff together would markedly improve recruitment to the technologies and encourage more women to enter them;

2 The quality of the new delivery systems (such as Open Learning), pioneered so successfully at Childwall would be further enhanced by the

facilities at Riversdale, (via a much larger Open Learning suite and the Olivetti Technology Centre, which would make available £250,000 worth of new information technology equipment);

3 The development of non-traditional provision in ceramics, art, photo-graphy and local history was inhibited at Riversdale because the College did not have the resources to provide these popular subjects at both campuses. Concentration would result in more opportunities for more people and more productive use of resources;

4 At Childwall, students of commercial subjects, such as word processing, were limited in their progression because of lack of facilities. The facil-ities at Riversdale would offer them extended progression. Women stu-dents, in particular, would be able to progress to higher levels in the fields of information technology;

5 The Childwall campus was badly served in educational support terms (in photocopying, audio visual resources, lecture theatre facilities, and sports and library facilities). Concentration of provision at Riversdale would inevitably result in marked improvement in this regard;

6 Whilst it was true that some students in the catchment area of Childwall might be inconvenienced by the move to Riversdale, College manage-ment felt there were large numbers of Liverpool residents (in Speke, Garston and Toxteth) being denied an appropriate education whilst cer-tain courses were based at Childwall;

7 Within further education provision it was possible to define a number of key areas which constituted a core curriculum — basic literacy and numeracy, information technology, technological awareness and pre-paration for the European Community of '1992'. The College would be in a markedly improved position to provide this core curriculum if all its staff, each with their special capacities, qualifications and experience, were brought together on one site;

8 It could be argued that, despite the progress of recent years, neither Childwall nor Riversdale had a reasonable balance of courses, students or staff. Riversdale was still, in essence, a technological College, Childwall was still, very largely, a general education College. Concentration would bring about a Community College with balanced provision;

9 At present some subject areas, for example, Mathematics, Science, Eng-lish and Technology, were insufficiently coordinated. Basic skills support for the study of science and technology was essential and would enable the College to improve service to the disadvantaged, including those

from ethnic minorities. The practical experience gained in providing the Open Learning Workshop at Childwall, where the overall retention rate had improved in recent years from 50 per cent to 69 per cent, would be invaluable at Riversdale;

10   The economic benefits resulting from concentration of provision at Riversdale (including improved utilization of teaching staff hours) could be used to improve the quality of educational provision.

Although the City Council's subsequent resolution to close the Childwall site was passed at the end of March, it was mid-July before the final decision was taken and College management was told to begin the relocation in preparation for a September start at Riversdale. Among the meetings which occurred between these dates were the following:

April 3 1989	Meeting of all Childwall staff for the Principal to pass on the information the College possessed;
April 4/5/6/7/10	Meetings with Childwall students to explain the situation;
April 7	Inaugural meeting of the Childwall Relocation Working Party (this included representatives of management and teaching and administrative staff. The April 7 meeting was the first of a number);
April 13	Further staff meeting addressed by the Principal;
April 14/20 and May 2/8/15	Further meetings of the Relocation Working Party;
April 19	Principal addressed Childwall students;

In addition, meetings of the staff and students were addressed by Liverpool City Councillors.

The Working Party established by College Management had completed its study and had concluded that all the courses located at Childwall could be relocated at Riversdale for the reasonably modest sum of £36,000. This could be found from within the College's budget for the 1989/90 Financial Year thanks to much improved allocation to the College on its Repairs and Maintenance line (and approval from the Authority for the necessary virement). A copy of the detailed study, together with its accompanying budgets and diagrams was sent on 18 May to the Chair of College Governors and to the Local Education Authority.

Mention has been made in Chapter 5 of the 'fierce sense of identity' which was among the first impressions that Liverpool made on Bishop David Sheppard and Archbishop Derek Warlock when they came to the City. They went on to speak of: 'the most intense loyalties which are themselves reflected in a strongly expressed possessiveness'.... and that 'Solidarity may find expression in the quickness, sharpness, wit and anger united in vigorous response to an enemy'.[2]

The management of the College now felt the force of such a 'vigorous response' from those staff and students located at the Childwall campus. Management tried hard to explain that even if resistance to change was not ascribed to this vigorous response and that their concern for the people in the Childwall catchment was taken at its face value, staff and students had to realize the social consequences of their actions. As has been mentioned in Chapter 5, when the issue was originally debated in the 1985–86 Session, the point had sensitively but forcefully been made that 'undue concern for a particular group of people might prove economically paralyzing to the College and prevent it from operating in a decisive and efficient way for the broader constituencies it had been set up to serve' (p. 80). Management also emphasized that provision was being made for local bus services to be extended to assist actual and potential students near to the Childwall campus to travel to Riversdale. Management was also of the firm view that, overall, there would be no loss of student numbers to the College. However, it was to no avail, and during the Summer vacation the closure of Childwall and transfer of the provision to Riversdale was carried through without opposing views on the subject being in the slightest degree reconciled.

Management's hopes, that unification of provision on the Riversdale site would have a positive effect on changing the culture and on the diversification and development of the College, were to prove well founded nevertheless.

Conceptual and Theoretical Constructs

Observing the marked progress and diversification now taking place, it was possible, when analyzing this conceptually to fit certain theoretical constructs into place. Drucker[3] for example when writing on the management of opportunities and risks has classified three kinds of opportunity and four kinds of risk. Using his typology of opportunities:

1   The 'additive' ones arise from chances to exploit more fully existing resources, for example, by establishing additional markets for existing products. Additive opportunities do not change the basic character of the organization, and an example for South Mersey here would be its drive to replicate on the Riversdale campus the successful programme of community courses in place at Childwall;

2   'Complementary' opportunities consist of the addition of new activities which complement existing provision and deliver a synergistic effect. These

opportunities do change the structure of the organization and require at least one new area of expertise. The establishment of education for special needs at the College is appropriate in this regard, but management did not immediately recognize the need for additional expertise; this generated problems as we shall see later;

3 'Break-through' opportunities change the fundamental characteristics of the organization and demand first-class resources, effort and expenditure on research and development. The College would claim that the clear need for training in information technology constituted a vast market opportunity for the College. The National Training Award had affirmed that its human resources were matched to the opportunity and the subsequent establishment of the Olivetti Centre had helped to ensure that its capital equipment was at an adequately high level.

Using Drucker's typology of risks is also a fitting way to delineate the College's approach to strategy.

1 The risks it had to accept were those associated with response to change in order to ensure survival. Resources had to be diverted towards new areas and away from old ones;

2 The risks it could afford to take, i.e. those where even the worst failures would not cripple the College, were those associated with strategies to increase enrolments on existing courses and to extend those courses on broadly similar lines so as to make the most productive use of the qualifications and experience of existing staff;

3 The risks it could not afford to take were those where it was unable to exploit success through lack of capital. It knew that there had been an upturn in the demand for marine engineering courses. Despite the knowledge that the other UK Colleges of Advanced Maritime Studies were keeping abreast of technological development, the College could not undertake the necessary expenditure. This was to have sad repercussions as will be explained;

4 The risks it could not afford not to take, i.e. where it could not afford to be left out of major new developments if it was to survive, relate to the break-through opportunity provided by the market for training in information technology, described earlier.

The 1988/89 Session also saw a major reorganization of the academic structure. As the book has developed it can be seen that management continually reappraised the structure and, where appropriate, reorganized it. This is what Mullins[4] has described as the contingency approach to organization structure, based on the view that there is no one absolute best design; rather, there is a multitude of possibilities and the best or preferred choice will be contingent on the situation being analysed. Situational factors should induce variations in structure and the rate of change of these structural variations depends on the rate of change of the situational factors.

The main focus of this book is to assess the contribution of management to the performance of the College during the four-year period under review. Drawing on other work, Oldcorn[5], writing of the 'futuristic manager', affirms the point that:

> The ratio of managers to workers will increase to handle the shift in the management orientation from the routine manipulation of material objects to the creation of ideas and the motivation of individuals to implement such ideas. Reflection and diagnosis will replace action as the primary activity of the manager.

He also draws attention to the view of Toffler[6] that organizations of the future will require people who can 'learn very fast' — to be able to understand novel situations and problems, and with imagination, to be able to invent new solutions.

It would be accurate to say that although College management at the highest level carried through a great deal of executive work and day-to-day decision making, it nevertheless saw its most important task to be the creation of ideas based on a continuing appraisal of the environment. Given the relatively small size of the management team, day-to-day administration was its first duty. But it was not its highest duty. Another area in which management gave a positive lead was in the development of the commercial approach and entrepreneurial activity as a firm element in organizational ideology. The seeking of partnerships was a key objective and the establishment of the Olivetti Technology Centre was the first major outcome.

Speaking of entrepreneurship in the service institution, Drucker[7] takes the view that 'public-service institutions find it far more difficult to innovate than even the most "bureaucratic" company', adding that 'most innovations in public-service institutions are imposed on them either by outsiders or by catastrophe.' In this context he lists three main reasons:

> First, the public-service institution is based on a 'budget' rather than being paid out of its results. . . . And 'success' in the public-service institution is defined by getting a larger budget rather than by obtaining results.

> Second, a service institution is dependent on a multitude of constituents. . . . A public-service institution has to satisfy everyone; certainly, it cannot afford to alienate anyone.

The most important reason, however, is that public-service institutions exist after all to 'do good'. This means that they tend to see their mission as a moral absolute rather than as economic and subject to a cost benefit calculus.

The experience of College management did not accord with Drucker's view, however. None of its constituents, internal or external, had dissented from the steer towards partnerships and external funding. At least they had not brought any misgivings to the notice of management. There appeared to be genuine support for, some pride even, in such achievements. Possibly, events after the reorganization of 1985/86 were seen as helping to maintain an FE service in being in the face of profound political and economic uncertainty.

However imperfectly, management also felt it was genuinely seeking participation in these efforts by, in Barham and Rassam's phrase[8] 'a more open organization, with freer and less status-conscious communication'. Informal communication was also important because of the time pressures obviating an adequate level of formal communication, the reasons for which were outlined in Chapter 6.

These same authors make the point that many management thinkers believe that change in the 1990s is going to be qualitatively different in that each environmental factor is undergoing transforming changes and that these changes are profound. One of the consequent major challenges is, therefore, logistical: management is confronted with too much information, too little time in which to digest it and with 'almost too much uncertainty to be able to make any meaningful plans about the future' (Barham and Rassam).[9] They believe that:

> Among the many routes to achieving success, two in particular stand out: introducing and managing effectively information technology and, secondly, building more responsive, more versatile organizations.[10]

College management would claim that the institution was making progress along both routes; first, as has been described earlier, within the network of data processing required by the Authority, the federal FE system and the DES and second, through a positive lead from management itself which saw its primary role as based upon the formulation of policy responses to its continual scrutiny of the environment.

John Adair's concept of 'the interaction of needs'[11] provides an appropriate insight into management's approach. He suggests that task, group and individual needs are always interacting with each other (see Figure 7.1). The circles overlap but they do not sit on top of each other. In other words, there is always some degree of tension between them.

Figure 7.1: *The interaction of needs: The three circles model*

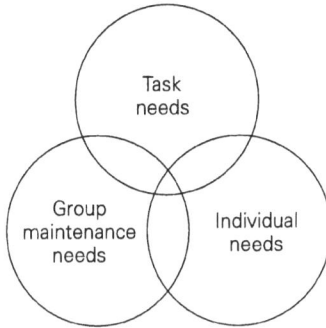

Effective leadership entails guiding the group to:

- achieve the common task
- work as a team
- respect and develop its individual membership (see Figure 7.2).

Figure 7.2: *The three circles model: The role of the leader*

However imperfectly, management understood the concept and tried to act upon it, recognizing that while the College had to succeed in absolute terms, it also had to succeed in providing opportunities for the personal and professional growth of its staff — this in addition to formal programmes of staff development initiated by the College and the Authority. It tried to do this by encouragement of, and delegation to, small groups and individual teachers on the production of ideas intended to serve the objectives of development and diversification.

The outstanding contribution of the staff to the success of the College must not go unremarked. Management firmly believed in the ownership of work, and minimum bureaucratic intervention, as powerful motivating forces.

Hence its readiness to let people 'run with their own ideas'. In their now classic work, *In Search of Excellence*, Peters and Waterman[12] found that two cardinal factors which distinguished the most successful organizations were product quality and the employee's sense of self-worth. In this last respect, these are their words:

> At the same time, however, each of us needs to stick out — even, or maybe particularly, in the winning institution. So we observed, time and again, extraordinary energy exerted above and beyond the call of duty when the worker (shop floor worker, sales assistant, desk clerk) is given even a modicum of apparent control over his or her destiny.

These authors discovered that 'one of the main clues to corporate excellence has come to be just such incidents of unusual effort on the part of apparently ordinary employees.' College management would support the efficacy of these findings in practice, though it would not conclude that its employees were in any sense ordinary.

Whilst the working relationships between the staff and management were good, it has to be said that the closure of the Childwall site brought the management into opposition with a considerable section of the staff. Buchanan and Huczynski[13] comment that two different views of conflict in organizations have been identified: the 'happy family' view, which considers conflict to be disruptive and thus to be avoided or eradicated if it erupts and the Marxist tradition which starts with stability and lack of conflict as the problem. These writers add a third view: that conflict within limits is held to assist evolutionary and not revolutionary change. Acting as a safety valve, it keeps organizations flexible to internal and external changes while retaining intact their essential characteristics such as the power distribution and the organizational hierarchy. They quote Lewis Coser[14] in support:

> ... conflict, rather than being disruptive and dissociating, may indeed be a means of balancing and hence maintaining a society as a going concern.... A flexible society benefits from conflict because such behaviour, by helping to create and modify norms, assures its continuance under changed conditions.

In retrospect, management was inclined to view the differences which arose over the Childwall closure more in terms of their benefits to relationships than their costs. We shall return to this topic in reviewing the 1989/90 Session. Perhaps O'Shaughnessy's comments on strategy-consensus building,[15] comes closest to the way in which management tried to perform its personnel function, and particularly in respect of the Childwall closure.

In his comments on strategy consensus-building and gaining acceptance for change, O'Shaughnessy's view is that active support for any strategy is generated by:

- education
- incentives
- indoctrination

Education is used to dispel any misunderstanding about job security and other perceived threats to interests — here, management tried to convey to the teachers that operating on a single site would make the College less and not more vulnerable to further change.

Incentives are used to compensate for losses. Opposition to suggested changes is often conditional: compromises can be reached, accommodations made, bargains struck etc., providing sufficient incentive is offered. In this respect, management had arranged for all Childwall provision and the staff associated with it to be housed together in adjacent blocks at Riversdale, though this had meant relocating a significant number of Riversdale staff to other parts of that campus. O'Shaughnessy adds that *participation* might be considered under incentives. The establishment of the Relocation Working Party had been an attempt to ensure that the views of the Childwall staff had been adequately represented.

Indoctrination is a term used more benignly by O'Shaughnessy than its normal currency would suggest. He says:

> Finally, *indoctrination* of values is needed to emphasize the importance of success and to stimulate commitment and active support. This does not mean that the strategy being proposed must become everyone's preference. All that is required is sufficient agreement to proceed in a coordinated way.

Again, on this definition of the term, indoctrination was a visible part of management's approach, not only through the importance placed upon success but also by the stress placed upon 'Childwall values' in making it possible. Whatever efforts management made, however, they were not sufficient to enable the staff and students at the Childwall campus to adjust to the prospect with equanimity.

Reverting to the issue of staff motivation, Steers and Porter[16] commend eight strategies to management in this regard. The sixth is that management should foster an organizational culture oriented to performance, and the seventh that it should stay close to employees and remedy problems as they arise. College managers felt they were communicating the sixth factor powerfully enough but had not performed so well on the seventh, mainly because of the external as well as the internal demands on management time. Certainly, the Principal felt that if his own visits to the Childwall campus had not been so episodic, the staff would have been better prepared for the Childwall closure and the operation might have been concluded with less opposition.

Mullins[17] reports the comparison of management style and practice in different cultural settings provided by Ouchi, who recommends a Japanese style 'Theory Z' environment in contrast to the more traditional, bureaucratic environment. The characteristics of a Theory Z organization are these:

- long term employment, often for a lifetime;
- relatively slow processes of evaluation and promotion;
- development of company-specific skills, and moderately specialized career paths;
- implicit, informal control mechanisms supported by explicit, formal measures;
- participative decision-making by consensus;
- collective decision-making, but individual ultimate responsibility;
- broad concern for the welfare of subordinates and co-workers as a natural part of working relationships, and informal relationships among people.

In Britain, Marks and Spencer has been seen to come closest to this type of organization. The management of the College were struck by the high degree of congruence between the Theory Z organization and some educational establishments including their own — even if the acquisition of some of these characteristics had been inadvertent! The Theory served to highlight the importance of those factors which tend to receive less attention than they deserved because of time pressures — notably the welfare aspects of managing people.

The other key element in management's frustration with its own performance lay in its continued inability to plan operations for the whole College in a regular, systematic way, (for example, after the approach suggested by Boyle[18] in Figure 7.3). Despite its continuing appraisal of the environment and its readiness to take initiatives in response to market opportunities, the absence of a systematic, comprehensive planning process left managers with the feeling of being carried along by events, if only to an extent, rather than actually shaping those events.

Writing of recent events, Cantor and Roberts[19] mention 'the bewildering and exponential character of the many changes which are shaping further education in England and Wales today'. They conclude that:

Indeed, the problem of coping with the 'management of change' is probably greater for further education than any other sector of our educational system. This is, perhaps, due to the fact that it has to be sensitive to, and respond quickly to, changes in industry and business and, indeed, in society at large. As part of the environment in which it has to operate, political pressures in the form of government policy

Figure 7.3:   The four elements of the planning cycle

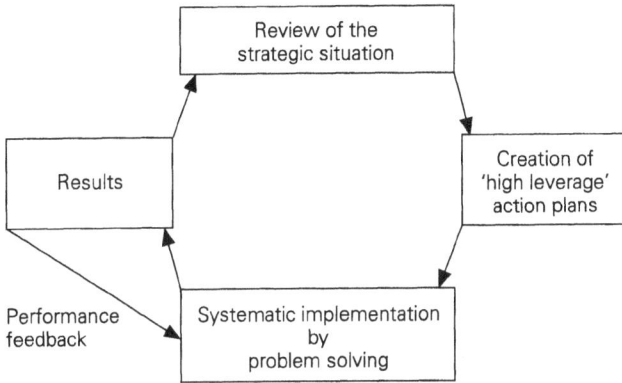

have played an increasingly strong part, so that it is being more and more required to ensure that it is financially 'accountable' and that its products are 'marketable'.

The management at South Mersey fully recognized the truth of these observations and indeed welcomed the challenge of operating in this milieu. Its disappointments stemmed from the difficulty of replicating the planning time and the planning processes typical of other commercial organizations. In a later part of their work, Cantor and Roberts[20] underscore the important role of mainstream adult education which is concerned with giving the individual the opportunity for fulfilment in a variety of ways, including creative, physical and social activity. They add:

> In any case, at a time when long-term structural unemployment seems to be becoming the norm, adult education of all kinds has a valuable part to play and is well equipped to do so, its provision being firmly set in local communities and, therefore, reflecting the educational and social needs of these communities.

'Broad-brush' though the College's overall planning might be, there were clear objectives concerning the development of its community education. In earlier pages, the progress being made in this regard is clearly evident. Senior management was convinced, however, that a higher public profile was both attainable and desirable. On the vocational side a great deal of media attention and publicity was attesting to the College's capabilities, with news of the National Training Award and the establishment of the Olivetti Technology Centre well to the fore. It was important that a powerful institutional image was projected on the adult and community side, and a series of public lectures was envisaged making use of the services of personalities of national and international standing who were acknowledged experts in their respective fields. Funding for the Lectures was obtained from the Sunley Educational Trust and the National Westminster Bank. The Sunley-NatWest Lectures, held at the Liverpool Town Hall, by permission of the Lord Mayor, were a pronounced success and among the well-known personalities taking part were Melvyn Bragg, Bamber Gascoigne, Michael Holroyd, Margaret Drabble, John Keegan and David Puttnam. Management believed in Olins' adage that 'corporate identity has emerged as a major communication discipline,'[21] that the controlled and explicit management of the ways in which the College's activities were perceived exercised a considerable influence on its future. Senior management, therefore, devoted a significant amount of time to it.

Not only was the external perception important, the way the College was perceived internally was germane to its progress. As Morgan[22] has pointed out, organizations are 'mini-societies', possessing their own distinctive patterns of culture and subculture. To appreciate the nature of culture and subculture it is useful to adopt the role of anthropologist and observe the day-to-day functioning of the organization, as if one were an outsider. (The author had adopted this participant observer role from the onset, when even a cursory examination had denoted that groups from different constituent colleges, different locations, and different subject areas were hardly likely to bring shared orientation to the new College unless mechanisms for change were rapidly devised and employed.)

In organizations, Morgan comments:

> ... there are often many different and competing value systems that create a mosaic of organizational realities rather than a uniform corporate culture.

The successful organizations observed by Peters and Waterman seem to have found ways of breaking down these divisions so that different professionals could guide their activities with reference to a common and integrated set of norms and priorities. Shared meaning, shared understanding and shared sense-making were all different ways of describing culture. Changing the culture was no fortuitous thing but the outcome of deliberate and sustained action. Management shared Morgan's belief[23] that where corporate culture is strong and robust a distinctive ethos pervades the whole organization: employees exude the characteristics that define the mission or ethos of the whole, for example, outstanding commitment to service, perseverance against the odds, or a commitment to innovation.

Publicity helped to establish the identity of the College — for the internal as well as the external viewer. Its publicized achievements, by the fact of publicity, were laid open to ownership by the whole College. In this way the whole College was able to participate in the construction of the new reality, the new culture.

Narrative: The 1988/89 Academic Session

Diversification and Development: Links with Employers

The creative alignment of the College with a rapidly changing environment was seen as a primary objective. Management believed that an important feature in achieving this was to strengthen existing links with employing organizations and to widen these links as much as possible.

The extent of the College's progress in this respect can be seen from the details provided in the Section in Appendix 16 which describes the College's 'Link with Employers'. The Senior Management was more than ready to provide the lead here believing in the importance of Sathe's[24] dictum of 'showing through deeds' as a means of achieving strategic change.

The reward for the College's efforts came quickly and in a highly tangible way for in December 1988 it secured the valuable and prestigious National Training Award. The highest awards organizations can win for their training, the National Training Awards, were introduced for industrial organizations in 1987 by the Training Commission. They are based on the idea that training can produce identifiable improvements in quality and output. In 1988, the Awards were extended to cover educational institutions as training providers.

South Mersey College was selected for an award for a customized training package in computer-related systems to support the installation of an automated production process at Baines Dairies Limited of Litherland. The Managing Director of the Company had expressed the view that:

> ... the training was effective because production, profits and the product range have all increased, management control has been maximized and our credibility with our bankers has never been higher.[25]

The Director General of the Training Agency emphasized that the winners (including the College) were selected after a detailed and rigorous assessment and judging process. Following the announcement of the Award on Channel 4 television in November 1988, the College was presented with the Award at a special ceremony in January 1989 by the Duke of Westminster. It also received a letter of congratulation for its efforts from the Prime Minister.

This recognition was tremendously important to the College in its efforts to develop and diversify. The success of the Riversdale Open Technology Centre (ROTeC) in obtaining the Award was of decided benefit to the whole College and the Principal declared that:

> The staff of the College are convinced that they can make an important contribution to the economic regeneration of Merseyside through their provision of training packages to firms in the area. This Award underlines the credibility of their views and is a tremendous boost to their efforts.[26]

The realism of this statement was made clear by the establishment, a few months afterwards, of the Olivetti Technology Centre. Appreciating that the capital equipment of the College would fail to keep pace with the accelerating rate of technological development, particularly if reliance rested solely on public funding, the College began to seek energetically funding partnerships with industrial and commercial organizations. As part of the College's commitment to client-centred development, the programme of visits to local, regional and national employers was stepped up, with the Senior Management travelling extensively to negotiate with their industrial and commercial counterparts.

An early result of these efforts was that, with substantial financial support from British Olivetti, South Mersey College was able to set up one of the most powerful microcomputer networks in the North West of England. The total installation comprised over forty microcomputers, twenty of which were networked, as well as desk-top publishing and computer-aided design facilities. At standard prices, the installation was worth £250,000. It was installed by British Olivetti for under £150,000, with advice on the design of the Centre and training for College staff being provided free of charge. The contract negotiated also provided for the periodic replacement of equipment in line with the technological development of microcomputing and other technology.

Beyond doubt, obtaining the National Training Award was of substantial help in the College's quest for sponsorships, and the establishment of the Olivetti Technology Centre attached a great deal of credibility to the drive to further develop the steadily expanding base of industrial and commercial clientele.

General Progress: Performance Indicators

In the Principal's Autumn Term report to the Governing Body (4 November 1988), the enrolments position to 30th September was set out, with the comparative figures for the previous two Academic Sessions.

Enrolments at 30th September	1986/87 Session	1987/88 Session	1988/89 Session
Faculty of Automobile Engineering	675	801	853
Faculty of Construction	1185	1164	1259
Faculty of General Studies	1200	2200	2516
Faculty of Maritime Studies	750	690	870
	3810	4855	5498

The Principal warned, however, that:

> ... whilst these signs are encouraging, we cannot be complacent. It has to be remembered that the above figures are for *enrolments*, many of which are part-time. In order to become a fully viable Burnham FE (Group 7) College, we must attract more *full-time students*. Progress *is* being made, with increased recruitment in Special Needs, Marine Engineering and Media Studies. However, we still have some distance to go and the staff in all Faculties are mindful of this.[27]

He also pointed out that, under the Premature Retirement Compensation (PRC) terms offered by the Authority, a number of teaching staff had left the College since September 1986; the current complement of full-time teaching staff was 178, compared with 198 on formation of the College. (It should be noted here that whilst a development-minded management took no satisfaction from this, it did mean a steady improvement in the College's student-staff ratio, which was a primary objective.) The Principal also reminded the Governors that the College continued to enrol throughout the Session, indicating that comparable full-Session data would be provided for the Governors' Summer Term meeting.

This data was incorporated in his report of 9th June 1989 and is reproduced here. It illustrates clearly the College's upward momentum.

Academic Session	*Full-time (equivalent) Students*	*Full-time (equivalent) Staff*	*Student/ Staff ratio*
1986–87	1601	208.74	7.67
1987–88	1742	209.88	8.30
1988–89	2208	215.20	10.26
1988–89 (revised Annual Monitoring Survey figures)	2334	212.18	11.00

To these figures, the Principal added:

> The fact that we are now in the vicinity of the required national 'norms', well ahead of schedule, does not obscure the fact that we still have much to accomplish and fully intend to do so. I feel it is right and proper, however, to pause in our activity and acquaint you with this picture of progress, accomplished through the ungrudging efforts of all levels and categories of staff.

Reports from the Faculties

Automobile Engineering

The start of the new Academic Year saw major changes in the Faculty, for:

1   The Special Needs Unit began its first full year as an established centre at Riversdale.
2   The transfer of vehicle body trades provision from City College, one of the further elements in the reorganization of FE in Liverpool, was completed.
3   As part of the same exercise, BTEC General Engineering courses and City and Guilds courses above Craft Level 1 were transferred to Sandown College.

Enrolments for the new Session allowed a continuing upward trend:

1986/87 Session	675	enrolments
1987/88 Session	801	enrolments
1988/89 Session	864	enrolments
(to October)		

It was particularly pleasing that 141 of these were full-time students (including fifty-one for Special Needs education) and that a high proportion of these attracted fees and other income for the Authority.

The College was now a managing agent for automobile engineering and aspired to having motor cycle and vehicle body trades provision as part of its agency. The full-time courses in auto management were redesigned to provide more 'in-fill' opportunities for part-time students and discussions with the Wirral Metropolitan College had resulted in students beyond Craft Part II and National Certificate level being referred to the College.

Unfortunately, the transfer of Vehicle Body Trades provision presented the College with a resources problem at the outset. The cost of transferring the provision had reduced the revenue budget available to the Faculty and the Industrial Advisory Boards were gravely disappointed that badly needed, up-to-date equipment had not been purchased. The National Conference of the Vehicle Body Repair Association had identified the need for improved training. It indicated that without an up-to-date body jig and spray booth, courses could not be properly serviced. Conference was seeking new national centres for this training. The Principal outlined to Governors and to appropriate City Councillors that for the required outlay of £25,000 the College could become such a national centre, with supplementary benefit to the income of its residential accommodation.

Lack of resources had also meant that vehicle refinishing had to remain at City College. This was straining relationships with Advisory Boards, Managing Agents and the Road Transport Industry Training Board. Also, the introduction of a full-time course was in abeyance. There were forty-three prospective evening students and numerous unemployed people on waiting lists for courses.

Subsequently the College's Vehicle Body Advisory Committee and the Motor Agents Association, among others, wrote to the Director of Education concerning the lack of capital equipment and other resources. By 9th June 1989, the Principal was able to report to the Governing Body that, with the approval of the City Council, the College had made available from its Revenue Estimates an allocation of approximately £81,000 to enable the Faculty to close the gap somewhat between itself and the industry in terms of up-to-date equipment. Included in the allocation was a sum to cover the acquisition of a body jig and spray booth for the Vehicle Body Section.

With regard to curriculum matters, the creation of two specialist workshops and a lecture room for the GCSE, CPVE and TVEI students of Automobile Engineering was proving most beneficial to the needs of the Schools Consortia in the Southern and Central Districts of the City. Vocational courses within the Faculty were undergoing the most significant changes seen in twenty years. Apart from workshop and laboratory services having to be reorganized to meet the introduction of continuous assessment and tests of competence, the syllabi of all full-time, and part-time day courses had been rewritten to meet the requirements of the National Council for Vocational Qualifications (NCVQ). The GCSE Examining Boards were also emphasizing the student-led learning approach. The consequence of all these developments was that by June 1989, the whole of the Faculty's workshop space had been re-designed and re-ordered.

With regard to income earning activities, the Road Transport Industry Training Board continued to make use of workshop space for skills-testing purposes, and over 360 student days of computer keyboard skills had been sold to the automotive industry. Visits and discussions with major manufacturers were continuing with positive results. A number of staff, including the College Principal, were taking part in this programme of visits. In addition to the donation of many costly items of equipment, enquiries for product-knowledge training, to be taught by College staff on behalf of the industry, were also being generated. In September 1988, the Faculty participated in the three-day Liverpool Motor Show at the City's Festival Park. This enabled the College to register its presence once again with the major franchise dealers and the general public and made its obvious contribution to the increase of enrolments. Heartened by this, the Faculty decided to devise a one-day seminar to be held at the Haydock Park Racecourse (Conference Suite) in October 1989 on 'Design and Repair Developments in Vehicle Engineering'. The seminar would be hosted by South Mersey College and was already creating a great deal of interest in the North West. Ten major national contributors including Ford Motor Company, Austin-Rover and Leyland-DAF had already been engaged to give presentations and delegates were rapidly taking up available places.

Special Needs Education

By November 1988, the Unit was providing for fifty-one full-time and thirty-three part-time students, fifteen subjects were being provided, ranging from training for independence to computing, but due to resource constraints four-fifths of the teaching was being done by part-time staff (twenty-five in total). The majority of the students would attend for forty-eight weeks each year, and thirty of them were being provided with daily transport.

By the Spring of 1989 interest in the College's Special Needs provision had grown significantly. An Open Day had attracted over 160 parents, young people and special schools staff. Expansion was limited by resource constraints but the Unit continued to draw a great deal of positive interest and support. Students from the Unit began to play an increasing part in the social life of the College and the College refectory, and other staff undertook a great deal of fund-raising activity on behalf of the Unit. More comment will be made on this at the end of the chapter.

Construction

Although development of the Faculty was somewhat restricted by shortage of staff and other resources, a steadily improving trend in enrolments was discernible:

Academic Session	Full-Time Equivalent (FTE) Students
1986–87	445
1987–88	482
1988–89	506

However, the most disturbing evidence to emerge from the latest enrolments was the Faculty's inability to provide, due to lack of resources, for the large number of unemployed persons applying for craft skills courses. Details of the waiting lists were as follows:

Brickwork	30
Plastering	35
Plumbing	36
Carpentry and Joinery	25
Total	126

One feature of the Faculty's development and diversification efforts had resulted in its being given conditional approval by the Incorporated Association of Architects and Surveyors for the establishment of a College-based diploma course. Also, the Construction Industry Training Board (CITB) had expressed a wish for the College to become the Merseyside centre for Studies in Construction Management. Firm proposals had been made for courses to begin in June and September 1989. After extended negotiations with the Institute of Maintenance and Building Management (IMBM) it had been confirmed that the College was to become the national centre for the Institute's courses and examinations. It was hoped that the IMBM courses would commence in September 1989.

As part of careers guidance development, the Faculty offered a series of two-day courses on Careers in Construction, for sixth-form pupils, and the Building Services Section established a new course in Gas Installation studies which it was hoped, along with other recent developments, would establish the credibility of the Faculty in the Gas Services training field. Cooperation between the Faculty of General Studies and the Faculty of Construction in providing a French course for technician students resulted in a student exchange visit by a group of French students from a Construction College at Tourcoing. It was hoped that this would initiate a long, beneficial development to assist students to face the challenge of '1992'.

With regard to Equal Opportunities, there was noteworthy development of courses in the Construction field for women. In the 1986/87 Session, provision had consisted of short 'taster' courses in Craft Skills. To these was added, in 1987/88, a Foundation Course in Craft Skills and in the 1988/89 Session a City and Guilds Course in Carpentry and Joinery had been a further addition. It had also been Faculty policy at all times to encourage female recruitment to the Faculty's established courses. The College believed that the two-year course in Carpentry and Joinery leading to the award of a City and Guilds Craft Certificate was probably the only one of its kind in the North West. The Faculty hoped that its links with Merseyside Skills Training Limited would lead to the development of technician type courses for black persons. The Faculty also had several schools-link 'taster' courses for girls, and these were well supported.

The Construction Industry Training Board had requested that the Faculty make increased provision for Heating and Ventilating block-release courses for the 1989/90 Session, and in late June 1989 the Faculty hosted the first Inter-College Surveying Competition. It was hoped that this would become an annual event. The Faculty had also planned a series of in-house staff development initiatives, mostly concerned with information technology and open learning. It was also actively participating in Local Education Authority staff development initiatives.

The effects of Government's changes in industrial training provision, the uncertain future of the Construction Industry and the emergence of Training and Enterprise Councils (TECs) were all environmental factors of importance to the Faculty, which it would monitor closely so as to adjust provision and respond to new opportunities as necessary. The Faculty was determined to be a centre of strength for both vocational and community provision, but development was being hampered by resource constraints. Whilst the Faculty appreciated it must bear its share of these, the deterioration of some of its accommodation was felt to be a particularly serious matter. Repairs and redecoration to Blocks A and B were long overdue. In order to maintain an adequate learning environment and in view of the increasing number of visitors (including monitoring teams and employers' representatives) coming to the College, it was essential that some priority be given to this.

General Studies

The marked increase in enrolments continued. Enrolments at the beginning of the Session (with previous years' figures for comparison) were as follows:

	September 1986	September 1987	September 1988
Total enrolments	1200	2300	2716

The Faculty was energetically pursuing an open access policy for all sections of the Community by promoting student-centred courses, by better marketing and publicity and by increasing Community links. For example, enrolment details for women and black students were as follows:

	September 1986	September 1987	September 1988
Enrolments (women)	700	1320	2095
Enrolments (black students)	100	148	387

Areas where enrolment had increased significantly included Community Education courses and Business Studies courses at the Riversdale Campus, and Access to Higher Education and Women's courses at the Childwall Campus. The Open Learning Workshops at Childwall had enrolled over 700 students (full or part-time). There were 500 enrolments for Basic Mathematics and 200 for English.

It was particularly pleasing that the number of women attending the Faculty's courses at Riversdale had risen from 200 in the year 1987/88 to 978 in 1988/89. Significant reasons for this included the provision of an excellent nursery and a much wider range of Community courses but, above all, a genuine commitment from all the staff to develop an 'open access' environment at the Campus by providing a welcoming atmosphere in classrooms, using supportive interviewing techniques and by using a less rigid attitude to formal entry qualifications.

Seventy of the 150 students on the 1987/88 Access to Higher Education course had gained degree course places at Universities and Polytechnics (to commence studies in October 1988). In 1988/89 180 students were enrolled on the Access course, including students on a new component which provided opportunities to enter the nursing profession, subject to satisfactory completion of the Nursing Authority's entrance test. It was planned to provide an additional component which would provide openings for people interested in Education for Special Needs.

Plans were being developed for an Access Teacher Training Course (in conjunction with the Liverpool Institute of Higher Education and the University of Liverpool). The Faculty was working with colleagues from the Technical Faculties to develop Access to Technology courses. One such course, planned for introduction in September 1989, was Access to Studies of the Built Environment.

The Faculty continued to offer a range of classes at 'outreach' centres in the south of the City. The twenty venues used included Libraries, Bail Hostels, Community Centres and Day Centres. Provision ranged from Basic English to Drama and Video for Special Needs students. The current enrolment totalled 224 students. It was intended to offer tuition in study skills, via the Open Learning Workshops, to all students. The acquisition of study skills, with competence in Mathematics and English, enabled students to progress more speedily on all types of courses.

Funding of a further £5000 had been made available by the US Embassy in London for the editing of a teacher/student pack on popular American culture, and following validation of its courses, the College had been accepted as a member of BASCELT (The British Association of State Colleges in English Language Teaching). It was hoped that as a result of inclusion in BASCELT publicity, advertisements in Hong Kong newspapers, and an extensive direct-mail campaign to relevant agencies, the number of overseas students attending College courses would increase markedly in the future.

As the Session progressed, it was clear that the increased range of Community Education courses at Riversdale was proving very popular. Classes included Local History, Art, Microwave Cookery, Horticulture and the new Basic Maths and English 'Workshop' courses. They had all attracted considerable interest. At Childwall, the wide range of community education courses running successfully included Stress Management, Co-Counselling, Interpersonal Psychology and a number of new women's options including Health and Fitness for Mothers and Toddlers, Health and Fitness for the Older Woman and Introduction to Science.

There were resource difficulties, and in the case of the Faculty of General Studies these were mainly centred on teaching staff. There was still an urgent need for a Senior Lecturer to co-ordinate the Access to Higher Education course and for a Lecturer, full-time, to teach Social Sciences on Access and GCE 'A' level courses. A recent HMI report on Non-Advanced Further Education (NAFE) courses in Business Studies[28] stated that where sections had more than 33 per cent of teaching hours being taught by part-time staff, considerable administrative and managerial problems occurred.

The Business Studies Unit at Childwall had over 60 per cent of its teaching hours being taught by part-time staff. Over ninety part-time teachers were employed this Session (to cover the two campuses) and, even recognizing the high standard of tuition provided by these colleagues, this imposed a severe organizational burden on the Faculty. More full-time appointments, particularly in English, Mathematics, Social Sciences and Business Studies, were urgently needed.

By the Summer Term, the Faculty was involved in a number of major developments. These included:

1 The proposal to close the Childwall site and move the provision to Riversdale;
2 The reorganization of the Faculty, with approximately twenty staff being transferred to the new Faculty of Organization, Information and Communication Studies, and the Special Needs section of the College being moved into the Faculty. (Both of these developments were seen as being fundamentally important to further growth and development.)

The Trades Union Education Unit developed an Open School to provide a flexible, opening learning facility which would offer advice, consultation, a range of study plans and access to information sources. In conjunction with the Unit, the College began to offer a number of 'workshops' for School Governors.

Maritime Studies

By the end of September, recruitment had shown an improvement over the previous two years:

September 1986	*September 1987*	*September 1988*
750 students	690 students	870 students

The most noteworthy improvement was the number of students enrolled for the first year of the Diploma in Marine Engineering course:

September 1986	*September 1987*	*September 1988*
19 students	17 students	45 students

It was important to bear in mind that all of the 1988 intake would be potential recruits for the Higher Certificate and Diploma course. However, a major disappointment had been the failure of the new Diploma in Maritime Technology/Transport Studies course. It had received as much marketing and publicity effort as the Diploma in Marine Engineering but had failed to attract sufficient students to justify its commencement.

By the Spring Term, two new Technical and Vocational Education Initiative (TVEI) courses in Craft, Design and Technology had been introduced (with a total recruitment of twenty-nine students). To mirror the format of the successful Diploma in Marine Engineering course, the Business and Technician Education Council (BTEC) had given permission to re-phase the long established Diploma in Nautical Science. This would enable unsponsored students to be enrolled for Deck Officer Training and become sponsored during the College-based period of their initial training. A formal submission had been made to the Training Agency for YTS places. By June, and after consultations with the recognized Union, the Department of Transport and the Merchant Navy Training Board, this funding had been agreed by the Training Agency. The College had also been approached by two major British Shipping companies to act as their Managing Agents under the Department of Transport Training Initiative. As these companies had a number of cadets on the HND course, the Faculty considered this to be an important vote of confidence from influential clients.

The Faculty's Diploma courses were being vigorously marketed and these efforts included contacts with shipping companies, careers officers (nationally and locally), regional schools and sea cadet units. Two Symposia for careers officers were held in the Autumn Term and the Faculty was represented at Careers Conventions throughout the region and on the Isle of Man.

Several other marketing and promotional efforts were meeting with success. Recruitment to first-aid courses had almost doubled and enrolments to Royal Yachting Association courses were maintained at their high level. The Offshore Survival courses had a waiting list of over 300 applicants, but this popular and well-regarded course then met with a serious setback. On the 9th June 1989, the Principal reported to the Governing Body that:

Due to the delay in the installation of the second set of davits required by the Offshore Petroleum Industry Training Board (OPITB) and equipment needed by the Merseyside Fire Authority, the OPITB have, since Easter, indicated to employers that they cannot 'recognize' the course. Consequently it has been necessary to close the course temporarily until all the equipment has been installed.[29]

The Faculty hoped that during the Summer recess the Board could be invited back for a validation re-inspection and that the courses would recommence in September 1989. In the event, the hope was not realized and much frustration and delay was in store.

Riversdale Open Technology Centre (ROTeC)

The Centre made most notable progress during the 1988/89 Session. Some of its main achievements were as follows:

1 Success in its submission for a National Training Award (based upon a programme provided for a local firm — Baines Dairies Limited);
2 An increase in flexible training in computer applications for both large and small businesses;
3 The acquisition, from the Merseyside Enterprise Board, of a further programme of Management Training for Small Business;
4 A successful bid to the Department of Trade and Industry for funding to develop its Computer-Aided Design facilities. An industrial standard system was obtained valued at £10,000;
5 The establishment of ROTeC as the North West Regional Pilot Centre for a new Certificate in Open Learning Delivery; operating on behalf of the City and Guilds of London Institute;
6 Success as a prominent Gateway Centre for the Open College and as a facility for BBC video previewing which had resulted in bringing a number of national organizations into the 'client orbit' of ROTeC;
7 Not least, the generation of adequate revenue from its activities to cover the Centre's operating costs and yield a surplus.

From the information set out in the foregoing Sections, it will be clear why, in his report of 9 June 1989, the Principal commented, 'As this Session draws to its close, I am able to report to Governors that the College's upward momentum continues'.[30] Key features of the Session's progress are listed below:

1 Management believed in the concept of a critical rate (or confidence level) of change. For this reason the College had been established with a hierarchical (as opposed to a more novel) form of structure, which would be reviewed in the light of experience. In the Spring of 1989 it had reviewed and revised this structure

- to assist diversification and development;
- to improve the pace of implementing Equal Opportunities policies;
- to increase the focus on student-centred learning;
- to extend Open Learning across all academic areas;
- to increase the pace of reducing or eliminating declining areas and assist the rise of new ones;
- to improve financial and decision support services for clearer and more cohesive planning and control.

2 Because of the news that the Local Education Authority would be carrying out a Further Education Review (announced towards the end of the Session), implying a further reduction in the number of Colleges, the institution of Cross-College Units — in Academic Planning and

Development and in the Administration of Resources and College Services — regrettably had to be suspended indefinitely;

3 Through its Position Statement on Quality Control and Institutional Effectiveness, the College affirmed its belief in user orientation. This emphasized the development of the quality of the service through an informed view of the needs of existing and potential users. In implementing the policy, the College was significantly increasing the number and type of its client organizations in industry and commerce, a strategy that was to serve it well;

4 The Session saw the completion of arrangements for the closure of the Childwall campus. The case for this had been argued on educational as well as economic grounds. Management hoped that concentration of provision at Riversdale would have a markedly positive effect on changing the culture;

5 Theoretical and conceptual constructs which had assisted strategic thinking during the Session had included Drucker on the management of opportunities and risks; Mullins on the contingency approach to organization structure; Barham and Rassam on the value of organizational openness and less status-conscious communication; the Adair concept of the interaction of task, group and individual needs; Peters and Waterman on the distinguishing characteristics of successful organizations and O'Shaughnessy on strategy consensus building and Theory Z organization (which emphasizes the welfare aspect of managing people);

6 Work on heightening the visibility of the College and the development of a positive public image continued, with the introduction of the Sunley-Natwest Lectures and the powerful symbolic publicity surrounding the National Training Award and the establishment of the Olivetti Technology Centre;

7 All the Faculties made notable contributions to the College's progress during the Session, at the end of which student enrolments had increased dramatically (1986/87 – 3810; 1988/89 – 5598) as had the student:staff ratio. (In 1986/87 the student: staff ratio was 7.67; by 1988/89 it had risen to 11.00);

8 Particularly notable had been the increased level of the College's provision in Education for Special Needs and the interest this had aroused both externally and internally. In the first respect, an Open Day had attracted over 160 parents, young people and special schools staff. Internally, this provision was making a significant contribution to beneficial change in the College's culture. One aspect of this derived from a great

deal of fund-raising activity being undertaken by staff on behalf of the Special Needs Unit. This brought together staff from all Faculties and also resulted in closer contact between a number of teaching and educational support staff. This effort, grounded in the generosity of spirit which typifies Liverpool people, provided opportunity for a diversity of staff to unite in the name of the new College — an opportunity which might not otherwise have occurred.

There was a second aspect to this cultural change. It was among the most significant features observed in this action research project. By demonstrating their keenness for social contact, their enthusiasm for learning, their gratitude for the service provided and their resolution in the face of personal disabilities, the special needs students acted as a powerful catalyst for change. The tonic effect they had on motivation and morale was perhaps best summarized by the Maritime Studies teacher, faced with a continuing decline in his work, who said, 'If I come here feeling sorry for myself, when one of these students comes up to me, smiles, asks my name and how I'm getting on, I feel a whole lot better.' As the benefits they brought to the new culture were becoming increasingly apparent, one senior manager concluded, 'They do more for us than we can ever do for them.'

Notes

1 WEST, J. *et al.* (1989) 'Proposed reorganization of the college academic structure 1989', Report of the College Management Team, South Mersey College, Liverpool, May, pp. 1–2.
2 SHEPPARD, D. and WARLOCK, D. (1988) *Better Together, Christian Partnership in a Hurt City*, London: Hodder & Stoughton, p. 42.
3 DRUCKER, P.F. (1964) *Managing for Results*, London: Pan Books, and in MULLINS, L.J. (1989) *Management and Organizational Behaviour*, 2nd Edition, London: Pitman Publishing, pp. 100–1.
4 MULLINS, L.J. (1989) Ibid., p. 147 ff.
5 OLDCORN, R. (1989) *Management*, London: Macmillan Education Ltd., p. 288.
6 TOFFLER, A. (1985) *The Adaptive Corporation*, London: Pan Books Ltd., p. 97.
7 DRUCKER, P.F. (1986) *Innovation and Entrepreneurship*, London: Pan Books Ltd., pp. 201–3.
8 BARHAM, K. and RASSAM, C. (1989) *Shaping the Corporate Future*, London: Unwin Hyman Ltd., p. ix.
9 BARHAM, K. and RASSAM, C. (1989) Ibid., p. 6.
10 BARHAM, K. and RASSAM, C. (1989) Ibid., p. 13.
11 ADAIR, J. (1979) *Action-Centred Leadership*, Aldershot, Hants: Gower Publishing Company Limited, p. 10.
12 PETERS, T.J. and WATERMAN, R.H., Jr. (1982) *In Search of Excellence*, London: Harper & Row, Publishers, p. xxiii.
13 BUCHANAN, D.A. and HUCZYNSKI, A.A. (1985) *Organizational Behaviour*, London: Prentice Hall International (UK) Ltd., pp. 433–35.
14 COSER, L.A. (1956) *The Functions of Conflict*, London: Routledge and Kegan Paul, pp. 137 and 154.

15 O'SHAUGHNESSY, J. (1988) *Competitive Marketing A Strategic Approach*, 2nd Edition, London: Unwin Hyman Ltd., pp. 398–99.
16 STEERS, R.M. and PORTER, L.W. (Eds) *Motivation and Work Behaviour*, 3rd Edition, New York: McGraw-Hill, pp. 642–43.
17 MULLINS, L. (1989) Op. cit., p. 241.
18 BOYLE, D. (1988) *The Strategic Planning Process* in 2nd Edition, *The Gower Handbook of Management*, Aldershot, Hants: Gower Publishing Company Limited, p. 33.
19 CANTOR, L.M. and ROBERTS, I.F. (1986) *Further Education To-Day, A Critical Review*, 3rd Edition (revised) London: Routledge & Kegan Paul, p. 249.
20 CANTOR, L.M. and ROBERTS, I.F. (1986) Ibid., pp. 257–58.
21 OLINS, W. (1988) 'Shaping the company image', in HELLER, R. (Ed.) *The Complete Guide to Modern Management*, London: Harrap Ltd., p. 212.
22 MORGAN, G. (1986) *Images of Organization*, London: Sage Publications Ltd., p. 121.
23 MORGAN, G. (1986) Ibid., p. 139.
24 SATHE, V. (1985) *Culture and Related Corporate Realities*, Irwin, in JOHNSON, G. and SCHOLES, K. (1989) *Exploring Corporate Strategy*, Hemel Hempstead: Prentice-Hall International (UK) Ltd., p. 310.
25 BAINES, G. (1987) *Winners '88*, Sheffield: The Training Agency (Employment Department), South Mersey College.
26 FRAIN, J.P.A. (1988) in *Liverpool Weekly Star*, Thursday, *December 1st.*
27 FRAIN, J.P.A. (1988) *Principal's Report to the Governors, South Mersey College, Liverpool*, 4 November, p. 1.
28 DEPARTMENT OF EDUCATION AND SCIENCE (1988) *Report by Her Majesty's Inspectors on a survey of some major full-time courses in NAFE Business Studies carried out 27 April to 9 June 1987*, London: DES.
29 FRAIN, J.P.A. (1989) *Principal's Report to the Governors, South Mersey College, Liverpool*, 9 June, p. 7.
30 FRAIN, J.P.A. (1989) Ibid., p. 1.

Chapter 8

The 1989/90 Session

Strategic Analysis : Environmental Turbulence

Along with other management theorists, Stoner and Freeman[1] have indicated that, over time, òrganizational environments tend to become more 'turbulent'. Ansoff,[2] a significant contributor to strategic management reasoning has described the organizational predicament as turbulence increases: events are less predictable, changes more frequent and past experience less relevant to current decision-making. These views were set out in Chapter 3 when the developing environment of the Liverpool FE Colleges during the four year period of the research was described. Within that description some of the key factors making for increasing turbulence were enumerated, namely:

- within the task or direct-action environment, the intervention of the Liverpool Education Authority and its establishment of a Federal System of FE operations and management;
- within the general or 'outer-layer' environment, governmental and quasi-governmental intervention culminating in the Education Reform Act, 1988; the Joint Efficiency Study, 1987; and the establishment of the National Council for Vocational Qualifications (NCVQ), 1986.

All of these influences were fundamentally important and had to be provided for, yet, because they coincided with management's attempts to steer the College through a process of significant change, they made that process more complex and multivariate than it otherwise would have been. Increased turbulence in the shape of the demands made on management time by the Federal System also increased management anxieties about those aspects of its responsibilities which were not receiving the attention they merited, particularly with regard to internal communication and the more detailed planning now required. The implications of the other environmental changes, and the other action taken in relation to them will now be outlined.

The Education Reform Act

Among the proposals relating to College Governing Bodies was the observation (para. 3.1) that:

> The Government attaches great significance to the role of governing bodies. . . . But to be fully effective they need to be independent and they need to be assured a worthwhile and clearly defined part to play in determining the conduct and direction of the institution. (DES, 1988)

The Instrument of Government of South Mersey College, approved by the Department of Education in pursuance of the Education Reform Act, set out the composition of the new Governing Body (which met for the first time on 22 November 1989). The twenty members were as follows:

> Nine members who were or have been engaged or employed in business, industry or any profession;
> One co-opted member with expertize in special educational needs;
> Four members nominated and appointed by the Authority;
> Two members representing the staff of the College (one member elected from the teaching staff, one member elected from the non-teaching staff);
> One member (elected) to represent the students of the College;
> One member drawn from a neighbouring educational institution;
> One member appointed by the Authority on the nomination of a local community organization
> The Principal of the College.

The management of the College fully subscribed to the idea of the role of the Governing Body, as described in the Act, and believed it important to ensure that the Governors in membership should be highly qualified and experienced in this regard. Accordingly, it devoted a great deal of time, thought and negotiating energy to compiling the list of invitees for submission to the Education Authority. The Principal and his colleagues felt their efforts had been amply rewarded when the composition of the Governing Body finally took shape.

For example, the industrial representatives included directors/senior managers from British Olivetti Limited, Esso Petroleum, Bibby Lines Limited, Tarmac Construction, Stewart Mechanical Services, BBC Radio Merseyside and J. Blake and Company, Ltd. (a large local vehicle distributor). Another Governor, representing the North West TUC, was a project engineer in the precision hydraulics field. The four representatives of the Local Education Authority were all experienced members of the Liverpool City Council, and one, who became Chair of the Governing Body, was also Chair of the City's Continuing Education Sub-Committee.

The other external members were the Deputy Headmaster of a large neighbouring community comprehensive school, a member of the Merseyside Community Relations Council (with a special interest in equal opportunities (race)); a Psychologist from the local Health Authority (with experience and interest in education for special needs) and a member of the Merseyside Police with long experience of community work in deprived areas of the City.

Despite the responsibilities and pressures of their own employment, the Governors took up their task with a high degree of energy and commitment. For example, by the provisions of the Instrument of Government (Section 10.1) they were required to meet as a Body at least once every term. In their first Academic Session (1989/90) they met five times in full session (22.11.89; 24.1.90; 30.3.90; 25.5.90; 20.7.90) instead of the customary three times. In addition, they formed a Finance and General Purposes Committee comprised of three members with industrial/business backgrounds, two members of the Local Education Authority, the Principal and Vice Principal of the College. Subsequent to the first meeting of the Governing Body, this Committee met on a number of occasions in preparation for the full meetings of the Governing Body.

This action research project describes the successful diversification and development of a College of Further Education over a four-year-period. Its primary focus is upon the role of management in that process, but management would readily acknowledge its own role as being only one element in the process. Among the other key actors were those members of the City Council and the Local Education Authority in close working relationship to the College, the members of the College staff and the members of the College Governing Bodies. The management had been grateful for the interest and support of the Governors who served it in the period from September 1986 to August 1989. These Governors had encouraged managers in their efforts, offered timely advice and had taken pride in the College's progress, but prior to the Education Reform Act their powers had been circumscribed. The new Governing Body gave clear indications of its intention to partner management in the governance of the College with vigour and enthusiasm. This made a positive contribution to morale at a time when the continuing financial problems of the City were adding to the administrative burdens of the further education service.

Kogan *et al.*[3] make the point that the administrative structure of the English education system is characterized by a lack of clear relationships between the various institutions and bodies. They add:

> The 1944 Education Act prescribed a diffusion of power and authority between the elements such that no single body was intended to assume a dominant position; instead, partnership and balance were to be the guiding principles determining the style of these relationships.

Although the context of their observations is the school governing body, what they describe also holds true for the further education sector. For

Figure 8.1: The College Governing Body and its network of relationships (adapted from Kogan et al.: Policy-Making in Education in McNay and Ozga)

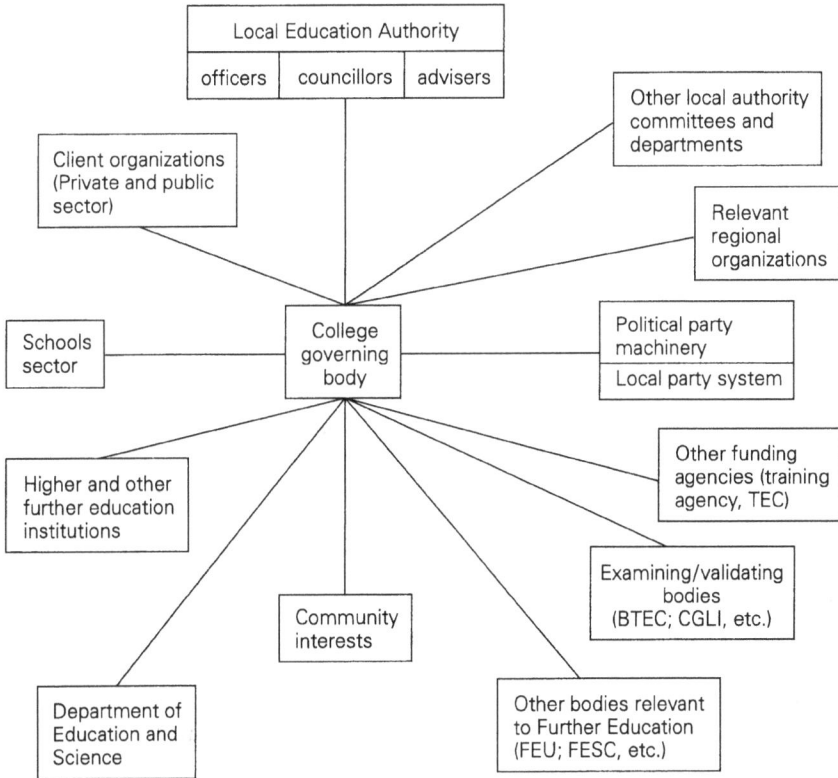

example, they describe the network of the several different organizations and groups underlying 'the concept of the local political-administrative system' and provide a schematic denoting the interaction between the different organizations and groups. Figure 8.1 is the writer's adaptation of that schematic as it might apply to a governing body in further education.

As Kogan and his colleagues point out, the concept of a policy-making or inter-organizational system, as depicted in Figure 8.1, is typically found in public administration. Clearly and insightfully they add:

It developed as a heuristic and analytical tool to portray 'government' as a series of different groups which impact upon each other and therefore form relationships. Implicit in this approach are, first, multiple linkages involving different types of influence and, secondly, the existence of complexity and at times ambiguity in these relationships. Although each body may have its own terms of reference, there is overlap between the functions performed and bodies become interdependent.[4]

The reader with experience in the management of further education will recognize the accuracy of the reference to 'complexity' and 'at times ambiguity' and perhaps support the view that in the past these have inhibited flexibility and responsiveness at the institutional level. In framing the Act, Parliament doubtless had this in mind with its prescription for the composition of Governing bodies and the notion of 'balance' in this regard. The best hope for the individual College was that its Governing Body, by dint of its collective qualifications, experience, capacities and commitment would quickly develop the professional self-confidence to act as a powerful mediating influence in the face of the complexities and the ambiguities. The capability of the Governing Body to act thus would directly affect the quality of the College's response to the market. In this, the management of South Mersey was not to be disappointed: a remarkable outcome if we bear in mind that shortly after its formation the new Governing Body learned that its own existence would be short-lived (for reasons we shall see later).

Moreover, despite the increasing turbulence in a period of already profound change, the College managers welcomed the provisions of the Act, particularly those relating to the delegation of financial powers and the ability to retain a sufficient proportion of income earned through full-cost courses. The College already earned a significant amount of money through courses designed for customer organizations and, in the opinion of management, this could be markedly increased. Thus the incentive provided by the Act would enable the College to solve deep-seated problems related to capital equipment. The rate of change of the technologies was such that these problems could never be overcome through normal (revenue estimates) funding. Also, whilst management was loyally committed to its ties with the Liverpool City Council and wished to remain very much a local authority College, it felt that the change in the role of responsibilities of Governing Bodies would bring its advantages. Through the attractions that increased influence would bring, the College was now able to invite senior executives from industrial and commercial organizations to join its Governing Body. This would undoubtedly influence the curriculum for vocational courses and the way the College's affairs were managed, strategically and tactically. It was also hoped that a Body in which employment interests featured so significantly would assist the College in its quest for benefactions and other sources of external funding.

The Joint Efficiency Study

The work of the Steering Group which produced this study has already been described in Chapter 3. In the 1989/90 Academic Session the College management had to devote some of its attention to the recommendations of the report, namely:

- The use of performance indicators to determine efficiency (notably the progression towards an S/SR of 11.4 by 1991/92);
- the setting of targets related to the performance indicators;
- the linking of performance indicators to the planning of provision and the setting of budgets;
- the establishment of 'comprehensive, integrated computerized management information systems for performance indicators and (other) FE data within 5 years' (from July 1987, that is).

A situation report[5] prepared in February 1990 by a member of the Senior Management Team indicated that:

- the College had progressed some way to meeting these requirements and had the capability to meet most of them by the required deadline if the freedom to develop systems independently of the LEA was agreed without delay; not enough work had yet been done on the establishment of performance indicators, other than the S/SR, although this was standing at 11.0 for 1989/90;
- with regard to the setting of targets related to performance indicators, except for the monitoring of enrolments against the recruitment targets and the logging of 'early leavers', no indicators had yet been set. Insufficient attention had been paid so far to reasons for student 'wastage', the setting of retention targets; progression or success rates; the monitoring of costs and resource utilization;
- progress *had* been made towards the allocation of budgets related to the attainment of targets set in the FE Development and Planning procedures (at the Authority level with the cooperation of the Colleges);
- the College was in a position to arrive at values for most of the performance indicators but only in a piecemeal manner. The installation of a Prime minicomputer and Oracle software had made it possible to anticipate the general nature of the integrated systems to be established, though much detailed work was needed to make it possible to monitor performance indicators related to expenditure accurately and comprehensively.

It was felt that the way forward was for the College to:

- Plan a system of budgetary control to monitor the expenditure of allocated finance across a range of defined cost centres and within specified budgetary headings;
- begin to implement this system by manual methods, converting to computerized systems as soon as resources were available;
- link budgetary monitoring to performance and efficiency criteria so as to inform the planning process, for example, determination of the

cost per FTE student — enrolling, completing, qualifying, succeeding — across the range of expenditure headings.

The National Council for Vocational Qualifications (NCVQ)

Chapter 3 contains an outline of the establishment of the Council. Its system of National Vocational Qualifications (NVQs) and the criteria for these was also described. This development presaged major changes in vocational qualifications and had wide implications for colleges of further education, including South Mersey. A paper prepared by a member of staff for the College Principal[6] outlined these implications clearly. In summary they were as follows:

- There was need for increased liaison with employers for a sufficiency of work placements, so that students might learn through experience.
- It was necessary to allocate resources for adequate guidance and counselling: procedures were required to help students prepare and present evidence of prior achievement; guidance facilities were required so that students could accumulate appropriate units.
- Development work was necessary to use NVQs as the basis for new forms of flexible learning and assessment using credit accumulation and the National Record of Vocational Achievement (NROVA).
- To be successful NCVQ had to be learner-led and time had to be provided for staff to guide and advise students and to visit industrial and commercial organizations to diagnose the skills and competences required.
- Record-keeping was an important part of NCVQ delivery, enabling students to be efficiently credited with their units of competence.
- The College had to treat the matter as urgent, for in many of the vocational areas, private agencies would be competing with colleges in the maintained sector.

The Contribution of College Staff

Despite an accelerating rate of change and the complexity of that change, diversification and development went ahead at a significant pace. The four-year long observation process revealed that this could not have occurred without the special qualities and the unstinting effort of the College staff. In making the point that to a large measure, the success achieved by the institutions of further education depends upon the quality of the staff who teach in them, Cantor and Roberts are heartened by the fact '... that the subject of teacher education and staff development has never received so much attention as in recent years'.[7]

While they add that the overall situation is still far from satisfactory[8], they draw attention to this very welcome increase (which occurred largely in response to the first report of the Haycocks Committee[9]) which brought about a situation whereby teacher training for further education, previously concentrated mainly in the former colleges of technical education had spread into polytechnics, colleges of higher education and the further education colleges. This had placed such training in a setting '... which encompasses the whole spectrum of education and so helps to break down its previous isolation'.

The management at South Mersey believed staff development to have been an influence in staff, hence College, performance, and that the context, very often the workplace, was as important as the content of training. The Local Education Authority must take much of the credit for this. Its interpretation of teacher training went far beyond the provision of two-year part-time courses leading to the Certificate of Education (FE). It made a continuing appraisal of the informational and skills needs of its teaching force and arranged intensive short-courses on a variety of topics including equal opportunities (race and gender), fair selection training, national vocational qualifications, open-learning and the Single European Act.

So staff development was an important element in the contribution of the staff to organizational change and development. But management would say that to discover why, in the generality, the staff maintained and increased their motivation for the tasks in hand, it is necessary to look primarily to the innate qualities of the staff itself. Dispassionate observation revealed that several circumstances could have contributed to a loss of appetite for College diversification:

- the continuing financial problems of the City;
- the recent reorganization of FE which had entailed changes of role and of location for very many;
- the changed status of the teacher (entailing what Stewart Ranson[10] has described as the loss of some of their traditional professional control of the 'secret garden' of the curriculum);
- the necessity to develop new skills, as in the provision of open learning and the implementation of new methods of assessment;
- the changing culture of the College.

Other factors should be added to this, in management's view. An insufficient level of communication, as management perceived it, has already been commented upon. This was unlikely to improve, particularly since management decided not to seek a replacement for one of the College's Vice Principals when he left the College. Admittedly, the objective here was to use the salary this saved in order to help create lower level posts, but the benefits this might have had on morale were denied the College, because of the Authority's budgetary problems prevented the savings being made available.

In spite of all this, the College diversified and its enrolments increased. The Principal, for example, would describe his own management style as iconoclastic, mainly because he refused to be burdened with detail. This was not what the staff were used to, and this issue could have caused great dissatisfaction. Fortunately, the staff were not captious; faced with the scale and complexity of change, they focused on the good of the students. Any teleology of South Mersey's success must find this at the heart of the matter. It was symptomatic of the generosity of spirit that many staff took on extra responsibilities knowing that the chances for financial recognition for these were, at the best estimate, extremely unlikely.

Conceptual and Theoretical Constructs

Changing the Culture

It may seem far-fetched to suggest that cultural anthropology has relevance and value for managers and for managerial tasks. Yet the clear link is established in the way culture is defined by cultural anthropologists. In their classic paper on culture, Kroeber and Kluckhohn[11] define it thus:

> ... patterns, explicit and implicit, of and for behaviour acquired and transmitted by symbols, consituting the distinctive achievement of human groups, including their embodiments in artifacts; the essential core of culture consists of traditional (i.e. historically derived and selected) ideas and especially their attached value; culture systems may, on the one hand, be considered a product of action, on the other as conditioning elements of further action.

Despite its prolixity, the definition is reasonable if we take culture to mean the shared orientations, norms and values that characterized staff activity before the reorganized college emerged in 1986, and changing culture to mean alterations in ideology and actions thereafter.

Some signposts of this changing culture can be found in the earlier parts of this book, for example:

1 the general concepts which conditioned management thinking:
    * systems theory and the notion of the College as an 'open system';
    * the marketing concept and its student-centred approach;
    * the model of course and curriculum development which emphasized feedback and the importance of behavioural outcomes (Chapter 4, Figure 4.5);
2 the restructuring of jobs and increased delegation of authority as a means of enriching work experience and increasing motivation and the allocation of resources to those areas where growth and development were already taking place (Chapter 6);

3   the requirement for the college to become more financially accountable (including the capacity to generate more of its own resources).
(Chapter 6)

The attitudes required for diversification and development were those to
be found in outward-looking, self-reliant, adaptable individuals, and it would
not be recondite to state that helping to develop these attitudes means
'changing the culture', as the cultural anthropologist would define it. Yet
again, management would not claim the credit for this. In the phraseology of
Francis[12] it had 'shared the compelling vision' and helped to 'turn perception
of threat into opportunity' (Chapter 6, Figure 6.2). It had demonstrated the
capacity to regularly review the organization structure in the light of external
changes acting upon the College and to modify it, if need be. But the capability of 'making things happen' as Harvey-Jones[13] describes it, was proving
not to be the exclusive preserve of management; here, management would
draw attention to the diligence with which, for example, the motor vehicle
department lecturers obtained significant resources in kind from the industry
and the speed at which other generic technologists devised and operated
recreation, leisure and other community courses, when it was explained to
them this would constitute a desirable change in the culture.

The organization structure was changed as the need arose and this assisted growth and diversification to take place, but it also called for greater
toleration of ambiguity. As Boisot[14] indicates '. . . the structuring and sharing
of information is the collective enterprise through which culture is built
up . . .' but as has been explained earlier, management felt its own performance to be lacking in this regard, if only because of the contribution it was
called upon to make to the 'federal' system, and hence, the pressures on its
time. Again, therefore, management would say that the way in which new
objectives were internalized and a new organization structure assimilated was
due in large measure to the innate qualities of the staff and its self-directedness.
Once it knew what the new codes were, it contributed more than its share to
building up the culture. A point of qualification here, perhaps. The increased
size of the organization and the expectations of management from those who
had been allocated cross-college roles did help to break down what Boisot
has termed 'clans'.[15] Of these, he writes:

Entry is restricted and individual players are expected to observe the
'club rules' that serve to disguise the extent to which they pursue
their own individual interest, and also impose upon them some minimum concern with the common weal. Such transactions are characteristic of *clans*.

Management selected those for appointment to cross-College roles with
some care, supported colleagues in those roles and, in spite of resource restrictions, timetabled a fair measure of interaction between the Childwall and

Riversdale sites. Key areas of provision were also moved from one site to another (for example, media studies and American studies from Childwall to Riversdale; motor cycle engineering from Riversdale to Childwall). In this way, entry became derestricted, the number of players per cognate area increased and any clannishness was mitigated. The uncodified norms and values that had previously acted as social cement thus lost their power to bind. New allegiances were struck attuned to the new culture.

Survival is more than simple adaptation to an external environment. The wider goal is to maintain the integrity and coherence of internal processes while doing so — internal coherence meaning the fit between technology, organization and culture. The seeds of the necessary change in this regard were down to management style, while the implementation of that change was down to the attitudes and the energies of staff.

Decision-Making

Although a primary objective of the research was to examine the role of management within an institution needing to adapt to a changing environment in order to survive, nothing has so far been said about decision-making, other than what can be deduced from the commentary on the evolution of the institution. The study of decision-making is at the core of a number of intellectual disciplines, including economics, systems analysis and psychology. If social science has any claim to systematically illumine how an organization can be understood as an intelligible entity, then the host of choices made by managers must, in the words of McGrew and Wilson[16] '... be ordered from their particular and concrete individuality and reduced to comprehensible patterns, or *explained*'. It is a daunting task to provide even a limited explanation of the process involved in the College being examined, for this entails analyzing and drawing from the vast amount of published work on decision-making and either fitting this to the observed realities or discarding it for its lack of explanatory value. Nonetheless some study of the process had to be undertaken, for without it, the research would have been defective. As Hall[17] has indicated, most normative statements predicate some ideally rational model of decision-making that may or may not be followed in an imperfect world. Most start from economics and its philosophical basis, grounded in nineteenth-century utilitarianism. The approach postulates the series of logical steps, abbreviated and set out below:

- Scan the environment — isolate the main problems.
- Set up a hierarchy of goals — edit to manageable proportions.
- Establish an inventory of available resources.
- Evaluate alternative approaches to goals — in terms of some common metric of costs and benefits.

- Estimate probabilities of different courses of action.
- Identify the preferred course — to maximize the net expectation.
- Translate to managerial action and implement.
- Monitor implementation, and modify appropriately.

As Hall points out, however, the rational model quickly becomes tempered by pragmatic considerations, namely:

- The rational model requires perfect information, which is often lacking.
- It is generally impossible to assess objective probabilities for outcomes — the best that can be done is to ask decision-makers for their subjective assessment.
- The model assumes all actors hold the same values, which, in complex decisions, is highly unlikely.
- Some objectives are readily quantifiable, some are not.
- There is no common agreement on an objective function which can be valued on a single scale, such as money values.
- The rational model parameters of the decision remain fixed, yet fluidity is the central feature of the real world, etc.

Here it is interesting to note that the management of the College set out with some belief in the organizing power of the rational model concept (see, for example, Chapter 5, p. 90). Yet as events transpired it began to be concerned that, in theoretical terms at least, management could be criticized for lack of in-depth planning, for lack of structured decision-making (see Chapter 6, p. 97). The reasons for this have also been touched on earlier: lack of time due to the pressure of 'federal' commitments, the incomplete development of an adequate data base, etc. Management would echo Hall's sentiments on the deficiencies of the rational model approach, as set out above, though its own experience ran counter to Hall's dictum on the lack of congruence in the value held by actors. Two examples might clarify this:

1 All members of the senior management team, and their departments, supported the decision that funding should be witheld from all departmental budgets to establish a College unit for information technology (IT) (located in one department, (Room E208)). The received doctrine in this regard[18] is that actors may well perceive that the greatest good for the greatest number may mean a loss to their own group;

2 The decision of the Principal not to seek a replacement for a retiring Vice-Principal in order that the funding so saved could be used for posts in the main lectureship grade was again supported by College

managers, although the decision clearly meant that their own pressures and responsibilities would increase in consequence.

Now it well may be that the situational factors, such as the College's struggle for survival, were sufficient to overawe the well-established theory on selective perception, but again, as the writer observed it, it also said something about the generosity of spirit to be found in the College's staff. This made for more than goodwill and adequate industrial relations. It was the Principal's view, for instance, that the decision to refurbish and equip E208 as the College's IT Unit markedly influenced the decision of British Olivetti to locate the £250,000 Technology Centre at the College.

How best then, can the College's decision-making processes be conceptualized? The 'incremental model', set out by Dahl and Lindblom[19] is a useful starting point for an explanation of the observed facts. These writers assume that decision-makers consider only incremental alternatives at any one time, together with a limited number of alternative means. Solutions will be considered only if they are realistic (i.e. appropriate to the available means). There is no clearly defined problem, no one decision; problems are never *solved*.

Hall[20] argues that this too is oversimplistic. He goes on:

> ... it ignores the fact that social change and innovation comes about through incorporation of new social values. Consequently, it has been claimed, the right mode of analysis is a kind of *mixed scanning*, which distinguishes fundamental *contextual* decisions from *individual item* decisions. Contextual decisions are made through a fundamental exploration of the main alternatives in the light of goals and objectives.... At this stage, details are properly omitted. Then, piecemeal incremental decisions are made within the context of the fundamental one.

These last comments depict accurately management's own view of its approach to decision-making. It had found a college badly in decline, within a complex further education service, in a burdened city. As a key area of expenditure to the Council further education was expected to play an important role in social reform, to help fuel economic recovery, to facilitate equality of opportunity and to afford some justice to the deprived. Policy objectives for further education were, in Ranson's[21] phrase, 'to bring a new world out of the old'. Management's communication to staff on the fundamentals of the situation had:

- emphasized the declining numbers of courses for the more traditional industries and the accompanying need for a wide range of courses to cope with training in the new technologies;
- indicated the increased demand for vocational education in the service sectors, such as the media industry;

- drawn attention to the increased demand for general and continuing education;
- emphasized the growing need for pre-employment (vocational preparation) courses which reflected youth unemployment.

Its broad precepts to staff were based upon 1) the efficacy of the 'open-system' and the marketing approach as aids to development and diversification, 2) the importance of heightening the visibility of the college through the assiduous use of publicity and public relations 3) the importance of the staff's 'ownership' of its work and of its participation in the decision-making process.

It also influenced incremental decision-making by its own actions at the tactical level. For example, the establishment of the IT Unit (mentioned earlier) helped to communicate to colleagues the importance of an adequate balance between investment and consumption expenditure. Similarly, it signalled the importance of plural funding by its readiness to explore the opportunities for industrial and other partnerships. The establishment of the Sunley-NatWest Lectures (Chapter 7, p. 136) not only brought a host of nationally and internationally known figures to the College and hence much welcome publicity, it also served to communicate to staff and students management's view of the contribution of the hidden curriculum. (Here management adopted Roland Meighan's [22] aphorism that, as a working definition the hidden curriculum can be defined as all the other things that are learnt in addition to the official curriculum).

A final example — Dennison[23] has remarked on the resistance some Non-Advanced Further Education colleges have shown towards the Manpower Services Commission (MSC) financed courses for 16–19 year olds when this may be their most effective route towards long-term growth. In some (though not all) sections of the College, management found this antipathy and set out to correct it by actions intended to illustrate that the MSC, subsequently the Training Agency, then the Training and Enterprise Council (TEC) was an important part of the plural funding mechanism.

The descriptive term 'mixed scanning' would therefore seem to define the approach adopted to decision-making. Etzioni,[24] a respected writer on organizational behaviour, claims that mixed scanning entails a decision-making process in two phases. Initially a broad sweep is made of policy options and these are assessed against stated values in general terms. Then, within this framework, decision-making proceeds incrementally in matters of detail. He adds:

> It is essential to differentiate fundamental decisions from incremental ones. Fundamental decisions are made by exploring the main alternatives the actor sees in view of his conception of his goals, but — unlike what rationalism would indicate — details and specifications are omitted so that an overview is feasible. Incremental decisions are

made but within the contexts set by fundamental decisions (and fundamental reviews).

Other Organizational Issues

Mention has been made earlier of management's endorsement of the open-system concept. An elaboration of the basic model of this concept which is particularly useful for understanding organizations is the 'congruence-model' developed by Nadler and Tushman[25] and depicted in Figure 8.2. An important feature of the model is that it expands upon the process by which inputs are transformed into outputs. The model incorporates three major elements:

1 the formal structural features of the organization;
2 the characteristics of the particular tasks being performed;
3 the informal social relationships that exist among work group members.

And to these is added a fourth critical element: the characteristics of the people performing the tasks in question. These writers propose that the outputs from an organization are the direct result of the way these four elements relate to each other. When they fit together well, a state of congruence is said to exist and desirable outputs can be expected. For example, if we consider the relationship between the characteristics of the tasks being performed and the people performing them — routine, repetitive tasks requiring little skill might fit reasonably well with an employee who has little formal education, few marketable skills and little, if anything, in the way of career aspirations. There would be no 'goodness of fit' if the employee was a university graduate or a professionally qualified person. It is probable such an employee would quickly become bored and quit the job. This point is taken up again below.

As Mitchell and Larson[26] have reported, a number of factors that are positively related to job satisfaction can be placed under the heading of job challenge. People seem to be more satisfied with their job when it demands something from them. Moreover, people tend to be more committed to the job and are more involved with their work when they are challenged by what they do. The opposite of challenge is boredom. Here, the concomitant phenomena are high levels of dissatisfaction, absenteeism and labour turnover. Challenge, or lack of it, can have both attitudinal and economic aspects.

Another major contribution to our understanding of motivation is that of Edwin Locke.[27] He argues that employees have certain goals they set for themselves and that an organization can have a strong influence on the work behaviour of its employees by influencing their goals. More specifically, goal-setting theory states that hard goals yield better performance than easy ones, as long as they are accepted by the employee (Eriz and Ziden).[28] Mitchell and Larson[29] conclude their review of employee motivation as follows:

Figure 8.2: The congruence model of organizations

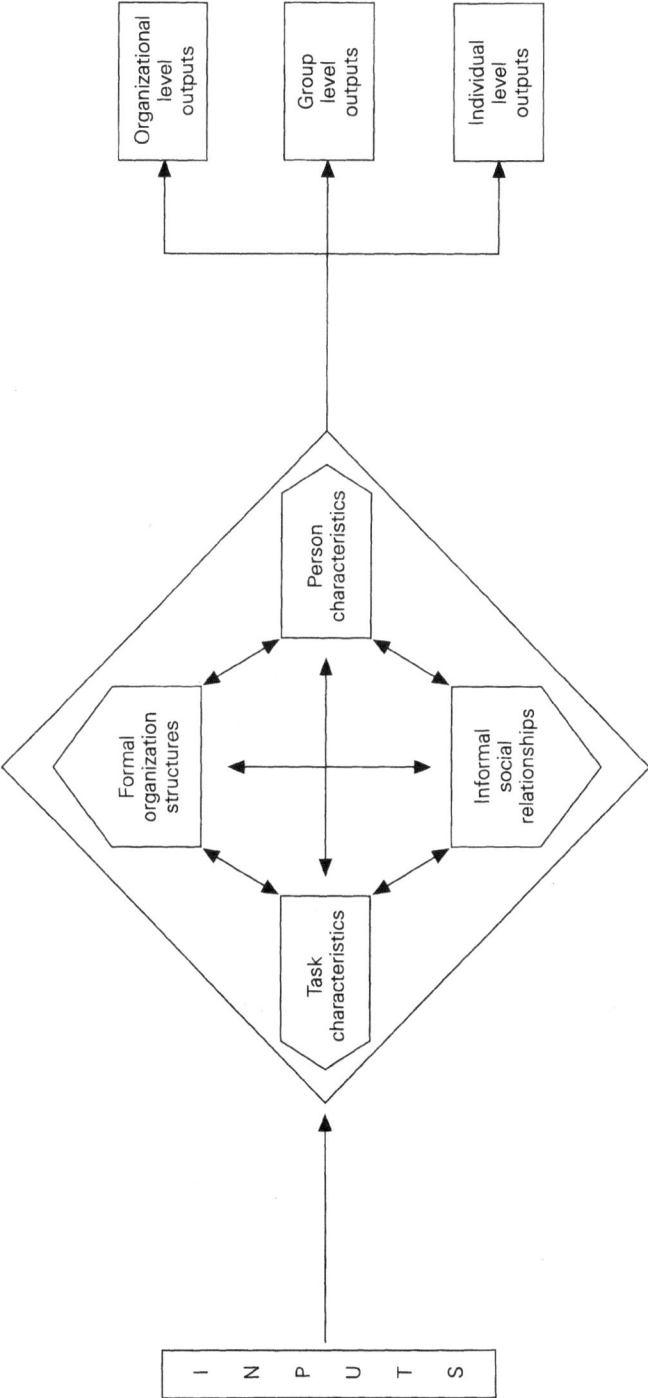

INPUTS

| Formal organization structures | Task characteristics | Person characteristics | Informal social relationships |

Organizational level outputs

Group level outputs

Individual level outputs

(Adapted from Nadler and Tushman, 1980)

167

In summary, the research evidence demonstrates rather convincingly that goals are a major source of work motivation. Goal setting is currently one of the most frequently tested theories in the field of organizational behaviour, and despite the caveats we have noted, it has received considerable support.

Group size can also be a significant factor in participation. A classic study by Ringmann[30] demonstrated that as a group size increased, the average contribution per person decreased. A related phenomenon is 'social loafing'; it appears that when people work in groups in which their individual contributions cannot be assessed, they work less hard than they would if working alone.

Finally, in their writing on communication, Mitchell and Larson[31] draw attention to the importance of external communication not only to enable the organization to assess and successfully interact with its environment but also for the internal functioning of the organization (through the communication of behavioural expectations by external role-set members).

In this Section then, a number of influences on productivity have been accentuated:

- organizational congruence
  (based on goodness of fit between tasks and employee characteristics)
- job challenge
- goal setting
- group size
- external communication

Through this observational study it was possible to discern that, while the innate quality of staff had a great deal to do with the successful diversification and growth of the college, these four factors were also part of the organizational context and made a distinct and positive contribution to success. Some explanation is now necessary.

Perhaps the most important single aspect of management's own credo was expressed laconically, 'a management that can't delegate is a weak management.' Its view was, for example, that the College would never have attracted over £333,000 in sponsorships in its short history, if management had allowed itself to be 'sucked into detail'. Its readiness to delegate enlarged the discretionary component of many jobs and particularly those of middle management. Providing a better fit between the education, background and training of staff and the tasks they were allotted had contributed to organizational congruence and also increased job challenge. Group size was a situational factor which, though not consciously planned for, brought its benefits. The Faculties might be large, but the sections and the course teams making them up were small, giving every opportunity to assess individual contributions and providing peer-group pressure on any evidence of 'social-loafing'!

So here were three influences at work for which management would take no credit but which, fortuitously, contributed to the common weal. Management would claim, however, with regard to the other two factors that it did set goals, that it did make its expectations of performance clear, faced as it was with the grave situation of the College in 1986 and that, especially, it did emphasize the importance of external communication and at the same time gave a clear lead by it own actions in that regard. Having made these points, however, management would again emphasize the fundamental contribution made by staff in 'turning round' the College's fortunes, particularly by those staff entrusted with supervisory and middle-management responsibilities. It is notable, for example, that Mitchell and Larson, quoting Locke's research finding that hard goals yield better results than easy ones (reference 27 q.v.), add 'as long as they are accepted by the employee'. Senior management was unable to recall a single instance of any member of staff refusing to accept a goal and its concomitant responsiblity for him or her.

A key objective of this study is to provide a narrative history of the life of South Mersey College during the period from 1 September 1986 to 31 August 1990. Three Sessions have been dealt with in earlier Parts of the work. The Section which follows completes the chronicle.

Narrative: The 1989/90 Academic Session

Reports from the Faculties

The information which follows is based upon an analysis of the Principal's reports to the College Governing Body for its meetings on 22 November 1989; 24 January 1990; 30 March 1990; 25 May 1990 and 20 July 1990.

Faculty of Adult and Community Education

It was difficult to give direct comparisons for total enrolments due to the change in the composition of the Faculty. However, comparisons for some of the major courses were possible:

	Total 1988/89 Enrolment	*Enrolment to 11 November 1989*
Special Needs courses (Full and part-time)	104	214
Access to Higher Education courses (Full and part-time)	200	196
GCE 'A' Level courses (Full-time)	50	72
GCSE courses (Full-time)	130	106

The early signs were, then, that there appeared to be little effect on enrolments resulting from the closure of the Childwall site. At the onset of the Session the Faculty enrolled 2239 students (59 per cent of its target). Through continued publicity and year-round enrolments the figure rose to 3489 (92 per cent of target) by April 1990, and subsequent further enrolments saw the target achieved. The target would have been well exceeded but for a 150 hours per week reduction in part-time teaching hours (the Faculty's allocated reduction as a result of the City Council's further reduction of the College's budget due to Council's continuing grave financial position).

The transfer of provision from Childwall caused some problems for the Faculty: classroom and staff accommodation was adequate but there were difficulties for craft provision, especially for Art and Pottery; in the delayed availability of the Campus Gymnasium at Riversdale (which had to be used for the storage of furniture); and in the provision of a student common room. These factors also militated against further growth in student numbers.

The Local Education Authority and the College regarded flexible learning opportunities as an increasingly important feature of the curriculum. In a 3-year period, the Drop-In Workshop at Childwall had developed into a facility catering for more than 700 students. It had been visited, admired and emulated by representatives of other Colleges in the area. The transfer to Riversdale, where the Unit was to occupy part of the Campus Library, a much larger space and the appointment of a Senior Lecturer to co-ordinate this provision, had been seen as a further significant step. In the event, the timing of the move from Childwall and a 'boundary dispute' on the space allocated to Open Learning and that allocated to the Library had affected the establishment of a comprehensive library service at Riversdale for the enlarged student body. This, in turn, had affected the quality of provision in the workshop. By the end of the Session, however, these difficulties were well on the way to being resolved and the Unit had attained no fewer than 628 enrolments to Open Learning, a total of nearly 30,000 student hours. Among the factors contributing to this outcome were:

- a review of timetabled hours, so as to ensure continuity of tutorial support;
- improvement to the decor and layout of the workshop;
- the acquisition of eighteen computers to provide a continuous support programme for students;
- the use of the workshop by students on vocational courses (which was expected to provide the opportunity for further marked expansion);
- the establishment of modules in study skills and job search techniques;
- the development of schemes of preparation for the entrance tests used by the various professions.

Special Needs provision continued to develop, and enrolments had increased from thirty-three in 1986/87 to 214 in 1989/90. This was testimony to the hard work and commitment of a team of dedicated staff, but due to the City's financial position, the College had been instructed not to fill the posts for the time being, of Principal Lecturer/Coordinator (Special Needs); Lecturer (Special Needs) and Care Assistant/Driver (Special Needs). It created difficulties in this area of provision and the Principal brought the matter to the attention of Governors in his 22 November 1989 report. He also outlined problems concerning transport and technician support for Special Needs courses. In the Spring of 1990 an Adviser conducted a survey of the College's provision on behalf of the Authority. This recommended that a Senior Lecturer and two Lecturers be appointed for Special Needs Education. Appointments were made immediately to two of these posts, and a Befriending Scheme (with Access students), a Carers' Liaison Group and an Advocacy Group were also established. The College was also selected for a three-year Pilot Project: Opportunities in Further Education for Adults with Learning Difficulties. It was to be established by the Health Authority in collaboration with Liverpool City Council and over the three-year period (commencing in September 1990) funding of £400,000 would be made available. As a result of this, the College was able to advertise in May 1990 for a Co-ordinator for the Project (Senior Lecturer), a Deputy Co-ordinator (Lecturer) and four Care Assistants. This noteworthy and much prized development was yet another feature of the marked diversification of the College from the former roles of its constituent Colleges.

It was safe to predict that, in Autumn 1990, approximately one hundred students from the Access to Higher Education course would proceed to Universities and other HE institutions. This meant that since its inauguration, 350 Access students would have entered Higher Education. Building on the success of the new Health Studies and Professional Studies options it was now planned to extend the range of vocational areas covered to include Construction and other technologies.

In 1989/90 there was a significant number of enrolments from the 50+ age group, particularly for Community and Basic Education courses. Consequently, the Faculty planned to extend its Active Retirement programme, with a significant number of students indicating that they would be attending for more than fifteen hours per week in the 1990/91 Session.

In March 1990 the Faculty completed an evaluation of its community provision using a questionnaire. A question on students' satisfaction with their course produced the following pattern of responses:

Satisfied	94 per cent
Dissatisfied	6 per cent

(NB: Dissatisfaction is related to language classes which catered for students with varying levels of ability within the same class).

Faculty of Construction

Enrolments increased by a margin of 14 per cent compared with the previous Session. Following the closure of the Childwall campus, part of the increase was due to the decision to place Horticultural provision within the Faculty. (In its combination with Building and Civil Engineering, this would provide opportunities for development in landscaping and land use, and the Faculty was determined to make the most of this opportunity). Nothwithstanding continuing resources difficulties, general progress was clear.

In addition to standard provision, the Faculty provided specialist courses for British Rail Maintenance staff; the Construction Industry Training Board (Site Levelling and Setting Out); the Lancashire County Council (Clerks of Works courses); and Haden-Young Limited (Heating, Ventilating and Air Conditioning). Links with British Gas were also being developed. Enrolments at 31.10.88 had totalled 1242. By 31.10.89 enrolments for the Session totalled 1427, but the recent decision by the Local Education Authority to suspend any new appointments gave serious cause for concern for appointments to its five vacant posts were essential to the continuance of current provision. Another of the Faculty's concerns hinged on the rapidly deteriorating state of its accommodation. The Principal's report to the Governors of 30 March 1990 emphasized the need to improve urgently the condition of Blocks A and B.

In spite of these problems, the Faculty continued to develop its operations in line with the changing context of further education. For example:

1 *Modes of delivery*. The Faculty was increasing its flexibility to enable students to select a programme of study suited to their individual circumstances;

2 *NCVQ*. The move to modularization of courses was being accelerated to align provision with the National Vocational Qualifications Scheme. The Faculty was also preparing itself to establish creditable schemes for workplace assessment — an important element of NVQs;

3 *European Dimension*. The Faculty had already forged links with two Colleges in France (at Tourcoing and Albertville), and it was currently involved in a funding bid under the PETRA scheme for extension of these links in order to broaden curricular provision. It was intended that exchange visits would become an established part of programmes of study;

4 *Pre-entry Advice and Guidance*. A development programme was under way to improve the guidance and counselling skills of staff to provide a better service to the student on entry and during progression to qualification;

5   *Equal Opportunities.* Developing its initiative in providing discrete courses for women in Construction Craft Skills, the Faculty was proposing to introduce a period of work experience as part of these courses in order to improve the employability of women in non-traditional skill areas. Positive Action Training was a key feature in the City Council's programme to improve employment prospects for the local black community. The Faculty was playing a very active part in the initiative with three groups of trainees at various stages of the special courses involved and the planned enrolment of additional students in September 1990. Courses for unemployed persons (Brickwork, Carpentry and Joinery, Plastering and Plumbing) were also continuing up to the very limit of available resources as were the popular schools link 'taster' courses for girls in Construction subjects;

6   *Staff Development.* Despite the pressure on manpower, most staff had received, by July 1990, training for Fair Selection, National Vocational Qualifications (NVQ), Quality Assurance, and Information Technology. Although some staff had taken part in anti-racist training, the number involved and the breadth of training would need to be increased, not least because of the Faculty's involvement with the City Council's Positive Action Programme. In 1990/91 it planned to participate in a variety of staff development programmes including basic teacher training, Fire Studies, various aspects and applications of Information Technology and Computer Aided Design.

The resource situation in general and the Summer 1990 announcement of a £600,000 further cut in the College budget were causing grave difficulties. The Faculty's materials budget would have to be reduced drastically and workshop time would have to be lowered for many craft courses. This negative but necessary step would have an adverse effect on the practical content of these courses. Because of the shortage of full-time staff in key areas, the Faculty had become heavily reliant on part-time staffing. This would now have to be reduced by 30 per cent in order for the Faculty to stay within its budget.

Notwithstanding all these difficulties, the Faculty's planning for the future continued with resolution. At the end of another successful Session, the Faculty was now not only the sole provider on Merseyside for courses in Wastes Management, Cleaning Science, Clerks of Works qualifications and Building Control Studies, it had also become a recognized centre for studies in Site Safety, Land Surveying, Gas Safety Training and Building Maintenance Management (for which it provided a national focus).

Faculty of Organization, Information and Communication Studies

The Faculty had been established at the end of the 1988/89 Session to provide courses in the following areas:

       Business administration, clerical and secretarial studies;
       Management studies, including European Languages;
       Information technology;
       Media studies;
       Trades union education;
       Income-earning courses for industry and commerce, through the
        Riversdale Open Technology Centre (ROTeC).

A situation report on the Faculty's early operations is set out below.

1 *Business administration, etc.* Unfortunately the closure of the Childwall campus had a negative effect on enrolments. Whole session enrolments for 1988/89 had totalled 1000 students. To November 1989, they were half this figure. Recruitment would continue throughout the year but would be constrained by staff shortages, even so. Nevertheless, there were grounds for optimism: a keyboard skills programme for ninety computer operators appeared to have met the sponsor's aims and was likely to result in follow-up work;

2 *Management studies.* This was a comparatively recent addition to the College's provision and the Faculty's first-term had been successful by any standards. Two significant contracts had been secured, the first to provide seminars and development kits for the Training Agency's Business Growth through Training Programme. It was a highly publicized national scheme, and forty managers of small/medium sized firms had quickly been recruited at the College. The second derived from connections with the training section of the former Merseyside Enterprise Board. The College had now become responsible for the delivery of its Strategic Management Programme (based on a model devised in collaboration with the Open University and the Cranfield Business School). In the Autumn term, fifty participants from local companies had attended residential weekend courses;

3 *Information technology.* Provision fell into two categories: computing courses, many of which were income-earning, and the incorporation of IT within the taught curriculum (in Construction, Auto-engineering, etc.). With regard to income-earning activity, the introduction of Computer-Aided Design facilities had opened up new markets. The Session would provide ample evidence of the revenue-generating capacity of this resource. These market opportunities stemmed from the partnership with British Olivetti. The Centre was markedly increasing the quality of standard provision and opening up excellent prospects for contract work;

4 *Media studies.* Enrolments had been as buoyant as usual (forty-five full-time students; fifty part-time students). The section was becoming increasingly well-regarded by media organizations on Merseyside. Although the

relocation of Media studies within the Riversdale campus (a secondary effect of the closure of the Childwall campus) had given rise to some problems, these were under continual review;

5 *Trades Union Education.* The programmes of this Section had recently received the commendation of Her Majesty's Inspectors. The courses were continually being developed and enrolments were constrained only by budgetary restrictions. Of particular note was the use of information technology as a delivery method. The Section was playing a distinctive role in the initiation and development of training for School Governors. There was also an increasing demand for trades union education from the schools sector now that 'the world of work' had become an important feature of the national curriculum;

6 *ROTeC.* The Unit continued to strengthen its connection with industry and commerce. It had now achieved its long-sought objective of becoming an in-house training facility for departments of Liverpool City Council. Its recent contracts included those with the O&M (Organization and Methods) Department, FE Section, Maintenance and Building Works Department, Promotion and News Unit (City Solicitor's Department) and City Estates Department. Additionally, negotiations were proceeding with the Merseyside Regional Health Authority, International Bio-Synthetics, Perris and Kearon, Advanced Resources and Training and the Brunswick Business Centre.

   ROTeC not only had the capacity to generate income, its 'brokerage' service to other Faculties of the College was also of great benefit. It was also an accreditation centre for the City and Guilds Certificate of Open-Learning Delivery, a Gateway centre for the Open College and a BBC Video Training Centre.

Other significant aspects of the Faculty's progress throughout the Session were these:

- the successful bid for an Urban Aid grant of £60,000 for the acquisition of Media Studies equipment over a three-year period;
- the development in combination with other institutions in the region, for a Certificate in Informatics course accredited by Sheffield University;
- the development of a range of Women's courses in information technology and operating small business;
- the establishment of a full-time BTEC Diploma course in Media Studies and a full-time pre-degree course in the same field, based on a combination of appropriate GCE 'A' levels.

It was clear that, but for staffing restrictions, the Faculty's development would be proceeding at an even faster pace.

Faculty of Transport

By the end of the Spring term, 160 courses had commenced with an enrolment of 2100 students. In the Summer term 481 students had been enrolled to undertake forty short courses in the Navigation School. New courses for the 1989/90 Session had included:

a BTEC National Certificate course in Motor Vehicle Engineering;
a BTEC First Diploma course in Motor Vehicle Engineering;
a BTEC Diploma course in Nautical Science;
a CGLI 383 course in Motor Vehicle Craft Studies;
and a CGLI course in Vehicle Bodywork.

In addition, recently introduced courses for the Institute of Automobile Assessors, the Marine Studies Foundation course and the McAlpine Offshore Pipelayers' Safety and Seamanship course had all progressed satisfactorily. The College had also been approached for a BTEC (Schools Link) Foundation course in Motor Vehicle Engineering Electronics. All course literature had been up-dated and distributed to industry, schools and the careers service and follow-up visits by staff to careers conventions and industrial contacts had been carried out. However, whilst the potential recruitment to Motor Vehicle courses was promising for 1990/91 the enquiries for Marine courses was fewer than in the past.

Senior executives from Honda (UK) Limited had visited the College following exploratory visits to the Chiswick Headquarters by the Principal. On the 15th March 1990 the College received confirmation that the Honda organization wished to establish a sponsored training facility at the College (this was officially opened on 7th November 1990). Coupled with the establishment and subsequent success of the Olivetti Centre, this could only heighten credibility with industrial and commercial organizations and would, hopefully, be another step in a series of similar ventures.

The installation of additional equipment to satisfy the Offshore Industry Training Board (OPITB), for the proposed re-establishment of the Offshore Survival course, had been completed. However, an inspection of the facilities arranged for 21 March 1990 had been postponed, for the Merseyside Fire Authority, the West Lancashire Authority and the Cheshire Authority were unable to conduct the fire-fighting training element of the course. Senior management was making exhaustive efforts to solve this crucial issue (and by the Autumn term of the 1990/91 Session negotiations were in hand with Liverpool Airport for the installation there of a suitable facility to be financed by a large loan from a shipping company).

Because of the need to deploy resources to areas of greatest need, after discussion with industrial contacts and HMI and considering the continuing decline of numbers for Maritime Studies courses, it became regrettably necessary that this department should close as soon as was practicable, with the exception of Offshore Survival courses, Yachtmaster courses and courses in Plant Maintenance. As a consequence of this policy, the only Marine Engineering courses operating in the 1990/91 Session would be the BTEC National Diploma (Year 2) and the BTEC Higher National Diploma/ Certificate. These would then be phased out in the following year.

Similarly, financial pressures made it inevitable that the Oldham Street Annexe in the City centre be closed at the end of the 1989/90 Session. It was hoped that the provision located there would not subsequently be lost, and arrangements were made to transfer the equipment and related materials to Workshop E110 at the Riversdale campus during the Summer recess (Workshop E110 had hitherto been used for Marine Engineering courses).

Though both of these decisions were taken with regret, particularly bearing in mind the history and reputation of Maritime Studies provision at Riversdale, they undoubtedly relieved the College of some financial burdens and enabled resources to be deployed to areas of actual and potential growth. Without these decisions, continued diversification and development in phase with market opportunities could only have been constrained.

The full-time Motor Vehicle Engineering courses had been redesigned to meet new industrial training requirements and, as has been noted earlier, new full-time BTEC Motor Vehicle courses had commenced in September. There was no doubt that these modular programmes would enhance the employment and career prospects of students. Recruitment into the first year of the Diploma and Certificate courses had increased by 40 per cent, and it was significant that an increasing number of young women (14 per cent) had enrolled. Recruitment from the Automobile Industry and the Training Agency to block-release and part-time day/evening courses, for BTEC National and Higher National Certificate courses and CGLI Certificate courses had also shown an increase on the previous year's enrolments. The new CGLI 383 Repair and Servicing of Road Vehicles course had been introduced as a pilot scheme this Session in preparation for full implementation from September 1990. Yet again, Royal Yachting Association (RYA) courses were very popular, and for the first time a third Yachtmaster class had been established. Plant Engineering and training courses for HM Customs and Excise were progressing in line with the planned forecast.

It was clear that in September 1990 there would be a significant increase in the number of students enrolling for motor cycle engineering provision. Following a limited amount of advertising, by 11 July 1990 the School had received thirty-seven applications to enrol on the new full-time course. The School of Automobile Engineering had completed, in the Summer term, a submission for funding in order to establish a Transport Management Centre. Bids had been forwarded to the Urban Programme Fund and to the Director of Education's Information Technology Budget for Colleges. If these were successful, the Faculty would gain a high-technology, computer-aided management centre. This would contain the type of equipment now coming into use within the 'lead bodies' of the motor vehicle industry.

By early Summer it was clear that the enrolment position for the 1990/ 91 Session would be more than satisfactory. Applications to enrol on first- year full-time motor vehicle courses already totalled fifty-two and were rising significantly. Interestingly, this figure included applications from Hong Kong, Trinidad, Bangladesh and the Maldives.

The 1989/90 Session was one in which the College's significant progress in diversification, development and a changed culture continued. A number of the Session's notable features are as follows:

- As a result of the LEA's federal FE system, the Education Reform Act, 1988, the Joint Efficiency Study, 1987, and the establishment of the Na- tional Council for Vocational Qualifications, the College's environment became more complex and turbulent, requiring a great deal of organiza- tional time and effort to adjust to it;

- The College welcomed the provisions of the Education Reform Act, par- ticularly the delegation of financial powers and the ability to retain the income earned through full-cost courses;

- The College had great hopes that its new Governing Body, through its collective qualifications, experience, capacities and commitment, would act as a powerful factor in its further growth and development (and it was not to be disappointed);

- Although work remained to be done on the establishment of performance indicators, the College made significant headway in meeting the require- ments of the Joint Efficiency Study (for example, a Student: Staff ratio of 11.0: for 1989/90 against the Study's target ratio of 11.4:1 by 1991/92);

- The requirements of the National Council for Vocational Qualifications (NCVQ) had been clarified for staff though there was urgent need to progress on a number of aspects. Work placements, guidance and coun- selling, new forms of flexible learning and of record keeping were among these;

- The benefits due to the changing culture of the College were becoming increasingly apparent. Much of the credit for this was due to the flexibility and energy of the staff and its capacity to innovate;

- In the Session, the value of certain conceptual and theoretical constructs in changing the culture again became apparent. Among these were open system theory, the marketing concept, job enrichment through job chal- lenge and increased delegation of authority, the 'mixed-scanning' model of decision-making and a number of influences on productivity, including organizational congruence, goal setting, group size and external commun- ication. Management played a distinctive part in this last aspect, but had great concern that it had not communicated internally to the extent that it should have;

- All Faculties made distinctive progress in the Session and despite the City Council's reduction of the College's budget by £600,000 (due to its own grave financial position), there were notable increases in student numbers which more than offset the slight reduction in some areas of work due to the Childwall closure. The College's progress in the field of Education for Special Needs resulted in its being selected for a three-year Pilot Project — Opportunities in Further Education for Adults with Learning Difficulties. Funding of £400,000 would be made available over the period of the project. Another development with significance for cultural change was the successful bid for an Urban Aid grant of £60,000 for the acquisition of Media Studies equipment. There were also two important contracts in the management studies field.

Sadly, there was a negative aspect to the changing culture; the continuing decline of student numbers for Maritime Studies courses had necessitated the termination of this provision. This development and the closure of the Oldham Street Annexe in the City Centre, while taken with regret, undoubtedly relieved the College of some financial burdens and enabled resources to be deployed to areas of actual and potential growth.

Notes

1 STONER, J.A.F. and FREEMAN, R.E. (1989) *Management*, 4th Edition, Englewood Cliffs, New Jersey: Prentice-Hall International, Inc., p. 72.
2 ANSOFF, I. (1981) *Strategic Management*, New York, New York: Halsted Press.
3 KOGAN, M., JOHNSON, D., PACKWOOD, T. and WHITAKER, T. (1985) 'School governing bodies and the political-administrative system' in McNAY, I. and OZGA, J. (Eds) *Policy-making in Education: The Breakdown of Consensus*, Oxford: Pergamon Press Ltd., p. 195.
4 KOGAN, M., *et al.* Ibid., p. 197.
5 WALKER, T.S. (1990) 'Meeting the objectives of "Managing colleges efficiently" ', an internal memorandum, South Mersey College, Liverpool, 21 February.
6 HOLLIDAY, P.M. (1989) 'The implications of NCVQ for staff in further education', an internal memorandum, South Mersey College, Liverpool, 21 June.
7 CANTOR, L.M. and ROBERTS, I.F. (1986) *Further Education Today A Critical Review*, 3rd Edition, London: Routledge & Kegan Paul, p. 256.
8 CANTOR, L.M. and ROBERTS, L.F. (1986) Ibid., p. 191.
9 ADVISORY COMMITTEE ON THE SUPPLY AND TRAINING OF TEACHERS (ACSTT), Further Education Sub-Committee, *The Training of Teachers for Further Education*, First Haycocks Report, 1975.
10 RANSON, S. (1985) 'Changing relations between centre and locality in education', in McNAY, I. and OZGA, J. (Eds) *Policy-making in Education: The Breakdown of Consensus*, Oxford: Pergamon Press Ltd., p. 111.
11 KROEBER, A. and KLUCKHOHN, C. (1952) *Culture: A Critical Review of Concepts and Definitions*, Papers of the Peabody Museums of American Archaeology and Ethnology, **47**, Cambridge, Mass.: Harvard University Press.

12 Francis, D. (1987) *Unblocking Organizational Communication*, Aldershot: Gower Publishing Company Ltd., p. 23 ff.
13 Harvey-Jones, J. (1989) *Making It Happen: Reflections on Leadership*, London: Fontana/Collins, p. 28.
14 Boisot, M. (1987) *Information and Organization: The Manager As Anthropologist*, London: Fontana/Collins, p. 49.
15 Boisot, M. (1987) Ibid., p. 99.
16 McGrew, A.G. and Wilson, M.J. (Eds) (1982) *Decision-making Approaches and Analysis*, Manchester: Manchester University Press in association with The Open University, p. 1.
17 Hall, P. (1980) —. *Great Planning Disasters*, Weidenfeld, —. and Nicholson.
18 Hall, P. (1980) Ibid., p. 42.
19 Dahl, R.A. and Lindblom, C.E. (1982) reported in McGrew, A.G. and Wilson, M.J. *Decision Making*, (reference 16) p. 4.
20 Hall, P. (1980) Op. cit., p. 42.
21 Ranson, S. (1985) Ref. 10, p. 103.
22 Meighan, R. (1986) *A Sociology of Educating*, 2nd Edition, London: Cassell Educational Ltd., p. 66.
23 Dennison, W.F. 'Education and the economy: Changing circumstances', in McNay, I. and Ozga, J. (Eds) *Policy making in Education: The Breakdown of Consensus*, Oxford: Pergamon Press Ltd., p. 30.
24 Etzioni, A. (1967 'Mixed scanning: A 'third' approach to decision-making, in *Public Administration Review*, **27**, p. 390, and reported in McGrew, A.G. and Wilson, M.J.) (reference 16) p. 120.
25 Nader, D.A. and Tushman, M.L. (1980) 'A model for diagnosing organisational behaviour: Applying a congruence perspective', *Organisational Dynamics*, pp. 35–51, and reported in Mitchell, T.R. and Larson, J.R., Jr. (1987) *People in Organizations*, New York: McGraw-Hill Book Company, pp. 65 ff.
26 Mitchell, T.R. and Larson, J.R., Jr. (1977) See reference 25, p. 140.
27 Locke, E.A. (1978) 'The ubiquity of the technique of goal setting in theories and approaches to employee motivation', *Academy of Management Review*, **3**, pp. 594–601. and reported in Mitchell, T.R. and Larson, J.R., Jr. (1987) See reference 25, p. 165.
28 Erez, M. and Ziden, I. (1984) 'Effect of goal acceptance on the relationship of goal difficulty to performance', *Journal of Applied Psychology*, **69**, pp. 69–78 and reported in Mitchell, T.R. and Larson, J.R., Jr. (1987) See reference 25, p. 165.
29 Mitchell, T.R. and Larson, J.R., Jr. (1987) See reference 25, pp. 165–6.
30 Ringmann study: summarized in Moede, W. (1927) 'Die Richtlinien der Leistungs-Psychologie', *Industrial Psycho-technick*, **4**, pp. 193–207. and reported in Mitchell, T.R. and Larson, J.R., Jr. (1987) See reference 25, p. 227.
31 Mitchell, T.R. and Larson, J.R., Jr. (1987) See reference 25, p. 299.

Chapter 9

1986/90: Review and Comment

Introduction

This book has described an action research project, the concept of action research challenging the view that analysis and practice (i.e. researching and educating) are distinct, separate activities requiring different skills and techniques and involving different perceptions of the establishments in which they take place. The research methodology was grounded in the non-reactive research approach of participation observation, supplemented by unobtrusive measures, such as documented statistical and financial data, used to provide a framework for the survey and to substantiate the findings yielded by participant observation. Because the confidentiality of the research was preserved throughout, a large number of formal and informal meetings became, in effect, proxy discussion groups in which hypotheses for testing by subsequent observation were formulated. The objectivity of the research was thus safeguarded by a triangulation of research methods — documentation, observation, discussion.

The population of a further education college is at least as pluralistic as that of any large human group, and while the objective of the research was to study the actions of management in changing the culture, this book offers glimpses of the powerful influences of the students and staff in bringing about the alignment of the college with its changing boundary conditions. With respect to the students, it can also be seen that the least advantaged of these, the special educational needs students, acted as powerful agents of change.

What this, and the contribution of the staff, demonstrates is that management does not change the culture, so much as liberates the new culture which is already within the organization struggling towards the light. This is a clear demonstration that, during the period of the research, the College adapted to a changed environment enabling it to develop and diversify. This was accompanied by improved use of resources (staffing, equipment and accommodation) and improved quality and relevance of the curriculum. The primary purpose of this study has been to examine the role of management in this process, testing its actions against the interpretive theories of that field of study commonly labelled 'management'.

In the words of a spokesman for the management team, 'we did not set ourselves up as conjurer men, but we did try to act in a bold, self-confident way and in changing the culture to one that was user-driven, we made use of some theoretical principles which seemed to us to be expedient.' A summary of these guiding principles is set out below.

- The value of open-system theory and the importance of sensitivity to changes in the environment;
- The value of the marketing approach emphasizing as it does the salience of the customer and the significance of productive use of scarce resources;
- The influence of expectancy theory on motivation and work behaviour and the influence of job enrichment and the notion of 'shared futures';
- The need to constantly reappraise organization structures to liberate creative energy and to align the structures with market opportunity;
- The importance of resisting the temptation to over-organize — seeing senior management's role as one of contextual decision-making only;
- The recognition that management's best contribution to changing the culture and overcoming resistance to change was to 'make things happen';
- The importance of the hidden curriculum for the educational experience of the student and of 'symbolic management' for heightening the visibility of the College and developing its institutional image.

The Contribution of Management

Testing the contribution of management against some of the concepts elaborated in the literature of management studies was a primary objective of the study. It can be seen that management intervened strategically in the social processes of the College organization. The generic term for this, embracing a wide range of intervention strategies, is 'organization development', defined in Mullins[1] as:

> ...a top-management-supported, long-range effort to improve an organization's problem-solving and renewal processes, particularly through a more effective and collaborative diagnosis and management of organization culture — with special emphasis on formal work team, temporary team and intergroup culture — with the assistance of a consultant-facilitator and the use of the theory and technology of applied behavioural science, including action research.

Whilst the processes in evidence in the College were neither planned nor formal, they did exhibit some of the features of organizational development (OD) outlined above. What was lacking was a formal work team as the key unit for development, although in the College Management Team itself, continuing emphasis was given to team development and the dynamics of small work group situations, if only through learning by doing. There was no consultant-facilitator (or change-agent or catalyst) in the strict sense of a third party internal or external consultant, though the Principal, with qualifications in applied psychology, observed and prompted in an informal sense, making suggestions for action which, though invariably *ad hoc*, derived from his formal training in this regard. Crucially, however, there was no process which involved the gathering of data from the client group, feedback and analysis of this data, and action by members of the client group to resolve problems.

What could fairly be said of management's role was that management was always trying, by example as well as precept, to get the College's culture consistent with its strategy and, as Stoner and Freeman[2] have pointed out, drawing on industrial and commercial examples, when culture is consistent with strategy, the implementation of strategy is eased considerably. Peters and Waterman[3] provide similar examples of organizational excellence through 'obsession with service', such as service to the customer. It is easy to discern the quality, reliability and loyalty in client relationships they speak of, replicated in the attitudes of staff to so many of the College's students and client organizations. Management had felt that one of its primary tasks was to further foster the client-led attitude already internalized by many staff.

Toffler,[4] whose writings have generated much interest and support, considers that organizations of the future will require people who can learn very fast — to be able to understand novel situations and problems — to have imagination, and to be able to invent new solutions. Additionally, the members of the Bullock Committee[5] in the conclusion of their report make the point that:

> ... the problem of Britain ... is not a lack of native capacity in its working population so much as a failure to draw out their energies and skill to anything like their full potential. It is our belief that the way to realize those energies, to provide greater satisfaction in the workplace and to assist in raising the level of productivity and efficiency ... is not by recrimination and exhortation but by putting the relationship between capital and labour on to a new basis which will involve not just management but the whole workforce in sharing responsibility for the success and profitability of the enterprise.

If the College management were to claim anything for its stewardship it would be a contribution along the lines advocated by Toffler and the Bullock Committee.

O'Shaughnessy[6] suggests there are three broad approaches to the implementation of strategy:

1 a central planning or bureaucratic approach;
2 a participative approach;
3 a combination of central planning and participation.

In describing the combination approach, he writes:

> The third approach combines elements of the other two approaches. Experts are used in studying the situation and drawing up a recommended strategy but, to make use of many others with ideas and perhaps further their interest and commitment, there is discussion on proposals at every level affected. Under the combination approach, plans often move up and down the various levels with committees and liaison managers acting as coordinators. All those affected by the strategy have an opportunity to participate, so the final version for implementation will emerge much more as a joint effort. This is becoming a favoured approach.

Although management would eschew the word 'expert', it is reasonable to suggest that its own approach was not a great deal different from O'Shaughnessy's combination approach. The proposition is in line with what may usefully be called its mixed-scanning approach to decision-making, outlined in Chapter 8. As has been said previously, management would also resist overclaiming for its planning activities, pointing out that the processes of objective setting (for the whole College) of strategy formulation and of organizational learning had not been established in the period 1986–90 to the extent that the management purist would seek. On the other hand, planning in conjunction with the Authority, rooted initially in the Work-related NAFE planning required by the Training Agency and developed for the LEA's delegated budgeting in relation to the Education Reform Act, did provide a useful planning framework for much of the College's operations. Figure 9.1, prepared by the College's Co-ordinator of Planning Services substantiates this point. Planning may not have been completely comprehensive, but much of the College's activities took place against the background of a formal mechanism, as indicated in Figure 9.1, together with less formal mechanisms at the levels of the College Academic Board and the Faculty Boards.

A related aspect where management perceived its own performance as incomplete is with regard to management information systems. Members of the management team would support, for instance, the view of Stoner and Freeman[7] that a computer-based information system has now become 'indispensable for planning, decision-making and control'. As has been pointed out, however, a management information system was established and was providing valuable data for financial control purposes and for the deployment of staffing (through the student:staff ratio). Management would echo the view that the student:staff ratio, being the only widely developed efficiency indicator in non-advanced further education was important and might

Figure 9.1:   Factors and processes in budgetary allocation

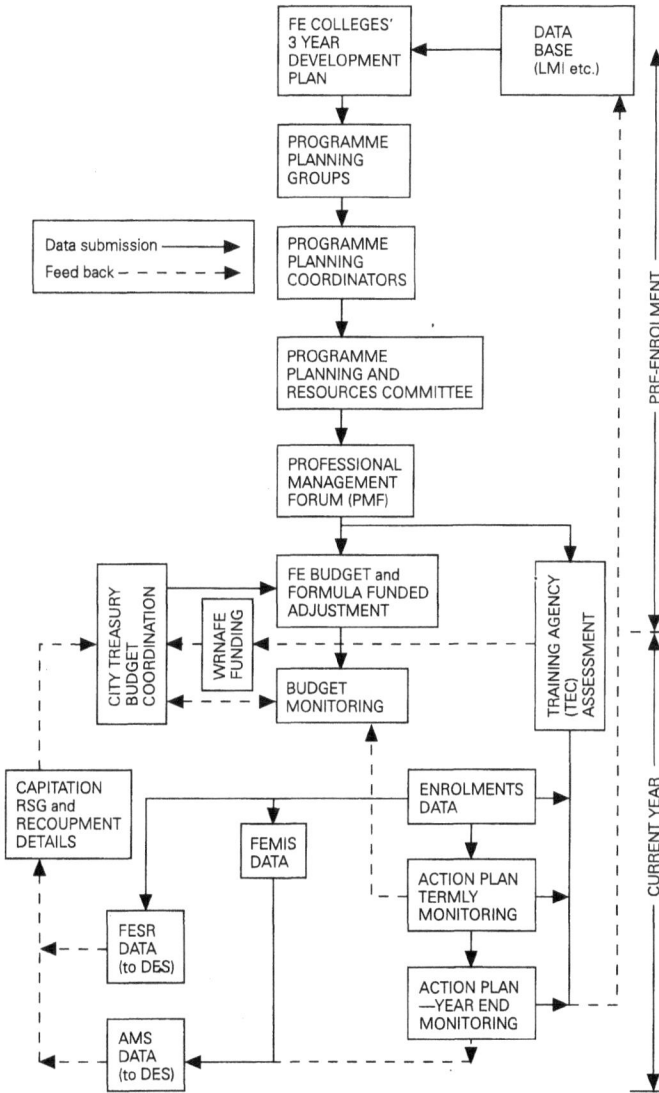

Legend

LMI — Labour Market Information
FE — Further Education
RSG — Rate Support Grant
AMS — Annual Monitoring Survey
FESR — Further Education Statistical Record
FEMIS — Further Education Management Information System
WRNAFE — Work Related Non Advanced Further Education

(*Source:* T. Walker, Planning Services Coordinator)

continue to be important. However, it took no account of non-teaching costs nor of the ultimate educational outputs of the College. Unit costs would provide better information on the resources utilized and when linked with sound indicators of output, they would provide better indicators of efficiency. Here, management supported the early introduction of the uniform costing system described in the Joint Efficiency Study[8] and looked forward to the early development of a decision-support system in which managers were linked via a real-time network to a data base of solid information for planning purposes. Even so, progress made in the control of resources during the period 1986–90 is worth highlighting. Upon the formation of the College, management found itself with three main sites (at Riversdale, Childwall and Oldham Street, in the City Centre) and with two residential hostels at Riversdale — Kinsman House and River House. It was immediately apparent to management that the type and level of work into which the College would hopefully diversify would provide no viable use for Kinsman House and that continued provision at Childwall and Oldham Street could scarcely be justified. All three facilities were accordingly closed, providing benefits to the City Council from the sale of the properties and significant reductions in the operating costs of the College.

In more than one sense, it would be fair to say that stewardship of the College had been conducted in accord with the Harvey-Jones dictum[9] that 'the prime management problem is "making it happen"'.

Considerations for the Future

Frequently, reports of research into organizational issues conclude with the observation that, if anything, this or that particular piece of research points up the need for further research. This writer had pledged to himself that he would avoid doing so, for apart from anything else, managers of Colleges in the FE service receive a constant flow of reports on some aspect of the operations and management of institutions. A random survey of recent publications reveals the following titles:

> *Opportunity 1992; Education and the Older Unemployed; Responding to the Demographic Challenge; Managing Quality Improvement; The Adequacy of Further Education Provision for the Community; The Assessment of Prior Learning and Achievement; Developing a Marketing Strategy for Adult and Continuing Education; Moral Competence; Towards an Education Audit; The Strategic Planning of Further Education; The Outreach College; Employment Training; The Implications of National Vocational Qualifications for Further Education; Coping with Crisis; Guidance and Course Provision for Unemployed Adults; Training and Enterprise: Priorities for Action 1990/91; Developing Access Routes for Unwaged Women; College Structures; Implementing Open Learning; Training and Development: An*

Evaluation of SKILLNET Quick Start Initiatives; *Promoting Further Education Enterprise*; *Planning a Curricular Response*; *Industry Needs You* (a guidance on meeting the changing needs of employers).

This list is by no means comprehensive and covers a limited period only (1989–90 in the main). The publications emanate from the Department of Education and Science, the Department of Employment and the Training Agency, the Further Education Unit (FEU), the National Institute for Adult and Continuing Education (NIACE), the National Council for Vocational Qualifications (NCVQ) and a number of other organizations, including individual Authorities and Colleges (where the reports in question are usually the outcome of funded research). So it is difficult to imagine any facet of the management of FE on which the findings of recent research are not available to a management in need of guidance. And, in the opinion of many, despite the criticisms levelled at it from time to time, the FE service has been quite flexible in meeting the challenge of the many environmental changes of the post-1945 period. One possible avenue for further research which does commend itself to this writer could be based on an organization development exercise, a long-range effort utilizing action research and the assistance of a consultant-facilitator (as described on p. 182). Set in the context of a single institution, such an exercise might generate data of much richness and variety to guide the processes of organizational renewal and problem-solving. At best, the research could be as useful as were the Glacier Project Papers[10] which recorded the outcome of such intervention strategies in an industrial setting.

Beyond this, however, there are two further reasons why this writer would not be intellectually comfortable in avoiding the statement that further research was necessary. They are, moreover, very powerful reasons. Firstly, as a result of its further review of the FE service the Liverpool City Council decided that the four Colleges established on 1st September 1986 would be reorganized into a single College. In the event, this new single institution, the City of Liverpool Community College, opened on 1st April 1991. One of the objectives of this present research project was to provide, for archival purposes, a narrative history of South Mersey College. It is an objective made poignant by the fact that despite its clear success as an institution, a success achieved moreover with even more momentum in the 1990/91 Session, the College was closed, along with its sister Colleges, on 31st March 1991. The resulting culture shock had to be absorbed not only by students and staff but by the new Governing Bodies, formed after the Education Reform Act of 1988, and now having to be disbanded (as briefly mentioned in Chapter 8). It is clear that as one of the largest colleges in the country, with 30,000 students enrolled, over 1500 staff and an annual revenue budget in excess of £30 million, the City of Liverpool Community College would provide a framework for a research project into culture, or a host of other aspects of organizational change, on a grand scale.

The other reason why further research may be desirable, or indeed necessary, is due to the intervention of HM Government which, in its Bill entitled Education and Training for the 21st Century (1991), announced its intention to change the composition of Governing bodies to remove the influence of Local Education Authorities and grant FE colleges corporate status, accompanied by their removal from local authority control. Funding will reach colleges via a Further Education Funding Council and will be directly related to student numbers. As corporate institutions, the colleges will require the application of management techniques at least as sophisticated as any other organization run for profit—a development rich in research possibilities.

Further Observations

Tracing the history of the South Mersey College through the four-year period has also enabled the writer to form some additional ideas about the future management of FE colleges and the FE service. He finds these views echoed in the current general literature on the management process. Boulden[11] for example, points out that while British industry and commerce have actually invested considerable amounts of time and money in management development over the years, reports (by Dr. John Constable and Professors Handy and Mumford) show very clearly that Britain lags far behind its main competitors. He adds:

> Training managers to manage and sending them back into traditional climates is a contradictory process, and conflict, frustration and abdication are inevitable consequences. They need to return to a climate which supports their new managerial behaviour.

This is good advice for College governors and for those with influential roles in the new funding councils.

Barham and Rassam[12] make the point that a simplistic approach to planning — detailed corporate strategy and long-term planning stretching far into the future — worked in a world which was relatively stable and predictable. The approach no longer fits the present rapidly changing environment. Interestingly they quote the view of Sir John Egan, former chief executive of Jaguar Limited, who believes that we have not coped very well with the present let alone the future. His philosophy is to do the things that are already being done 'better and better in order to become superlative, rather than getting hung up on issues that are more problematical'. Again, these words seem pertinent in an educational context. On its own admission, the management of South Mersey College paid no heed to demographic trends, trends which were even more marked in the City of Liverpool. They reasoned that participation rates were more important than demographic trends and succeeded in increasing student enrolments from 5000 to 12,500 in the period reviewed. It may be because of preoccupation with, at best, tenuous long-term trends that so many acts of planning in the FE service (including college closures) seem to have an infinite regress of consequences.

In discussing the strategic planning process, Boyle[13] states his belief that successful development depends on 'the creation of high leverage action plans'. Based upon the strategic review diagnosis top management should focus on those actions critical to their winning strategy. This restates Boulden's opinion on allowing managers to manage. It is the conviction of John Woolhouse[14] that the chief executive and those of his colleagues who share his responsibility for the direction of an enterprise perform four basic functions. They must:

1 Define strategy;
2 Specify the methods, technology and resources by which that strategy is to be achieved;
3 Prepare plans and programmes;
4 Create and manage an organization through which those plans and programmes will be implemented.

The reality in the FE service of the past is that senior managers had to devote a significant amount of their time to minor bureaucratic details. They had to attend many meetings on subjects of only peripheral impact on their organizations. It follows then that funding councils and governing bodies can influence the responsiveness of colleges by allowing managers to manage. The best talent will surely be attracted to those senior management roles which provide scope for strategic energies and skills.

Given that the environment in which further education operates will continue to be turbulent, adaptiveness to change will remain an important criterion for success (though it has to be said that the recent experience of FE practitioners in this regard should stand them in good stead). The management literature on the change process is extensive, so practitioners in need of guidance will not find it hard to come by. The 7-S McKinsey framework (reported by O'Shaughnessy)[15] provides a neat summary in this regard. Drawing on their work with McKinsey and Company, the international consultancy organization, Waterman, Peters and Phillips (1981) argue that effective organizational change depends 'on the effective alignment of seven variables', which comprise the 7-S McKinsey framework, namely:

- structure
- strategy
- systems (and procedures)
- style (i.e. management style)
- staff (i.e. people)

- skills (corporate strengths/skills)
- shared value (superordinate goals)

A brief word on each of these, in turn.

- *Structure*. Whilst preserving the shape of the underlying organization structure, successful large firms commonly use temporary structural forms, such as task forces, to accomplish specific strategic missions;

- *Strategy*. Inability to execute a strategy frequently arises from faults in the other dimensions of the 7-S framework than in the organization structure;

- *Systems* (e.g. capital budgeting, training, cost accounting, etc.) is the one variable in the framework that threatens to dominate the others. The development of systems to support a change in strategy can be therefore a major and critical undertaking;

- *Style*. One element of style which is emphasized is how a manager chooses to spend his or her time (for example, to reinforce a message, to nudge thinking in a desired direction, etc.);

- *Staff*. Waterman, *et al.* emphasize the importance of management development and socialization. Employees constitute a pool of resources to be 'nurtured, developed, guarded and allocated';

- *Skills* are the organization's dominating attributes or capabilities. They make up what has been referred to as the organisation's thrust;

- *Superordinate goals/shared values* are the fundamental values, aspirations and ideas underlying the broad notion of future direction which senior management wish to infuse throughout the whole organization.

In this writer's opinion, the 7-S Framework is a useful tool to structure thinking about the management of change and its convenient shorthand approach may well appeal to busy managers of the corporate colleges.

Well before the Education Reform Act and the Bill of 1991 advertisements for Principals and other college managers stressed entrepreneurship as a sought-after quality. Bearing in mind the theory of entrepreneurship's psychological roots, put forward by McClelland, who found that 'need-achievement', a social motive to excel, tends to characterize successful entrepreneurs, this raises the question of how the selection process typically employed to fill educational management posts can be applied to discriminate between candidates on the entrepreneurial dimension. Perhaps even more intriguing, with respect to considerations for the future, is the fact that entrepreneurs are not the only agents of change. Invoking industrial/commercial practice, Stoner and Freeman draw attention to the role of the 'intrapreneur'. Corporate entrepreneurship, called 'intrapreneuring', is a process whereby an organization seeks to expand by exploring new opportunities, through new combinations of its existing resources. Since resources will presumably be no easier to come by than in the recent past, FE colleges might usefully apply this approach. The starting point is the question of what new opportunities may be derived from the existing resource base. Perhaps the systematic study of the issue might provide a gainful occupation for a member of staff with appropriate qualifications and experience. The value of the role could conceivably be increased through examination of resource utilization using the techniques of value analysis. Here the approach is to examine all aspects of resource conversion with two questions in mind:

1 How do we obtain improved performance for the same cost?
2 How do we maintain existing performance for a lower cost?

Since a college's unit costs will have a decisive influence on its competitiveness, the stewardship of resources is a factor whose significance for performance will, if anything, increase further. 'Intrapreneuring' and comparing costs with functions through the value-analysis approach may well have much to contribute.

In reviewing twentieth century education, Boyd and King[16] remark upon the new ideas about educational effectiveness encouraged by developments in media of mass communication (television, distance learning programmes, cassettes, etc.) and allude to how this gave rise to 'an attitude of partnership and interaction beyond anything so far found in formal education'. Doubtless these trends will gather greater momentum as more intensively local media networks develop, so that by the next century, the FE college as we now know it may alter radically in form and size. Such concepts as the accreditation of prior learning may broaden the markets significantly enough for the FE college in its traditional form to find the competition (including that from employers devising their own in-house training programmes) will intensify. This will mean that innovation will become an increasingly critical competitive tool.

The organizations that survive and prosper in the face of increasing pressure to innovate will possess nimble leadership and will establish an organization-wide creative and innovative culture. Again there are precedents to be examined for their value. The authors B. and R. Richardson,[17] in their work on strategic management, explain how IBM and other organizations have discovered that speedier new product development, appropriate attention to innovation, reduction of nervous interference from line managers and the development of a motivated, communicative and entrepreneurial environment can all be brought about by the creation of a separate innovative function. Colleges might consider the point when evaluating their present structures. At the least, the capacity to innovate should not be stifled because of a desire to protect sacred organizational cows.

In the matter of structures, the service might perhaps bear in mind the support of Harvey-Jones[18] for the concept of 'added-value' in an organizational sense. Every level in the organization should exist only if it has some unique role, responsibility or capability to add to that which people below it are capable of doing. Such circumspection may not only result in leaner organizations with an increased capacity to innovate, they may also, through the task-force or working group approach, enrich the jobs of staff at a time when opportunities for career progression will otherwise be reduced.

As Britain becomes more fully integrated with her European partners there may also be advantage in studying the wider structures within which the FE service operates. For example, D.L. Parkes[19] writes:

> The Germans have a front-loading system which creates co-ordination among the various competing and conflicting interests in the system. The English do not have such co-ordination. They have semi-autonomous institutions, with shallow freedoms over curricula, method and resources. They have many different local authorities warring with central government. They have a wide variety of examining and validating bodies established by central government but without legal authority. Germany is an example of a decentralised federal country creating an effective training programme which appears, at least at a distance, to be more successful than ours.

Perhaps the provisions of the new Bill, will move the British system towards that of Germany, a key European partner. Finally, the extent to which the FE service will succeed in its future mission will largely depend upon the people who staff it. As Harvey-Jones[20] has said, the one enduring feature of any enterprise is its people and the skills that they possess. Individuals have to be constantly stimulated if they are to continue to contribute. He adds that it is only recently, since the publication of such books as *In Search of Excellence*[21] that attention has really been focused on the values and spirit that can be built up in an organization. It is hoped that this short history of one college demonstrates the quality of response that was forthcoming when management shared its responsibility for changing the culture.

Notes

1 MULLINS, L.J. (1989) *Management and Organizational Behaviour*, 2nd Edition, London: Pitman Publishing, p. 485.
2 STONER, J.A.F. and FREEMAN, R.E. (1989) *Management*, 4th Edition, Englewood Cliffs, New Jersey: Prentice-Hall International, Inc., p. 247.
3 PETERS, T.J. and WATERMAN, R.H., JR. (1982) *In Search of Excellence*, London: Harper & Row, Publishers, p. 171.
4 TOFFLER, A. (1985) *The Adaptive Corporation*, London: Pan Books, p. 97.

5 THE BULLOCK COMMITTEE (1977) *Report of Committee of Inquiry on Industrial Democracy*, London: HMSO, conclusion para. 2.

6 O'SHAUGHNESSY, J. (1988) *Competitive Marketing A Strategic Approach*, 2nd Edition, London: Unwin Hyman Ltd., pp. 401–2.

7 STONER, J.A.F. and FREEMAN, R.E. (1989) Op. cit. (reference 2), p. 653.

8 DEPARTMENT OF EDUCATION AND SCIENCE (1987) *Managing Colleges Efficiently*, (EDUC/280/1987) *The Joint Efficiency Study*, London: DES/Local Authority Association Officers report, 1987.

9 HARVEY-JONES, J. (1989) *Making It Happen Reflections on Leadership*, London: Fontana Paperbacks, p. 28.

10 JAQUES, E. (1951) *The Changing Culture of a Factory*, London: Routledge & Kegan Paul. (One of a number of volumes which became known as The Glacier Project Series).

11 BOULDEN, G. (1988) 'How to develop managers', in HELLER, R. (Ed.) *The Complete Guide to Modern Management*, London: Harrap Ltd., pp. 267–8.

12 BARHAM, K. and RASSAM, C. (1989) *Shaping the Corporate Future*, London: Unwin Hyman Ltd., p. 3.

13 BOYLE, D. (1988) 'The strategic planning process', in LOCK, D. and FARROW, N. (Eds) *The Gower Handbook of Management*, 2nd Edition, Aldershot, Hants: Gower Publishing Company Limited, p. 34.

14 WOOLHOUSE, J. (1988) 'Organization development', in *The Gower Handbook of Management*. See reference 13, p. 43.

15 O'SHAUGHNESSY, J. (1988) Op. cit. See reference 6, pp. 405–6.

16 BOYD, W. and KING, E.J. (1975) *The History Of Western Education*, 11th Edition, London: A. and C. Black (Publishers) Ltd., p. 500.

17 RICHARDSON, B. and RICHARDSON, R. (1989) *Business Planning, An Approach To Strategic Management*, London: Pitman Publishing, pp. 206–7.

18 HARVEY-JONES, J. (1989) Op. cit. See reference 9, p. 235.

19 PARKES, D.L. (1985) 'Competition . . . and competence? Education, training and the roles of the DES and MSC' in MCNAY, I. and OZGA, J. (Eds) *Policy Making in Education*, Oxford: Pergamon Press Ltd., p. 170.

20 HARVEY-JONES, J. (1989) Op. cit. See reference 9, p. 314.

21 PETERS, T.J. and WATERMAN, R.H., JR. (1982) Op. cit. See reference 3.

Appendices

Appendix 1

Programme Working Party

Terms of Reference

1 To take responsibility for the final drafting of the LEA's non-advanced further education (NAFE) Development Plan and Programme for presentation to the Professional Management Forum;
2 To respond to comments on the NAFE Development Plan and Programme from interested groups in the City and other agencies including the MSC;
3 To consider and make recommendations to the Professional Management Forum on College course proposals within the NAFE Development Plan and Programme;
4 To ensure the review of existing courses on a regular basis and make recommendations to the Professional Management Forum as appropriate within the context of the NAFE Development Plan and Programme;
5 To recommend course provision where appropriate and in accordance with the NAFE Development Plan and Programme;
6 To consider and make recommendations to the Professional Management Forum on the need for rationalization or expansion of areas of work in the Colleges and to do so in the context of planning and programming;
7 To receive recommendations from the Marketing, Development and Resources Working Parties and act thereon as appropriate;
8 To supervise and coordinate any project work in its area of activity;
9 To establish such sub-committees and working parties as are appropriate to the effective and efficient discharge of its terms of reference.

Membership:

Presidents or Vice Presidents	4
Representatives of Academic Boards	4
Senior Assistant Director (Further and Higher Education)	1
Assistant Education Officer	1
Representatives of LCP	1
Representatives of the Careers Service	1
Representative of Local Education Authority Inspectorate (or Advisory Panel) + power to invite, for example, Manpower Services Commission	1

Chair:

Senior Assistant Director (Further and Higher Education)

Secretary:

Assistant Education Officer

Meetings:

Every 6 weeks

Appendix 2

Marketing Working Party

Terms of Reference

1 To take responsibility for publicity and marketing of the Development Plan and Programme on behalf of the Professional Management Forum;
2 To publicize and market NAFE provision within the City to interested groups and other agencies;
3 To consider and make recommendations to the Professional Management Forum on publicity and marketing matters;
4 To ensure the review of publicity and marketing activity on a regular basis and make recommendations to the Professional Management Forum as appropriate;
5 To consider and make recommendations to the Professional Management Forum on publicity and marketing matters as they affect NAFE provision;
6 To receive recommendations from the Programme, Development and Resources Working Parties and act thereon as appropriate;
7 To provide appropriate inputs to the NAFE Development Plan and Programme;
8 To supervise and coordinate any project work in its area of activity (e.g. PICKUP);
9 To establish such sub-committees and working parties as are appropriate to the effective and efficient discharge of its terms of reference.

Membership:

Ps or VPs	4
Rep. of Academic Boards	4
SAD(FHE)	1
AEO	1
Rep. of LCP	1
Careers	1
Adviser	1
+ power to invite, e.g. MSC	

Chair:

AEO

Secretary:

Adviser

Meetings:

Every 6 weeks

Appendix 3

Development Working Party

1 To take responsibility for initiating and supporting curriculum innovation and development within NAFE in the City as requested by the Professional Management Forum;
2 To take responsibility for staff development matters within NAFE in the City and to report thereon to the Professional Management Forum;
3 To consider and make recommendations to the Professional Management Forum on certification/validation matters;
4 To ensure the review of existing courses on a regular basis and make recommendations to the Professional Management Forum as appropriate within the context of the NAFE Development Plan and Programme;
5 To recommend and develop new course provision where appropriate and in accordance with agreed budget provisions;
6 To consider and make recommendations to the Professional Management Forum on matters within its area of activity;
7 To receive recommendations from the Programme, Marketing and Resources Working Parties and act thereon as appropriate;
8 To provide appropriate inputs to the NAFE Development Plan and Programme;
9 To supervise and coordinate any project work in its area of activity;
10 To establish such sub-committees and working parties as are appropriate to the effective and efficient discharge of its terms of reference.

Membership:

Ps or VPs	4
Rep. of Academic Boards	4
SAD(FHE)	1
AEO	1
Rep. of LCP	1
Careers	1
Adviser	1

+ power to invite, e.g. MSC

Chair:
  SAD(FHE)
Secretary:
  Adviser
Meetings:
  Every 6 weeks

Appendix 4

Resources Working Party

Terms of Reference

1 To take responsibility for matters relating to finance and administration, including appropriate information systems, for NAFE within the City;
2 To provide appropriate inputs to the NAFE Development Plan and Programme;
3 To consider and make recommendations to the Professional Management Forum on financial and administrative matters, including issues relating to resourcing;
4 To ensure the review of practices on a regular basis and make recommendations to the Professional Management Forum as appropriate;
5 To receive recommendations from the Programme, Marketing and Development Working Parties and act thereon as appropriate;
6 To supervise and coordinate any project work in its area of activity;
7 To establish such sub-committees and working parties as are appropriate to the effective and efficient discharge of its terms of reference.

Membership:

Ps or VPs	4
Rep. of Academic Boards	4
CAOs	4
SAD(FHE)	1
AEO	1
Chief Assistant (Admin.)	1
Principal Administrative Officer	1
Personnel Officer	1
plus power to invite	

Chair:
AEO
Secretary:
SAD(FHE)
Meetings:
Every 6 weeks

Appendix 5

Principal's Diary Dates

18.04.88	Consortia meeting
20.04.88	Equal Opportunities meeting
25.04.88	NATFHE Deputation meeting
27.04.88	Equal Opportunities meeting
28.04.88	Work Experience meeting
06.05.88	Meeting with MEB
09.05.88	Anti-Racist meeting
10.05.88	Meeting with Authority Officers
11.05.88	Professional Management Forum meeting
12.05.88	Meeting with MEB
17.05.88	Meeting with LEA
18.05.88	Meeting with Authority Officers
19.05.88	Meeting with LEA
23.05.88	Meeting with Authority Officers
24.05.88	Meeting with LEA
25.05.88	Meeting with Authority Officers
01.06.88	Meeting with LEA
02.06.88 (a.m.)	Meeting with HMI
02.06.88 (p.m.)	Meeting with LEA
03.06.88	Meeting with City Estates Surveyors
08.06.88	Meeting with Authority Officers
14.06.88	Meeting with LEA
15.06.88	Meeting at Canning Place
17.06.88	Meeting with Authority Officers
22.06.88	NATFHE Liaison meeting
27.06.88	Consortium Co-ordinating meeting
28.06.88	Visit to University of Liverpool
01.07.88	Meeting with LEA
17.07.88	Visit to MSC
20.07.88	Visit to Radio Merseyside
21.07.88	Meeting with Authority Officers
26.07.88	Meeting with Authority Officers
05.09.88	NATFHE meeting
09.09.88	Meeting with LEA
13.09.88	Meeting with Authority Officers
14.09.88	Visit to LADSIRLAC
15.09.88	Meeting with Authority Officers
19.09.88	Meeting with Authority Officers
26.09.88	Visit to MSC
27.09.88 (a.m.)	NATFHE meeting

27.09.88 (p.m.)	Meeting with Authority Officers
04.10.88	NATFHE meeting
06.10.88	Meeting with Authority Officers
10.10.88	Meeting with Authority Officers
14.10.88	Access Review meeting
18.10.88	Consortium Co-ordinating meeting
19.10.88	Meeting at Hardman Street
17.10.88	Visit to London
20.10.88	Visit to London

Appendix 6

FEDERAL STAFF TRAINING PROGRAMME
at
South Mersey College
Aulis House

1992 and FE -- Getting it Right

29th March 1990
1.30 - 4.30

WORKSHOP

Brian Bonney - Cambridgeshire L.E.A.
'The Single European Market - Opportunities and Implications For the Further
Education Sector'

Followed by Workshops

Plenary Session and Questions

If you wish to attend this Workshop, please give your name to your College Contact:

SOUTH MERSEY COLLEGE - Madelene Gunny
CITY COLLEGE - Steve Cophall
SANDOWN COLLEGE - Rosanna McKeane
MILLBROOK COLLEGE - Neil Hannah

As soon as possible, closing date: Tuesday 20th March 1990.

Appendix 7

South Mersey College
Faculty of Automobile and General Engineering
Proposed Structure for September 1986

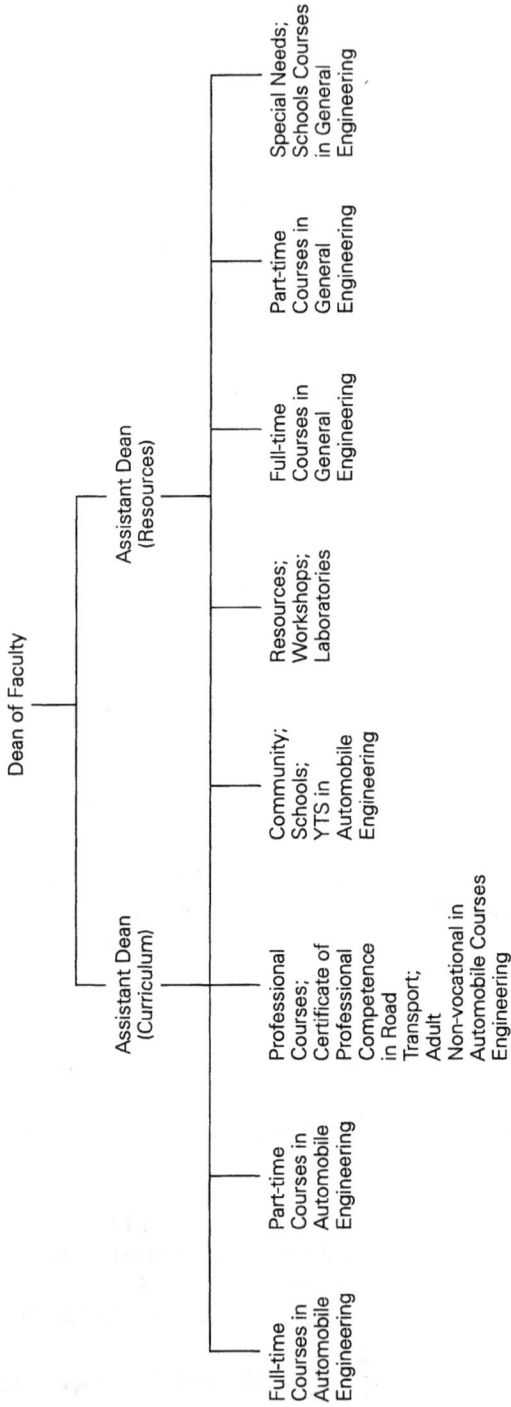

Dean of Faculty

Assistant Dean (Curriculum)

Assistant Dean (Resources)

Full-time Courses in Automobile Engineering

Part-time Courses in Automobile Engineering

Professional Courses; Certificate of Professional Competence in Road Transport; Adult Non-vocational in Automobile Courses Engineering

Community; Schools; YTS in Automobile Engineering

Resources; Workshops; Laboratories

Full-time Courses in General Engineering

Part-time Courses in General Engineering

Special Needs; Schools Courses in General Engineering

Appendix 8

South Mersey College
Faculty of Construction
Proposed Structure for September 1986

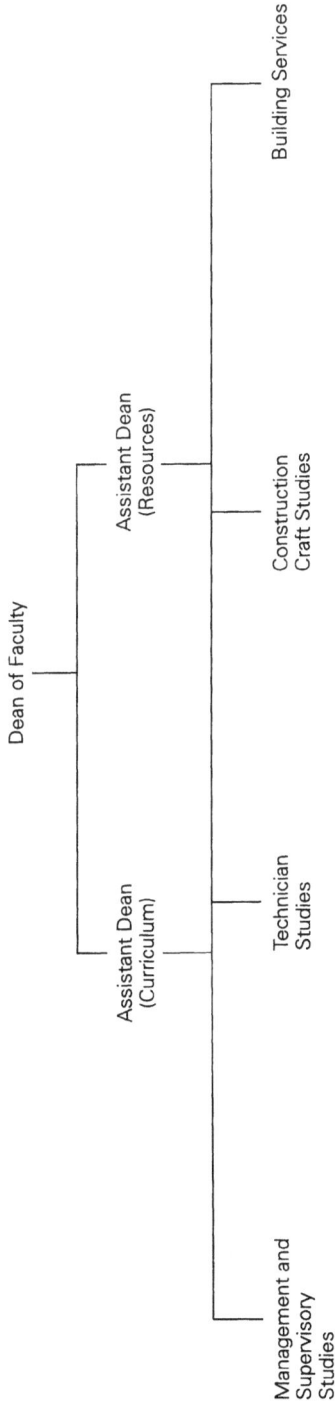

Dean of Faculty

Assistant Dean (Curriculum)

Assistant Dean (Resources)

Management and Supervisory Studies

Technician Studies

Construction Craft Studies

Building Services

Appendix 9

South Mersey College
Faculty of General Studies
Proposed Structure for September 1986

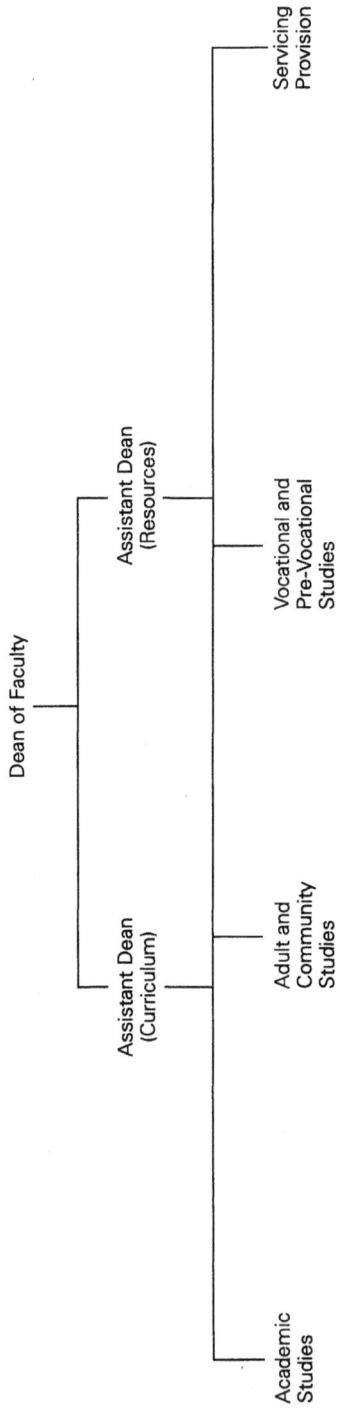

Dean of Faculty

Assistant Dean (Curriculum)

Assistant Dean (Resources)

Academic Studies

Adult and Community Studies

Vocational and Pre-Vocational Studies

Servicing Provision

Appendix 10

South Mersey College
Faculty of Maritime Studies
Proposed Structure for September 1986

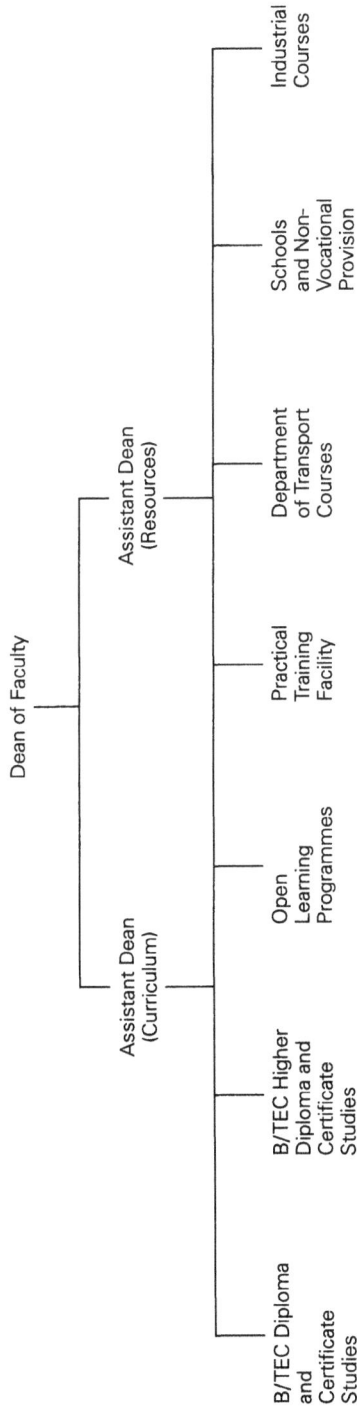

Dean of Faculty

Assistant Dean (Curriculum)

Assistant Dean (Resources)

B/TEC Diploma and Certificate Studies

B/TEC Higher Diploma and Certificate Studies

Open Learning Programmes

Practical Training Facility

Department of Transport Courses

Schools and Non-Vocational Provision

Industrial Courses

Appendix 11

South Mersey College
Faculty of General Studies (June 1988)
Revised Organization Structure

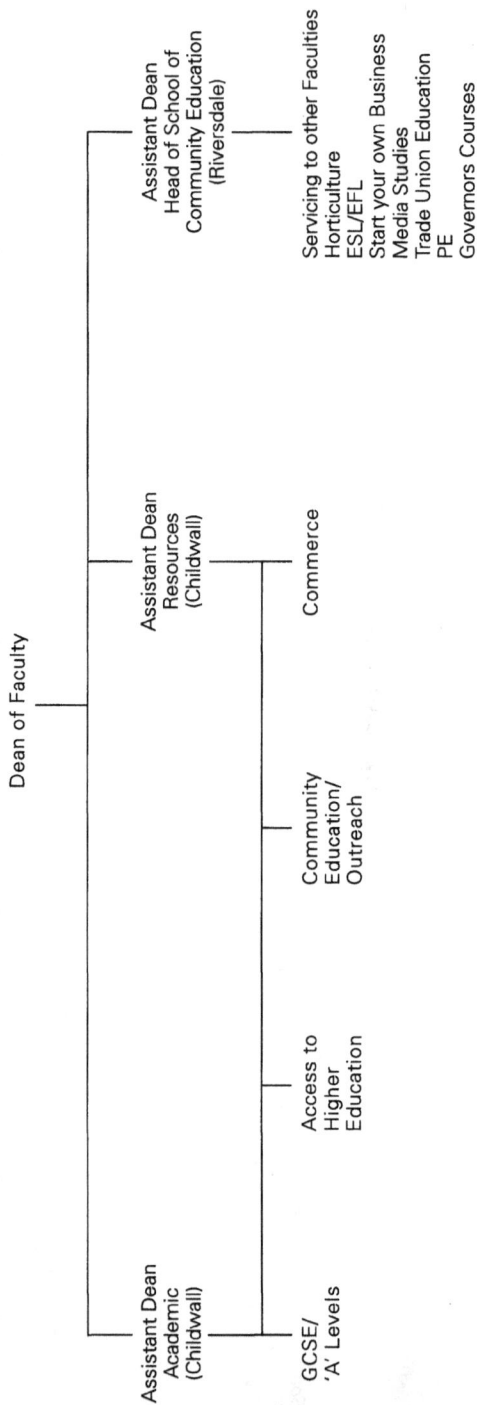

Dean of Faculty

Assistant Dean Academic (Childwall)

Assistant Dean Resources (Childwall)

Assistant Dean Head of School of Community Education (Riversdale)

GCSE/ 'A' Levels

Access to Higher Education

Community Education/ Outreach

Commerce

Servicing to other Faculties
Horticulture
ESL/EFL
Start your own Business
Media Studies
Trade Union Education
PE
Governors Courses

Appendix 12

SOUTH MERSEY COLLEGE

Principal
Dr. John P. A. Frain M.A., M.Tech., Ph.D., Dip.M., FIE.x.

We are pleased to welcome you to the inauguration of our American Studies Resources Centre. Today's programme has been generously sponsored by the Save & Prosper Educational Trust.

The Resources Centre has been established with the aid of a grant from the Government of the United States and with the support of the British Association for American Studies (BAAS).

The following pages outline the programme of today's events and provide further information about the work of the Centre.

Once again, welcome.

City of Liverpool Education Committee
Director of Education: K. A. Antcliffe

LIVERPOOL COLLEGES
CITY·MILLBROOK·SANDOWN·SOUTH MERSEY

SOUTH MERSEY COLLEGE
AMERICAN STUDIES RESOURCES CENTRE (NORTH)

INAUGURATION CEREMONY

12.30 p.m. Invited guests to assemble at Aulis House for a buffet luncheon, followed by conducted tours of the American Studies Resources Centre.

1.45 p.m. Guests assemble in the Conference Room, Aulis House for the formal proceedings and opening ceremony as detailed below.

2.00 p.m. **Dr. John P. A. Frain,**
Principal of South Mersey College.

Welcome to guests;
The incorporation of the American Studies Resources Centre within South Mersey College.

Councillor Thomas McManus,
Chairman of Liverpool City Council.

The American Studies Resources Centre in the context of Liverpool.

Councillor Ian Scott,
Chairman of the Further Education Sub Committee of Liverpool City Council.

The contribution of the Resources Centre to the Educational service.

Mr. John Shelley,
Director of the Save & Prosper Educational Trust.

The co-operation of Private and Public organisations for facilities on Merseyside.

Dr. Ronald Clifton,
Cultural Attaché at the Embassy of the United States of America, London.

Dr. Clifton will address the audience and declare the American Studies Resources Centre officially open.

Guests will then proceed to the Sports Hall for the Concert to be provided by the Royal Liverpool Philharmonic Orchestra, which commences at approximately 2.45 p.m.

CONCERT BY MEMBERS OF THE
ROYAL LIVERPOOL PHILHARMONIC ORCHESTRA

The Royal Liverpool Philharmonic Society and Orchestra

In the centre of Hope Street, Liverpool, between the city's two great cathedrals, stands the Philharmonic Hall, the home of the Royal Liverpool Philharmonic Orchestra. Concert-going has been an established custom in Liverpool since the Society was formed in 1840. The Society is among the oldest concert societies in the world, together with the Leipzig Gewandhaus, the Vienna Gesellschaft, the Royal Philharmonic Society and the Paris Conservatoire. At home and abroad, the Royal Liverpool Philharmonic Orchestra receives critical acclaim. A typical review followed the Orchestra's concert in the Berlin Philharmonie in April 1981: "Liverpool is the home of an orchestra which deserves to be ranked as one of the leading orchestras."

The Royal Liverpool Philharmonic Orchestra

EDWARD PEAK, Conductor

LESLEY GWYTHER, Leader

Today's programme consists of a musical journey illustrating the popular light music of America, Britain and Europe from the days of J. P. Sousa in America, and the Strauss family in Vienna, via Eric Coates and Leroy Anderson, to Lerner and Loewe; calling at one or two interesting stops on the way!

STARS AND STRIPES	Sousa
WO DIE CITRONEN BLUH'N	Strauss
'AMERICANA' SUITE	Thurban
TEDDY BEAR'S PICNIC	Bratton
GET OUT AND GET UNDER	Pether
ON THE QUARTER DECK	Alford
GIPSY PRINCESS SELECTION	Kalman

Interval for refreshments 15 minutes

LONDON SUITE	Coates
SYNCOPATED CLOCK	Anderson
MUSIC EV'RYWHERE	Coates
PAINT YOUR WAGON SELECTION	Loewe
PLINK PLANK PLUNK	Anderson
MY FAIR LADY SELECTION	Loewe

Edward Peak was born in 1951 on the Wirral and started to play the piano at the age of five. Later he took up the double bass which he studied at the Royal Manchester College of Music before joining the RLPO bass section in 1973. An interest from an early age in light music prompted him to start arranging and conducting. Many of his works have been broadcast, in particular for the BBC Radio 2 programmes 'Melodies for You' and 'Friday Night is Music Night'. As a conductor he has worked with the RLPO several times and also the BBC Concert Orchestra, with whom he has recorded programmes for the Sunday morning series 'Melodies for You'. Early next year he will conduct the RLPO again in a gala concert of symphonic film music, featuring the music of Miklos Rózsa, the composer of the music for such epics as *El cid*. This concert is to be broadcast by BBC Radio 2.

● Exhibits in the Sports Hall by kind permission of the National Museums and Galleries on Merseyside.

SOUTH MERSEY COLLEGE

AMERICAN STUDIES RESOURCES CENTRE (NORTH)

The Resources Centre aims to support and advise teachers in developing the study of the United States of America in British Secondary schools and Further Education colleges. The Centre offers an advice and information service providing audio-visual materials on loan to support classroom study. An extensive reference library is also available to teachers and students visiting the Centre.

The Centre organises conferences and workshops on United States related issues. These reach into many areas across the curriculum, to include geographical, historical, political, literary, economic and socio-cultural topics. The Centre has already operated as the venue for a successful schools conference on the American Civil War. In-service training workshops for American Studies teachers and further schools conferences will also be taking place in the forthcoming academic year.

The Centre receives advice and assistance through its U.K. Advisory Panel and its expert panel of U.S.A. based Advisers. Working in conjunction with the Resources Centre at the Polytechnic of Central London, the Resources Centre (North) provides a comprehensive service in an important and valuable area of study. We believe that an increasing number of educationalists will take full advantage of this important new venture on Merseyside.

SOUTH MERSEY COLLEGE
American Studies Resources Centre
Riversdale Campus
Riversdale Road
LIVERPOOL
L19 3QR

Telephone Number: 051 427 1227

Prestel: 517 225 705

CENTRE DIRECTOR: IAN RALSTON B.A.(Hons.), Cert.Ed.

Appendix 13

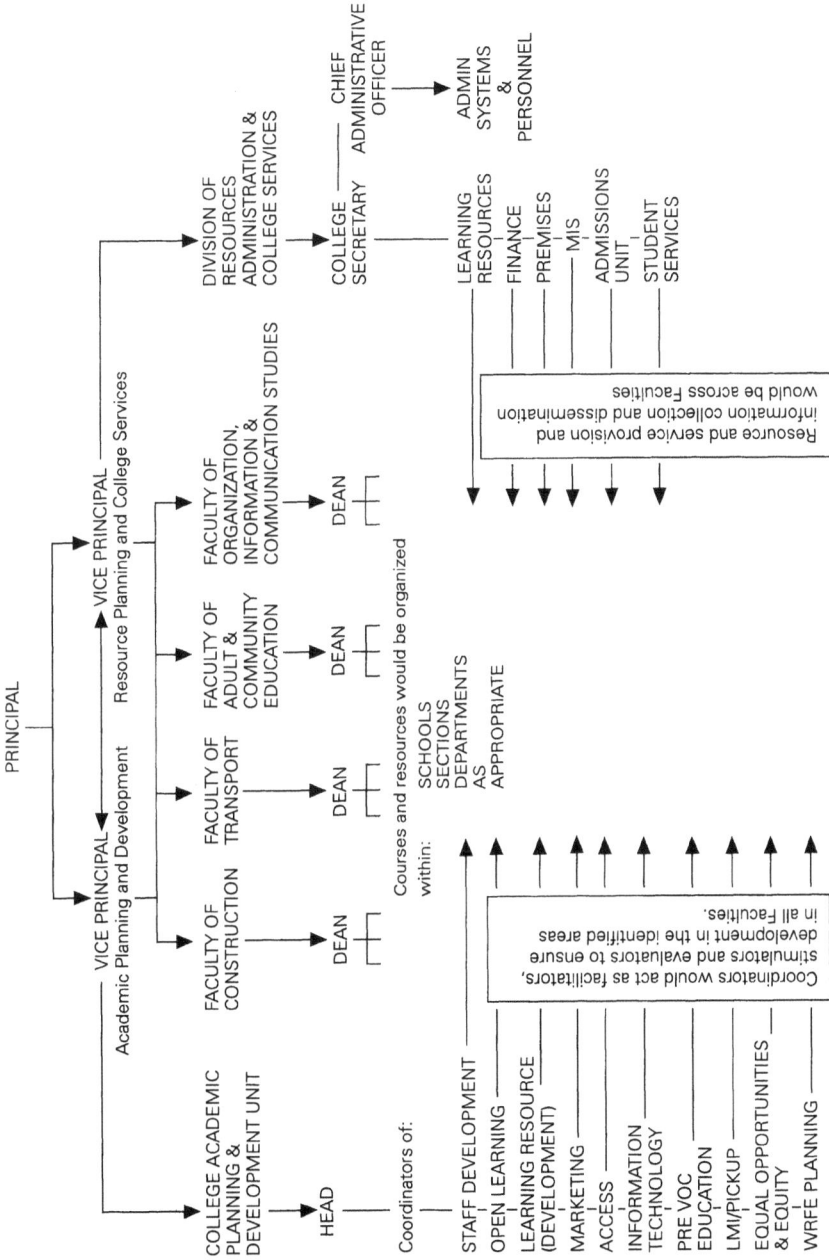

PRINCIPAL

VICE PRINCIPAL — Academic Planning and Development

VICE PRINCIPAL — Resource Planning and College Services

COLLEGE ACADEMIC PLANNING & DEVELOPMENT UNIT

HEAD

Coordinators of:

- STAFF DEVELOPMENT
- OPEN LEARNING
- LEARNING RESOURCE (DEVELOPMENT)
- MARKETING
- ACCESS
- INFORMATION TECHNOLOGY
- PRE VOC EDUCATION
- LMI/PICKUP
- EQUAL OPPORTUNITIES & EQUITY
- WRFE PLANNING

Coordinators would act as facilitators, stimulators and evaluators to ensure development in the identified areas in all Faculties.

FACULTY OF CONSTRUCTION — DEAN

FACULTY OF TRANSPORT — DEAN

FACULTY OF ADULT & COMMUNITY EDUCATION — DEAN

FACULTY OF ORGANIZATION, INFORMATION & COMMUNICATION STUDIES — DEAN

Courses and resources would be organized within:

SCHOOLS
SECTIONS
DEPARTMENTS
AS APPROPRIATE

DIVISION OF RESOURCES ADMINISTRATION & COLLEGE SERVICES

COLLEGE SECRETARY

CHIEF ADMINISTRATIVE OFFICER

ADMIN SYSTEMS & PERSONNEL

- LEARNING RESOURCES
- FINANCE
- PREMISES
- MIS
- ADMISSIONS UNIT
- STUDENT SERVICES

Resource and service provision and information collection and dissemination would be across Faculties

211

Appendix 14

1986 Management Structure

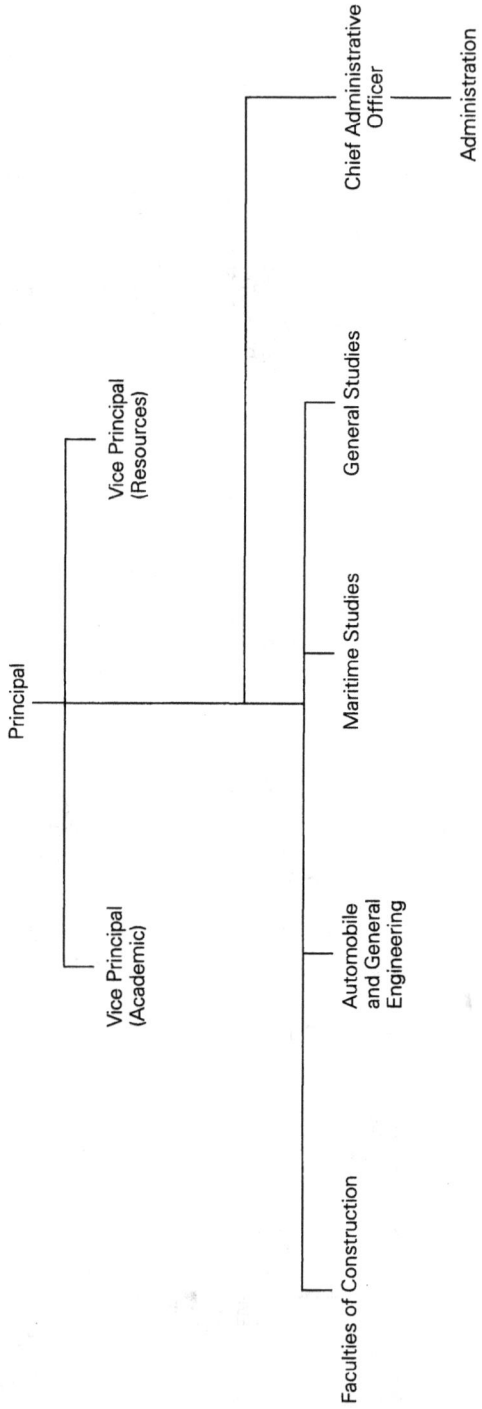

```
                                    Principal
                                        |
        ┌───────────────────────────────┼───────────────────────────┐
   Vice Principal                  Vice Principal          Chief Administrative
    (Academic)                      (Resources)                 Officer
                                        |                          |
   ┌────────────────┬──────────────────┼───────────────┐     Administration
Faculties of   Automobile        Maritime Studies   General Studies
Construction   and General
               Engineering
```

Appendix 15

1988 Management Structure

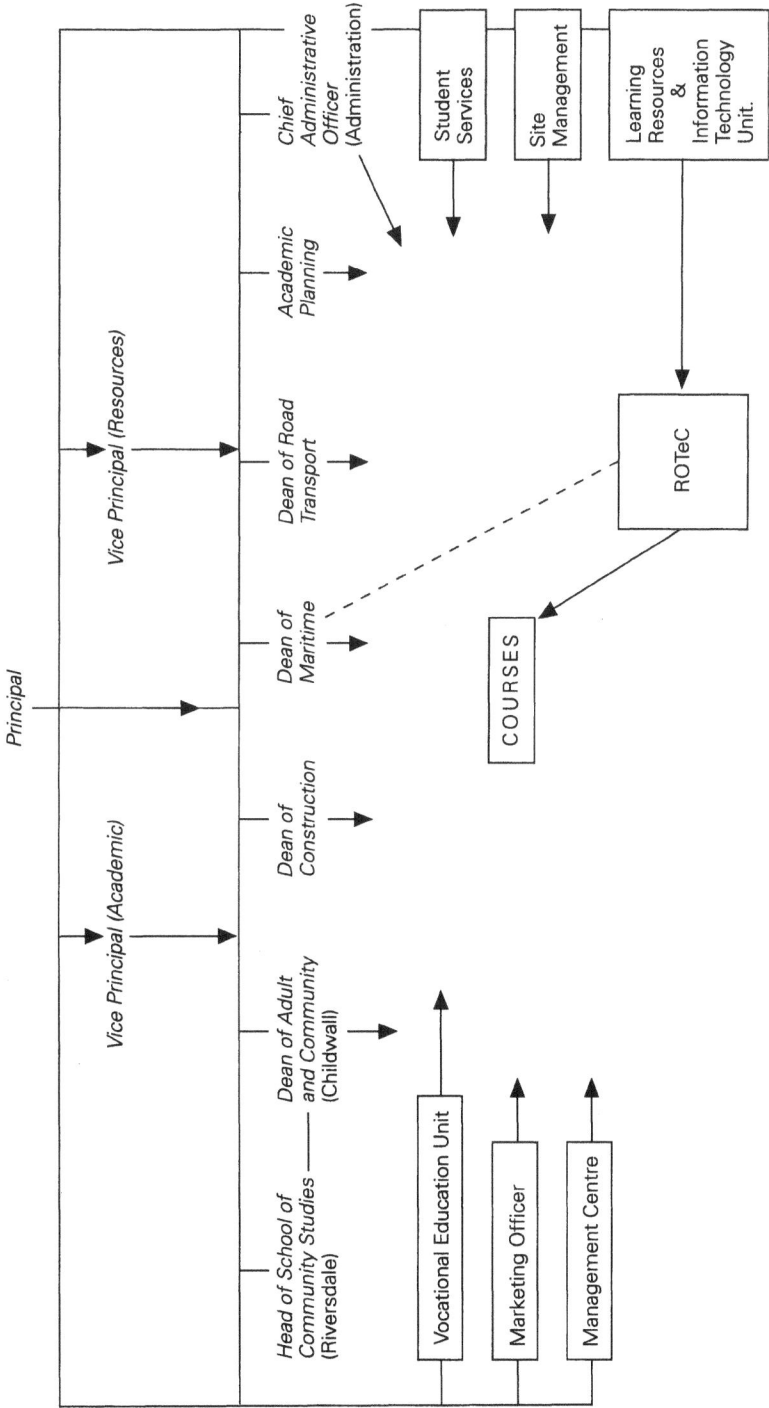

Appendix 16

South Mersey College

Quality Control and Institutional Effectiveness — Position Statement

1   Introduction

   1.1   The LEA draft mission statement puts emphasis on comprehensiveness and relevance of its Further Education service through an informed view of the needs of existing and potential clients. The statement further acknowledges the duty to provide entitlement, access and the opportunity for progression, by the removal of arbitrary and artificial barriers, giving equal opportunities to all regardless of race, gender, disability of age.

   The LEA is committed to ensuring that appropriate measures of quality and value are developed and applied;

   1.2   Within the broad LEA mission statement the College acknowledges the entitlement of the student to:

        equality of access
        equality of respect
        equality of opportunities and
        equality of esteem.

   The curriculum and the institution together with its resources both physical and human must reflect this entitlement, with the primacy of the individual being given the highest priority. The necessary support systems of guidance, counselling, assessment and communications must be put in place;

2   College Aims

The College aims to continue developing its learning opportunities to attract and retain client groups by developing as its clients would wish and support. Thereby it would open up new client areas and ensure maximum market penetration by:

   a)   adapting and developing management information systems to provide information concerning the present and potential student population and the needs of industry and the community;

   b)   developing procedures for curriculum evaluation which will measure the extent to which learning programmes are relevant to particular client groups;

c) developing learning provision both in curriculum and support systems to meet identified and perceived needs;

d) implementing an appropriate staff development pro- gramme.

The College further aims to improve its operational efficiency by maximizing its earning potential through full cost courses, consul- tancy, use of its premises and staff by industry and close monitor- ing of its resource allocations and utilization.

3 *Background*

At the Altrincham conference the issues of Industry, Equity and Client-centredness were picked up, and they were further devel- oped at the Adelphi conference. It is proposed to use these headings as foci for an action plan. Each member of the Princi- palship was given responsibility for one of the above areas. These are summarized in the next section.

4 *Industry Links*

4.1 The three technical faculties, Automobile and General, Construction and Maritime Studies have traditionally had links with local industry and the training boards through employer led day-release and full-time courses, but as part of our commitment to client-centred development, we have initiated a programme of contacts with national employers with the Principal and/or Vice Principal(s) together with the Deans travelling to industry's head of offices to talk to senior management. Visits which have taken place or are proposed include Jaguar, Austin Rover, British Rail, Ford, Toyota, Rockwell, Volvo, Vauxhall, Nissan, McAlpine, J. and F. Nelson, Tarmac, Northern Counties, Saab, Olivetti, Bibby, Esso, Shell, Cadbury Schweppes. A copy of the document prepared for Jaguar Cars Limited is attached to this Action Plan and a follow-up presentation visit is being arranged in Coventry. Following the reciprocal visit of one of their sen- ior executives, the Austin Rover Company has confirmed it will be using the College as a training resource in the future.

4.2 Positive moves are being made in contacts with the relevant training boards or employer bodies, RTITB, CITB, The Sea Fish Industry Board, the IMBM, the IAAS, IBCF and through various trade organizations in order to develop courses for small firms. All this activity is being co-ordinated with a view to accurately determine skill shortages as per- ceived by employers which will lead to jobs. It will also en- able the College to design retraining packages for existing work forces as technology develops. We also plan to de- velop a wide range of open learning packages for industry and to offer IT through the new Olivetti Centre to all branches of industry.

4.3 Consultancy and the use of College facilities by industry as for example in dealer training will be expanded to enhance income generation.

5 *Equity and Equal Opportunity*

5.1 Despite the dramatic increase in traditionally under-represented sections of the community:

	Sept. 1986	*Sept. 1987*	*Sept. 1988*
Female students	1005	1780	2678
Black students	215	341	602
Special needs students	40	72	155

the College still recognizes that it has a long way to go to ensure equality of opportunity in the more traditional areas because, of the 2678 female students, 2095 are in General Studies, and 387 of the 602 black students are in General Studies. However, it is interesting to note that the percentage recruitment of women to full-time courses in Automobile Engineering is significantly higher than the percentage recruitment to employment in the industry itself. It proposes, therefore, to improve and extend the childcare facilities at Riversdale. The impending closure of the Childwall site will assist this process but will in turn impose additional needs *re* capacity and staffing.

More generally, the College will set targets and examine through surveys whether times and patterns of attendance could be varied. It will continue to expand its drop-in workshop and outreach facilities and investigate modes of learning to provide mixed delivery patterns.

5.2 The curriculum is to be evaluated through working groups to see if it can be made more user friendly and less forbidding to the community at large, particularly with relationship to sexism and racism.

5.3 The proposed restructuring of College Faculties and the outcome of current applications for PRC should hopefully provide more opportunities for women staff to be appointed, preferably to senior posts. The serious imbalance of males and females at Riversdale will partially be rectified with proposed closure of Childwall and the transfer of female staff.

5.4 The policy of appointing or promoting women will be pursued (seventeen out of the last nineteen teaching appointments have been women; one PL, two SL, fourteen Lecturers).

5.5 Although there is a noticeable shift in attitude by employers (for example, there are more opportunities for women in maritime occupations, in the construction trades and automobile engineering) entrenched attitudes still exist. College staff are being encouraged, through professional bodies and employer links, to do everything possible to reduce this prejudice and the College has a positive drive to recruit more women to these areas.

5.6 The College intends to increase the number of staff with equal opportunity responsibilities and increase the spread of clear and relevant information by way of workshops and seminars for staff and students. The College's commitment to enforce the LEA's policies in this area will be made manifest.

6 *Client Led Developments*

6.1 To present a more welcoming aspect to the College Campus we have established a small working group, reporting to the Academic Board, which continuously monitors the decoration of premises and the pictures, posters and signs displayed. This accommodation working group is investigating the feasibility of transferring the College entrance for students from Riversdale Road to Mersey Road. The main entrance to the campus and the entrance to each teaching block will be made more attractive with pictures and posters, having an equal opportunity theme, being displayed. As previously indicated, childcare facilities will be improved and a proposal to extend childcare to younger children will be investigated. The Authority has agreed that £6000 earmarked for modifications to accommodate the nursery at Childwall and £4000 allocated for equipment at Childwall can be diverted to Riversdale thus allowing the Riversdale provision to be greatly enhanced.

In addition, student common rooms would be provided in A and C Blocks at Riversdale. Toilet facilities for women need to be enhanced at Riversdale and any offensive graffiti or display material monitored and removed.

6.2 In line with the policy to provide more learning support and guidance and counselling, it is proposed to seek two additional student admissions officer posts on the non-teaching staff. In the meantime, it is proposed to divert teaching staff time for this purpose. This will ensure a full-time year-round presence. Faculties are to be asked to supply detailed availability of academic staff to assist in guidance and to ensure that Faculty telephones are always manned.

6.3 It is further proposed to establish an Information/

Intelligence Recruitment Unit based in specifically designed accommodation with comprehensive information
on course provision located there.

6.4 Following the SPOC/EPOC training programme, designated
trainers from the College will 'cascade' the training into the
Faculties. Pilot evaluations will start in the summer term
using these and other relevant methods.

6.5 Alternative methods of assessment and accreditation are
being investigated. In conjunction with the CITB and RTITB
we are examining the modularization of courses in preparation for NVQ and will extend the range of 'pick and mix'
opportunities which exist. We will be participating in the
LEA NROVA project.

6.6 The Olivetti Technology Centre will be used to develop and
pilot a modular course comprised of a core module of IT,
numeracy and communication. Study skills will be incorporated in the course together with modules in specialist skills,
for example design, word processing, CNC and PLC clearly
related to potential employment areas.

The Training Agency have indicated that they will fund
a course of this nature through YTS.

6.7 The development of an enhanced open learning facility at
Riversdale is being investigated and this is to be integrated
into more traditional areas of the curriculum extending the
range of learning opportunities. This will be achieved by
incorporating the existing library facilities and open learning
workshop in H Block into a greatly enhanced Open Learning Centre.

6.8 Access courses for vocational areas will be developed. Access to the Built Environment is already under discussion
with the Polytechnic and an Access to Technology course is
being examined with a view to providing a variety of progression routes from our own Marine Diploma to courses in
the Polytechnic and University. When the move from
Childwall is completed the design of Access on a modular
basis with core and vocational skill units will be facilitated.
Training in Access teaching for vocational staff will be initiated.

7 *Conclusions*

7.1 The Governors have agreed to recommend to the Authority
that the proposed restructuring should go ahead which should
facilitate College development, particularly in curriculum and
equal opportunity.

7.2 The closure of the Childwall campus and the resultant transfer will facilitate:

a) enhanced learning provision in both content and modes of delivery at Riversdale;
b) improved childcare facilities;
c) a significant shift in the gender balance in both staff and students;
d) accelerated development of student centred learning particularly for adults.

8 *Other Factors*

It will be essential to keep the following factors under constant review as they all will have significant, if differing, influence on the College's development:

a) Premature Retirement and its effect on staffing levels;
b) The Education Reform Act and delegated powers;
c) Changes in the Governing Body;
d) Reviews and possible further rationalization of FE in Liverpool;
e) Revised conditions of service;
f) LEA policies on the 16–19 curriculum and Adult Education;
g) Changes in funding mechanisms and budget allocations;
h) Changes in accreditation and validation of learning;
i) Government policies on lecturer numbers and alternative education/training providers;
j) City Council responses to Government initiatives (such as ET and TECs).

April 1989

South Mersey College

Links With Employers

An illustration of the importance the College attaches to employer links is characterized by its recent National Training Award. In 1988, the College became one of the first winners of this valuable and prestigious award, for a training package devised in response to a request from a local firm, Baines Dairies Ltd. of Bootle (in connection with the automation of its processing plant). The Managing Director of the firm expressed the view that 'the training was effective because production, profits and the product range have all increased, management control has been maximized, and our credibility with our bankers has never been higher.' Other satisfied customers for similar services from the College include Prudential Assurance, Ward Blenkinsop, Goodlass Wall, Merseyside Enterprise Board and Wirral Council.

The College is also energetically seeking funding 'partnerships' with industry, and with substantial financial support from British Olivetti has recently set up one of the most powerful microcomputer networks in the North West of England. The whole installation involves over forty microcomputers, twenty of which are networked, as well as desk-top publishing and computer-aided design facilities. At standard prices, it is worth over a quarter of a million pounds and was installed by Olivetti for under £150,000 with free training also being provided for College staff.

The technical Faculties of the College have well-established links with business organizations, and the Training Boards, through employer-led day-release and full-time courses, but as part of the College's commitment to client-centred development, the programme of visits to local, regional and national employers has been stepped up, with the Senior Management of the College travelling extensively to negotiate with their industrial and commercial counterparts.

Visits which have taken place or are proposed include those to Jaguar, Austin Rover, British Rail, Ford, Toyota, Rockwell, Volvo, Vauxhall, Nissan, McAlpine, J. and F. Nelson, Tarmac, Northern Counties, Saab, Olivetti, Bibby, Esso, Shell and Cadbury Schweppes. Following the reciprocal visit of one of their senior executives, the Austin Rover Company has confirmed it will be using the College as a training resource in the future, whilst the Ford Motor Company has recently made it a gift of expensive equipment.

Positive moves are being made, in contacts with relevant training boards or employer bodies, such as the Road Transport Industry Training Board, the Construction Industry Training Board, the Sea Fish Industry Board, the Institute of Maintenance and Building Management, the Institute of Automobile Assessors, the Institute of Building Control and with various trade organizations, in order to develop courses for small firms. All this activity is being co-ordinated with a view to the accurate determination of skill shortages, as perceived by employers, which will lead to jobs. It will also enable the College to design retraining packages for existing work forces as technology develops. The College also plans to develop a wide range of open learning packages for industry and to offer information technology courses, through the new Olivetti Centre, to all branches of industry.

Consultancy and the use of college facilities by industry (as for example in dealer training) is also being expanded to enhance the generation of income. Substantial expenditure is also being committed to up-date and augment the provision of auto-technology and offshore survival training.

Bibliography

ADAIR, J. (1979) *Action Centred Leadership*, Aldershot, Hants, Gower.

ADVISORY COMMITTEE ON THE SUPPLY AND TRAINING OF TEACHERS (ACSTT) (1975) Further Education Sub-Committee, The Training of Teachers for Further Education, First Haycocks Report.

ANSOFF, H.I. (1975) *Corporate Strategy*, Harmondsworth, Middlesex, Penguin Books.

ANSOFF, H.I. (1981) *Strategic Management*, New York, Halsted Press.

ARGYLE, M. (1972) *The Psychology of Interpersonal Behaviour*, Harmondsworth, Middlesex, Penguin Books.

ARMSTRONG, P. and DAWSON, C. (1981) *People in Organizations*, Huntingdon, Cambridge, E.L.M. Publications.

BARHAM, K. and RASSAM, C. (1989) *Shaping the Corporate Future*, London, Unwin Hyman.

BARNARD, C.I. (1938) *The Functions of the Executive*, Cambridge, MA, Harvard University Press.

BARNARD, C.I. (1948) *Organization and Management*, Cambridge, Massachusetts, Harvard University Press.

BELL, D. (1976) *The Coming of Post-Industrial Society*, Harmondsworth, Middlesex, Penguin Books.

BOISOT, M. (1987) *Information and Organizations, The Manager as Anthropologist*, London, Fontana/Collins.

BOOT, R.L., COWLING, A.G. and STANWORTH, M.J.K. (1982) *Behavioural Science for Managers*, London, Edward Arnold.

BOWMAN, C. and ASCH, D. (1987) *Strategic Management*, Basingstoke, Hants., Macmillan Education.

BOYD, W. and KING, E.J. (1975) *The History of Western Education*, 11th Edition, London, A and C Black.

BOYD-BARRETT, O., BUSH, T., GOODEY, J., McNAY, I. and PREEDY, M. (1987) *Approaches to Post-School Management*, London, Harper & Row.

BOYLE, D. (1988) 'The strategic planning process', in LOCK, D. and FARROW, N. (Eds) *The Gower Handbook of Management*, 2nd Edition, Aldershot, Hants, Gower.

BUCHANAN, D.A. and HUCZYNSKI, A.A. (1985) *Organizational Behaviour,* London, Prentice-Hall International.

BULLOCK COMMITTEE, THE. (1977) *Report of Committee of Inquiry on Industrial Democracy,* London, HMSO.

BURNS, T. and STALKER, G.M. (1968) *The Management of Innovation,* 2nd Edition, London, Tavistock Publications.

CAMPBELL, D.T. and FISKE, D.W. (1959) 'Convergent and discriminant validation by the multi-trait-multimethod matrix', *Psychological Bulletin,* **56**.

CANTOR, L.M. and ROBERTS, I.F. (1986) *Further Education To-Day A Critical Review,* 3rd Edition (revised), London, Routledge & Kegan Paul.

CHISNALL, P.M. (1986) *Marketing Research,* 3rd Edition, Maidenhead, Berks., McGraw-Hill.

COSER, L.A. (1956) *The Functions of Conflict,* London, Routledge and Kegan Paul.

DAVIES, P. and SCRIBBINS, K. (1985) *Marketing Further and Higher Education,* London, Longman for Further Education Unit (FEU) and Further Education Staff College (FESC).

DEARBORN, C. and SIMON, H. (1968) 'Selective perception: A note on departmental identification of executives', *Sociometry,* **21**.

DENNISON, W.F. (1985) Education and the economy: Changing circumstances', in MCNAY, I. and OZGA, J. (Eds), *Policy-Making in Education: The Breakdown of Consensus,* Oxford, Pergamon Press.

DEPARTMENT OF EDUCATION AND SCIENCE (DES) (1987) Managing Colleges Efficiently *The Joint Efficiency Study,* (EDUC/280/1987), London, DES/ Local Authority Association Officers.

DEPARTMENT OF EDUCATION AND SCIENCE (DES) (1987) *Maintained Further Education: Financing, Governance and Law,* London, DES, August.

DEPARTMENT OF EDUCATION AND SCIENCE (DES) (1988) *Education Reform Act 1988,* London, HMSO, Chapter 40.

DEPARTMENT OF EDUCATION AND SCIENCE (DES) (1988) *Report by Her Majesty's Inspectors on a survey of some major full-time courses in NAFE Business Studies, carried out 27 April to 9 June 1987,* London, HMSO.

DEPARTMENT OF EMPLOYMENT/DEPARTMENT OF EDUCATION AND SCIENCE (1984) *Training for Jobs,* Cmnd. 9135, London, HMSO.

DICKINSON, A. (1988) 'Communication by public relations', in HELLER, R. (Ed.) *The Complete Guide to Modern Management,* London, Harrap.

DRUCKER, P. (1978) 'Technology management and society', reported in BOOT, R.L., COWLING, A.G. and STANWORTH, M.J.K. (Eds), *Behavioural Sciences for Managers,* London, Edward Arnold.

DRUCKER, P.F. (1986) *Innovation and Entrepreneurship,* London, Pan Books.

DRUCKER, P.F. (1964) *Managing for Results,* London, Pan Books.

EBBUTT, (1985) in HOPKINS, D. *A Teacher's Guide to Classroom Research,* Milton Keynes, England, Open University Press.

EMERY, F. and TRIST, E. (1965) 'The causal texture of organizational envir-onments', *Human Relations*, **18**, August, pp. 124–51.

ETZIONI, A. (1967) 'Mixed scanning: A "third" approach to decision-making', *Public Administration Review*, **27**.

EVERSLEY, and BEGG, (1987) 'Deprivation in the inner city', in Liverpool City Council, *Past Trends and Future Prospects Urban Changes in Liverpool 1916–2001*, February.

FOLLETT, M.P. (1920) *The New State*, London, Longman.

FOLLETT, M.P. (1924) *Creative Experience*, London, Longman.

FOLLETT, M.P., METCALF, H.C. and URWICK, L.F. (Eds) (1941) *Dynamic Administration*, London, Pitman.

FORD, J. (1988) 'Managing change', *North West Business Monthly*, July.

FREAN, D. (1977) *The Board and Management Development*, London, Business Books.

FRAIN, J. (1986) *Principles and Practice of Marketing*, London, Pitman.

FRAIN, J. (1988) *Principal's Report to the Governors*, South Mersey College, Liverpool, 4 November.

FRAIN, J. (1989) *Principal's Report to the Governors*, South Mersey College, Liverpool, 9 June.

FRANCIS, D. (1987) *Unblocking Organizational Communication*, Aldershot, Hants, Gower.

GALBRAITH, J.K. (1977) *The Age of Uncertainty*, London, British Broad-casting Corporation, Andre Deutsch.

GIST, R.R. (1971) *Marketing and Society: A Conceptual Introduction*, London, Holt Rinehart Winston.

GOULDNER, A.W. (1957) 'Cosmopolitans and locals: Towards an analysis of latent social roles', *Administrative Science Quarterly*, **1**.

HANDY, C.B. (1983) 'The organizations of consent', in BOYD-BARRETT, O., BUSH, T., GOODY, J., MCNAY, I. and PREEDY, M. (Eds) (1987), *Approaches to Post-School Management*, London, Harper and Row.

HARVEY-JONES, J. (1989) *Making It Happen, Reflections on Leadership*, London, Fontana.

HELLER, R. (1988) *The Complete Guide to Modern Management*, London, Harrap.

HERZBERG, F. (1968) 'One more time: How do you motivate employees?', *Harvard Business Review*, **46**.

HERZBERG, F., MAUSNER, B. and SNYDERMAN, B.B. (1959) *The Motivation to Work*, New York, John Wiley.

HEWTON, E. (1987) 'Inside knowledge: Rethinking education change', in BOYD-BARRETT, O., BUSH, T., GOODEY, J., MCNAY, I. and PREEDY, M. (Eds), *Approaches to Post-School Management*, London, Harper and Row.

HOLLIDAY, P.M. (1989) 'The implications of NCVQ for staff in further edu-cation', South Mersey College, Liverpool, internal memorandum, 21 June.

HOPKINS, D. (1985) *A Teacher's Guide to Classroom Research*, Milton Keynes, England, Open University Press.

HUGHES, Q. (1964) 'Seaport', *Architecture and Townscape in Liverpool*, London, Lund Humphries.

JAQUES, E. (1951) *The Changing Culture of a Factory*, London, Routledge & Kegan Paul.

JAQUES, E. (1956) *The Measurement of Responsibility*, London, Tavistock Publications.

JAQUES, E. (1982) *Free Enterprise, Fair Employment*, London, Heinemann.

JOHNSON, G. and SCHOLES, K. (1989) *Exploring Corporate Strategy: Text and Cases*, Hemel Hempstead, Prentice-Hall.

KATZ, D. and KAHN, R.L. (1970) 'Open-systems theory' in GRUSKY, O. and MILLER, G.A. (Eds) *The Sociology of Organizations*, New York, The Free Press.

KOGAN, M., JOHNSON, D., PACKWOOD, T. and WHITAKER, T. (1985) 'School governing bodies and the political administrative system', in McNAY, I. and OZGA, J. (Eds) *Policy-making in Education: The Breakdown of Consensus*, Oxford, Pergamon Press.

KOTLER, P. (1971) 'Metamarketing: The furthering of organizations, persons, places and causes', *Marketing Forum*, July–August, pp. 13–23.

KOTLER, P. (1972) *Marketing Management: Analysis, Planning and Control*, 2nd Edition, Englewood Cliffs, New Jersey, Prentice-Hall

KROEBER, A. and KLUCKHOHN, C. (1952) *Culture: A Critical Review of Concepts and Definitions*, Papers of the Peabody Museums of American Archaeology and Ethnology, **47**, Cambridge, Massachusetts, Harvard University Press.

LAWLER, E.E. (1973) *Motivation in Work Organizations*, Belmont, California, Brooks/Cole.

LIVERPOOL CITY COUNCIL (1987) *Past Trends and Future Prospects, Urban Change in Liverpool 1961–2001*, Liverpool, City Planning Officer.

LIVERPOOL CITY COUNCIL (n.d.) *Social and Economic Change in Liverpool*, Liverpool, Public Relations and Information Unit

LIVERPOOL EDUCATION AUTHORITY (1984) *Further Education Management Audit Studies: 1984–5, HMI and District Audit Studies An Overview of the College Surveys*, Liverpool, Liverpool Education Department, Further Education Section.

LIVERPOOL EDUCATION AUTHORITY (1987) *National Council of Vocational Qualifications*, (Educ/278), Liverpool, Liverpool Education Department, Further Education Section, 24 September.

LOCK, D. and FARROW, N. (1988) *The Gower Handbook of Management*, 2nd Edition, Aldershot, Hants, Gower.

LOCK, E.A. (1978) 'The ubiquity of the technique of goal setting in theories and approaches to employee motivation', *Academy of Management Review*, **3**.

LUPTON, J. and TANNER, I. (1987) *Achieving Change — A Systematic Approach*, Aldershot, Hants, Gower.

MACLURE, S. and LISTER, D. (1985) 'Demanding value for money', London, England, *The Times Educational Supplement*, 14 June.

MADGE, C. and HUXLEY, J. (1937) 'Mass Observation', in WORCESTER, R. and DOWNHAM, J. (Eds) (1986), *Consumer Market Research Handbook*, 3rd Edition, London, McGraw-Hill.

MANGHAM, I. (1979) *The Politics of Organizational Change*, London, Associated Business Press.

MASLOW, A.H. (1954) *Motivation and Personality*, New York, Harper.

McGREGOR, D. (1960) *The Human Side of Enterprise*, New York, McGraw-Hill

McGREW, A.G. and WILSON, M.J. (1982) *Decision-making Approaches and Analysis*, Manchester, Manchester University Press in association with The Open University.

McNAY, I. and OZGA, J. (1985) *Policy-making in Education: The Breakdown of Consensus*, Oxford, Pergamon Press.

MAYON-WHITE, B. (Ed.) (1986) *Planning and Managing Change*, London, Harper and Row.

MEIGHAN, R. (1986) *A Sociology of Educating*, 2nd Edition, London, Cassell.

METCALF, H.C. and URWICK, L.F. (1941) *Dynamic Administration*, London, Pitman.

MILES, R. and SNOW, C. (1978) *Organizational Strategy, Structure and Process*, Maidenhead, Berks., McGraw-Hill.

MINTZBERG, H. (1978) 'Patterns of strategy formation', *Management Science*, May.

MINTZBERG, H. (1983) 'The mind of the strategist(s)', in SRIVASTA, S. and ASSOCIATES (Eds), *The Executive Mind*, San Francisco, Jossey-Bass.

MITCHELL, T.R. and LARSON, J.R. (1987) *People in Organizations*, New York, McGraw-Hill.

MOEDE, W. (1927) 'Die Richtlinien der leistungs — Psychologie', *Industrielle Psycho-technik*, **4**.

MORGAN, G. (1986) *Images of Organization*, London, Sage.

MOSER, C.A. and KALTON, G. (1971) *Survey Methods in Social Investigation*, 2nd Edition, London, Heinemann.

MULLINS, L.J. (1989) *Management and Organizational Behaviour*, London, Pitman.

NADER, D.A. and LAWLER, E.E. (1979) 'Motivation: A diagnostic approach', in STEERS, R.M. and PORTER, L.W. (Eds), *Motivation and Work Behavior*, New York, McGraw-Hill.

NADER, D.A. and TUSHMAN, M.L. (1980) 'A model for diagnosing organizational behaviour: Applying a congruence perspective', *Organizational Dynamics*.

NATIONAL COUNCIL FOR VOCATIONAL QUALIFICATIONS (NCVQ) (1989) *Towards A Qualified Society*, London, NCVQ, September.

OLDCORN, R. (1989) *Management*, London, Macmillan.

OLINS, W. (1988) 'Shaping the company image', in HELLER, R. (Ed.) *The Complete Guide to Modern Management*, London, Harrap.

O'SHAUGHNESSY, J. (1988) *Competitive Marketing A Strategic Approach*, 2nd Edition, London, Unwin Hyman.

PEEKE, G. (1987) 'Role strain in the further education college', in BOYD-BARRETT, O., BUSH, T., GOODEY, J., MCNAY, I. and PREEDY, M. (Eds) *Approaches to Post-School Management*, London, Harper and Row.

PETERS, T.J. and WATERMAN, R.H. (1982) *In Search of Excellence*, London, Harper and Row.

PLANT, R. (1987) *Managing Change*, Aldershot, Hants., Gower.

POWELL, G. and POSNER, B.Z. (1978) 'Resistance to change reconsidered: Implications for managers', *Human Resource Management*, **17**.

PUGH, D.S., HICKSON, D.J. and HININGS, C.R. (1983) *Writers on Organizations*, 3rd Edition, Harmondsworth, Middlesex Penguin Books.

PYM, D. (1968) *Industrial Society-Social Sciences in Management*, Harmondsworth, Middlesex, Penguin Books.

RANSON, S. (1985) 'Changing relations between centre and locality in education', in MCNAY, I. and OZGA, J. (Eds), *Policy-making in Education: The Breakdown of Consensus*, Oxford, Pergamon Press.

RANSON, S., TAYLOR, B. and BRIGHOUSE, T. (1986) *The Revolution in Education and Training*, Harlow, Essex, Longman.

RICHARDSON, B. and RICHARDSON, R. (1989) *Business Planning, An Approach to Strategic Management*, London, Pitman.

ROBERTSON, I.T. and COOPER, C.L. (1983) *Human Behaviour in Organizations*, Plymouth, Macdonald & Evans.

ROETHLISBERGER, F.J. and DICKSON, W.J. (1949) *Management and the Worker*, Cambridge, Massachusetts, Harvard University Press.

SOUTH MERSEY COLLEGE (1989) *Proposed Reorganization of the College Academic Structure 1989*, Liverpool, report of the College Management Team, May.

SOUTH MERSEY COLLEGE (1989) *The Implications of NCVQ for Staff in Further Education*, Liverpool, internal report, 21 June.

SOUTH MERSEY COLLEGE (1990) *Meeting the Objectives of 'Managing Colleges Efficiently'*, Liverpool, internal memorandum, 21 February.

SRIVASTVA, S. and ASSOCIATES (1983) *The Executive Mind*, San Francisco, Jossey-Bass.

STANKIEWICZ, R. (1986) *Academics and Entrepreneurs: Developing University-Industry Relations*, London, Frances Printer.

STEERS, R.M. and PORTER, L.W. (Eds) (1983) *Motivation and Work Behaviour*, 3rd Edition, New York, McGraw-Hill.

STEWART, D.M. (Ed.) (1987) *Handbook of Management Skills*, Aldershot, Hants, Gower.

STONER, J.A.F. and FREEMAN, R.E. (1989) *Management*, 4th Edition, Englewood Cliffs, New Jersey, Prentice-Hall.

TILLEY, K. (1968) 'A technology of training', in PYM, D. (Ed.), *Industrial*

Society: Social Sciences in Management, Harmondsworth, Middlesex, Penguin Books.

TOFFLER, A. (1971) *Future Shock*, London, Pan Books.

TOFFLER, A. (1985) *The Adaptive Corporation*, London, Pan Books.

TRAINING AGENCY, THE (1989) *Winners 1988*, Sheffield, The Training Agency.

WALKER, T.S. (1990) 'Meeting the objectives of "managing colleges efficiently" ', South Mersey College, internal memorandum, February.

WEST, J. *et al.* (1989) *Quality Control and Institutional Effectiveness-Position Statement*, South Mersey College, internal paper, April.

WOOLHOUSE, J. (1988) 'Organization development', in LOCK, D. and FARROW, N. (Eds), *The Gower Book of Management*, 2nd Edition, Aldershot, Hants, Gower.

Index

For Product Safety Concerns and Information please contact our EU
representative GPSR@taylorandfrancis.com
Taylor & Francis Verlag GmbH, Kaufingerstraße 24, 80331 München, Germany

www.ingramcontent.com/pod-product-compliance
Lightning Source LLC
Chambersburg PA
CBHW070401270326
41926CB00014B/2657